Lawrence F Devlin

 W9-CMN-176

# An introduction to the world's Gemstones

# An introduction to the world's
# Gemstones

## E H Rutland

Doubleday & Company, Inc.
Garden City, New York

To my wife, who put up nobly with being a gem widow.

*Acknowledgements*
I am very grateful to the Institute of Geological Sciences for
permission to photograph many of its magnificent gemstones and for
the assistance so readily given by its staff. Particular thanks are due to
E. A. Jobbins and Miss P. Statham for their help and advice; to
M. Pulsford for his skill and artistry in producing splendid pictures;
to the Gemmological Association of Great Britain for the use of their
excellent library; to Dr E. Gübelin for supplying transparencies of
inclusions; and to B. W. Anderson and R. Webster who taught me
gemmology.

E.H.R.

Published by
The Hamlyn Publishing Group Limited
London · New York · Sydney · Toronto
Astronaut House, Feltham, Middlesex, England
Copyright © The Hamlyn Publishing Group Limited 1974

ISBN 0 600 33925 4
ISBN 0-385-05191-3 Doubleday
Library of Congress Catalog Number 73-19294

Filmset by London Filmsetters Limited
Colour Separation by Colour Workshop Limited, Hertford
Printed in Great Britain by Butler and Tanner Limited, Frome and London

# Contents

What are Gemstones? 6

The Origin of Gemstones 13

The Structure of Gemstones and their Imitations 35

The Gem Species 58

The Gemstone Industries 108

The Evolution of Gems and Jewels 138

The History and Lore of Gemstones 154

Collecting and Looking after Gems 172

Data Table 185

Bibliography 187

Acknowledgements 188

Glossary 189

Index 191

# What are Gemstones?

Gemstones are one of nature's rarest products. Centuries of search and exploration have now shown that well over 2 000 different kinds of minerals make up the solid crust of the earth on which we live. Only a minute fraction of these are capable of use as gems. While a few gem-forming minerals are relatively common, most are rare and only occur in small numbers, scattered over the world in a few, sometimes remote and inaccessible, localities.

In any case, only a tiny proportion of the minerals mined will ultimately yield stones that would grace a piece of jewellery, and when we think of really fine gemstones, the world's entire stock is reduced much further, almost to mere handfuls.

This may seem odd when we admire the cascades of jewels that adorn a large jeweller's windows, an occupation that always seems to attract a congregation of devotees. But notice how small each stone really is and how the goldsmith has used his art to enhance the importance of the stones with elaborate settings and embellishments. A specially small unit of weight, the carat, had to be devised to weigh the stones adequately.

The mineral beryl, for instance, which includes emerald and aquamarine among its varieties, is mined to the extent of a few thousand tons annually. All this is, however, completely useless for gem purposes. The material is greyish and opaque; it is used entirely to extract the rare metal beryllium, named after the gemstone. Gem-quality beryl is found only in a small number of areas where the yield is counted in pounds, not in tons, although many tons of soil have to be mined to win the gemstones. Even then most of the gem beryl will be wasted – either discarded as inferior in quality or lost in fashioning the gemstones. True emeralds of a sort can be bought for a very few pounds sterling or dollars; stones of a similar size but fine in colour and flawless, or nearly so, could fetch as many thousands. Value ranges of this order are by no means uncommon among the really precious stones and the rarity of outstanding specimens determines their value.

Ruby and sapphire come from a much commoner mineral, corundum. In its non-precious forms it is largely an ore of the metal aluminium and of the abrasive, emery. Gem material is only found in a very few places, mainly in Burma, Thailand and Ceylon. Most of the stones mined are quite unprepossessing – they do not even reach the stage of being cut as gems – but, as in biblical times, a fine ruby is still among the rarest and most valuable of ornaments.

Two of the greatest rarities have been discovered fairly recently. In 1945 an Irish gem dealer, Count Taaffe, came across a pale mauve stone which differed from the others in the parcel in one small particular, noticeable only to a trained gemmologist's observation. It turned out to be an entirely new mineral, previously unknown to science, and it now holds the distinction of being the only new mineral ever first discovered as a cut gemstone. In spite of extensive search only four other cut taaffeites have so far been reported – mainly small stones of unknown provenance. Chinese sources claim that the mineral has now been found in that country but none of it has yet been seen outside China.

Even rarer is painite, an attractive orange-red stone from Burma. So far it exists only as two uncut crystals on show at the British

Museum of Natural History in South Kensington, London. It was first described in 1957, having been found by Mr A. C. D. Pain who at that time managed the ruby mines near Mogok in Burma. In this case the locality is known precisely but the area is infested by bandits and little, if any, mining is now possible. More of this material may become available when exploration and mining is resumed.

Artificial restrictions have also made another attractive recent discovery somewhat rare. In 1967 the mineral zoisite, named after an Austrian geologist, Baron Zois von Edelstein (*Edelstein* means gemstone), was found in Tanzania in a hitherto unknown form. Instead of the usual opaque shapeless masses of green, pink or grey rock, it now appeared as transparent crystals of a most exquisite purplish-blue. Its other properties made it highly desirable as a gem and it was mined with vigour. More recently the Tanzanian Government put an embargo on exports and by 1971 the stones were very scarce indeed, so their price has risen rapidly.

2  New discoveries, however, can also affect the rarity value of a stone adversely. This has happened to fine amethyst. Until the eighteenth century this stone ranked among the most precious gems, the prerogative of kings and high dignitaries, particularly of the church. An amethyst necklace was among the most highly treasured possessions of Queen Elizabeth I. With the opening-up of the South American continent, large deposits of amethysts of superb quality were discovered in what is now Brazil and Uruguay. The stone became more and more common and its value fell so that it is no longer regarded as precious.

A word needs to be said at this point about the definition of a 'precious' stone. As has been illustrated, gemstones tend to move in and out of this category, largely according to the dictates of fashion and rarity. Their ranking within the precious group is also subject to vagaries, though in all cases only specimens of good quality can be truly precious. Some countries arbitrarily decree that certain kinds of

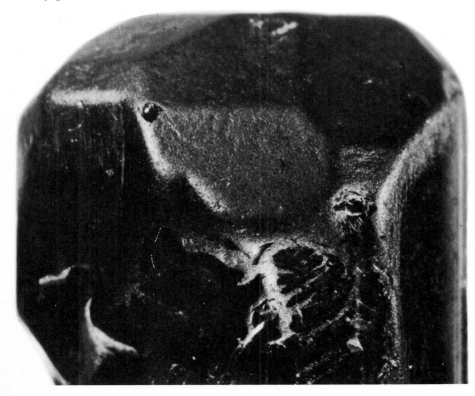

Painite—one of the only two crystals of this gem quality material so far recovered.

stone shall be regarded as precious—usually these include diamond, ruby, emerald, sapphire, opal and natural pearls. Special import or export duties are levied on these stones, irrespective of quality. Clearly, this is not a sensible procedure since a ruby of poor quality will fetch a much lower price per carat than a good quality stone of a semi-precious kind. It remains true, however, that the best quality stones of the types just mentioned will normally be sold for a higher figure than strictly equivalent stones from the semi-precious group.

The modern tendency is to disregard the somewhat arbitrary division into precious and semi-precious and to group all stones that are rare, beautiful, hard and capable of being cut and polished, as gemstones. Stones that are attractive but lack transparency and are rarely, if ever, faceted should be classed as 'ornamental stones'. No slur is necessarily implied by this classification; jade is an ornamental stone but translucent Imperial jade is extremely valuable.

Apart from rarity there are at least two other attributes that a gemstone must possess. Chief among these is beauty. This may be beauty of colour, often linked to transparency, as in ruby or emerald or it may be one of several delightful optical effects produced by some gemstones.

Most of us react emotionally to clear rich colours though we may find it impossible to say why we do so. It is certain that even in prehistoric times people were attracted by pretty pebbles and when these combined translucency or even transparency with colour, they were highly prized.

Its colour is a gemstone's most important and individual characteristic. Even now many dealers rely largely on their colour sense to identify stones although this is becoming an ever less reliable guide. Many new gems have been introduced from many new localities and the development of synthetic stones has been phenomenal. Although a person who relies on his colour sense alone to judge stones nowadays courts disaster, it still constitutes an essential first guide to identification. Some people have this colour sense developed to an uncanny degree; when this is combined with an appreciation of the lustre and brilliance of a stone, they seldom prove to be wrong, at least so far as the more popular stones are concerned.

The most desirable and valued colour for each variety of gemstone is discussed in the chapter dealing with individual gems. At this point it is sufficient to say merely that the colour should be rich—not so pale as to give the stone an anaemic appearance, nor so deep as to make it look dark or even black, particularly in artificial light. Too dark a colour reduces transparency and it is essential that a stone should retain a lively look with some sparkle. All this is achieved by skilful cutting and faceting.

In many stones the distribution of colour is uneven. When this results in clear-cut divisions, as in agates or in particoloured tourmalines, this is an effect that is much sought after. The blending of the various colours or tints of the same colour and the curious patterns and designs, produced as they are by nature, give such stones an individual appeal and make each one unique.

Rather less desirable is a certain patchiness of colour which gives the stone an indistinct, washed-out appearance. It occurs, for example, in some sapphires from Ceylon. The colour may be concentrated in a single spot or layer, the rest of the stone being almost colourless, or two colours may intermingle in an indefinite way. While some interesting patterns may thus be formed, such stones are not normally regarded with as much esteem as those where the colour is clear and even or where it falls into definite patterns. Skilful cutting can reduce the worst effects of uneven colouring.

There is another colour effect which is much sought after and which adds greatly to the value of the stones concerned. This is the change of colour observed when the stone is viewed in daylight and then in artificial light, particularly the light of a candle or a tungsten lamp. It occurs above all in alexandrite, a variety of chrysoberyl. These stones appear green in daylight and mauve or even red in artificial light. Some sapphires from Ceylon also show such a change from a purplish-blue by day to a magenta-red by night. So attractive is this phenomenon that artificial imitations of these stones have been made in vast numbers. Natural stones showing a colour change are very rare and it is wise to be wary of their imitations. These usually change from blue in daylight to a rather brash red in lamplight.

A more subtle effect is that shown by some stones in which two colours are always present (dichroism). When these colours are well developed and markedly different, the stone may show them either both together or alternatively, as it is moved from side to side. The effect can be very pleasing and intriguing in some alexandrites and andalusites, both of which are green with reddish reflexes, but in other stones there are merely two shades of the same colour – one light and one dark. Unless such a stone is orientated most carefully in its cutting, the chances are that the poorer colour may obtrude and spoil the general effect. This could happen particularly with tourmalines, corundums and iolites.

Even rough industrial diamonds (R.I. 2.42) stand out by their much higher lustre against most other minerals (here fluorite, R.I. 1.43).

Next to colour, lustre and sheen are the most prominent factors in affecting the appearance of a gemstone. A high lustre is indeed an essential attribute of a good stone – nobody wants a dull-looking gem. Lustre refers to the quality of the light reflected from the surface of a stone while sheen is the technical term that embraces a multitude of effects produced when light is reflected from within. Diamond, for instance, owes its pre-eminent position among gems to its incomparable lustre, brilliance and fire. Even in the rough state its surface lustre is rather more shiny than would be, say, a similar piece of glass. This, together with its extreme hardness, is what intrigued the ancients. Their hardness prevented diamonds from being cut adequately until the seventeenth century, so that their true fire and sparkle were not realized until then.

Most often stones have a lustre that is described as 'vitreous' or glassy. Some, like amber and hessonite garnet, are more appropriately credited with a 'resinous' lustre, while turquoise and some opals, for example, are described as 'waxy', but these terms are to a large extent subjective and cannot be measured with any exactness. Lustre is not, however, what gives a stone its *brilliance*. This is produced by the skilful cutting of the back facets of transparent stones in such a way that they reflect the incident light like mirrors, making the whole stone bright and shining when viewed from the top. In certain gemstones brilliance is linked with fire, where the reflected flashes of light are coloured by the dispersion of light. Fire and brilliance are outstanding attributes of diamonds and some of their recent imitations.

Various pleasant and curious effects are comprised together as the sheen of a stone. Pre-eminent among these is the play of colour shown so well by precious opal. This is also caused by the breaking-up of white light, but the physical causes and the resulting phenomena are somewhat different. Play of colour causes large patches or innumerable specks of vividly coloured light to be reflected from layers just beneath the surface of the opal. Other stones, notably labradorite and 'fire marble' also exhibit variants of the same effect. Play of colour is caused by the presence of minute globules within the stone. Sometimes crystalline layers are present which give rise to *schiller*, a subtle silvery or bluish sheen seen particularly well in some moonstones which are a variety of feldspar.

Other forms of sheen which greatly enhance the value of gemstones are the *cat's-eye* and *star* effects. These are produced in stones cut as cabochons (that is, with a rounded top) by fine fibrous crystals or channels within the stone. These inclusions give the stone a moving line of light across its centre (cat's-eye) or, when two or more such lines intersect in the middle, the appearance of a four-, six- or even twelve-rayed star.

These are the main characteristics which give gemstones their unique appearance and which distinguish them from the great mass of other minerals. There is, however, yet another attribute which gemstones should possess and which by no means all other minerals can claim: permanence.

Gemstones and the jewels in which they are set are treasured possessions intended to last a lifetime or even longer. Some jewels surviving to the present day have a history which can be traced back over hundreds and even thousands of years. Even this may represent only a minute fraction of the time during which the stones set in them have existed; in constant daily wear they are exposed to much greater risks than when they were safely embedded in their original rocks. They

must therefore be able to stand up to the knocks, abrasion and (possibly quite unintentional) ill-treatment they receive.

The most desirable quality under this heading is resistance to abrasion. Exposure to abrasion depends largely on the kind of setting in which a stone is used and on the frequency with which it is worn. Stones set in rings are particularly prone to damage and should therefore be chosen from the hardest and toughest gems. This is what makes diamonds the ideal choice for an engagement ring which rarely leaves the wearer's finger. Next to them come rubies, sapphires and chryso-beryls, all of which have very respectable degrees of hardness.

Some stones, although hard, are also somewhat brittle or they may be liable to cleave or fracture relatively easily. Set in a ring, a zircon will soon lose its sharp edges and opal (which is in any case a softish stone) will have its brilliant colours dimmed. This can be remedied by having the stones repolished. This is not a costly or difficult operation but it is better to avoid the problem by wearing the softer stones and those liable to fracture elsewhere than in a ring. Less damage is likely to come to them in brooches, earrings and necklaces while bracelets occupy an intermediate position. To prevent abrasion it is also very much recommended not to let pieces of jewellery rattle in a drawer where they can rub against each other. Stones that are liable to break easily at a sharp blow or on impact with a hard object include emerald, opal and topaz.

As will be explained in chapter three, a rough-and-ready scale divides all minerals into ten degrees of hardness. Most gemstones are well in

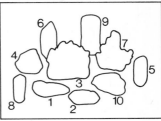

Minerals comprising Mohs' Scale
1 talc
2 gypsum
3 calcite
4 fluorspar
5 apatite
6 orthoclase
7 quartz
8 topaz
9 corundum
10 diamond

the upper half of this scale but not even diamond, at the top of the scale, should be exposed to any kind of abrasive ill-treatment. There used to be a misconception to the effect that 'real' gemstones would withstanding shattering, even when struck with a hammer; needless to say, even a diamond can be crushed with no great effort. Yet many a good and precious stone has fallen a victim to this 'test'.

Another misconception is that only diamond will scratch glass. Almost any self-respecting gemstone is able to do this, though a diamond does it with consummate ease.

There are several minerals of a pleasing colour and good transparency which cannot be used as gems because they are too soft or too liable to deteriorate from some other cause. Vivianite, for example, is a beautiful green mineral, but it is both soft and liable to cleavage, and on exposure to light and air gradually oxidizes to an opaque grey form. Ulexite can be cut to show a clear cat's-eye on a white or pale grey ground, but it is much too soft to wear. In spite of this, collectors sometimes have stones cut from soft minerals, including calcite, dolomite, barite and many others. Provided such stones are kept in a soft packing and are not worn, there is no reason why they should not be cut, especially if no beautiful crystal has been destroyed in the process. Soft stones are difficult to cut and even more difficult to polish. They are therefore often regarded as a challenge by lapidaries.

Fire is another hazard for stones. All will be irretrievably damaged by it, including diamond which, being pure carbon, will burn above a temperature of 800°C in air. Most other stones will crack and turn black.

Chemical damage by acids in the air or in the wearer's skin can be caused to stones such as turquoise (which for this reason is often covered with a protective layer of wax) and particularly to pearls.

To sum up, it is clear that if a stone is to be counted as a gem, it must possess three essential attributes: it must appeal by its colour, lustre or sheen, it must not be of common occurrence and it must be sufficiently hard and tough to withstand wear over long periods. Some of these attributes are uncommon in the mineral kingdom; taken together they distinguish gemstones from all other minerals and place them among the rarest and most precious products of nature.

# The Origin of Gemstones

Gemstones, apart from the properties peculiar to them outlined in chapter one, are just like other minerals. They are created in the same manner and occur within the common rocks that form the crust of the earth. They are formed by physical and chemical processes which have been active on earth for thousands of millions (billions USA) of years and which continue to operate to the present day. The effects of these processes are in most cases imperceptible: millions of years are required for mountain chains to be levelled. Elsewhere geological processes operate with catastrophic suddenness and violence, as in earthquakes and volcanic eruptions. The earth's crust, apparently so solid and changeless, is in fact undergoing perpetual change under the influence of unimaginably powerful internal stresses and strains, and of erosion by water, wind and weather. These influences transform the crust, altering its structure, breaking down old rocks and changing them into new ones. It is still not known how and when the process started. It seems likely that a solid crust, possibly formed from the molten state, first covered the earth some 3 000–4 000 million years ago. Methods have recently been devised to measure the age of rocks. Some rocks in central Canada are among the oldest so far discovered; it is believed that they were formed well over 3 000 million years ago.

These particular rocks contain no gemstones, but is is probable that most of the gems in use today were formed many millions of years ago; some may be hundreds or even thousands of millions of years old, which ought to satisfy the ambitions of even the most demanding collector of antiques. A precise age can rarely be assigned to a particular gemstone, partly because it may have been carried over considerable distances and into entirely new environments several times in the course of the transformations of the earth's crust. It is possible to estimate the period at which most rocks were formed but not always that at which some of the minerals composing these rocks originated.

Geologists make an important distinction between rocks and minerals. Rocks are the solid materials of which the earth's crust is composed. They are mainly hard and strong and extend both over the dry land surface and under the sea, but soft clay is also a rock and the mud and gravel in a river estuary are rock in the making. Even superficial inspection shows that rocks are made up of innumerable particles which may vary in size from the microscopically small to units measured in yards and weighing tons; minerals are these particles. A rock may consist wholly of a single kind of mineral; for example, there are entire mountains of marble, labradorite and other ornamental stones. Much' more often, however, rocks are composed of mixtures of several kinds of minerals, easily distinguishable from each other.

Each kind of mineral has its own peculiar and consistent structure and composition by means of which minerals have been classified into mineral species. The physical, chemical and crystallographic properties of each mineral species can be measured and described accurately; they usually vary only within narrow limits. Occasionally two or more closely related species may merge into each other by degrees, entailing a gradual transition in properties; or an admixture of impurities may lead to variations in colour and transparency as happens, for instance, in many gem species.

Well over 2 000 different mineral species have been discovered so far and further species, previously unknown, are constantly being added. Even so the field of mineralogy is in this respect much narrower than that of other natural sciences which may number their species in hundreds of thousands. With few exceptions, gemstones are minerals and are therefore also classified into species. Unless released by weathering, they are tightly held within rocks – rather like raisins or candied peel in a fruit pudding – surrounded by minerals of other, non-gem, species.

The association of specific mineral species with each other is not, however, a matter of chance. An environment that favours the development of one species also favours that of its associates, at the same time inhibiting the emergence of other species that tend to form under different conditions. This tendency of minerals to occur in limited associations implies that it is possible to classify rocks according to the mineral species composing them. This is the province of petrology, the study of rocks, and is not relevant here, though a few ornamental materials, such as certain jades and lapis lazuli, are composed of several minerals and are therefore more properly regarded as rocks. As every prospector knows, gems must be looked for in certain environments only and in association with a well-defined range of other minerals, that is, in rocks or deposits of a specific type.

An important characteristic of most minerals, and hence of most gems, is that they occur as *crystals*. On cooling from the molten state or from hot solutions they form shapes which are unique to each mineral species and are one of the most useful means of identification. It may not be obvious that every piece of jade, turquoise, agate or even every flint pebble, is crystalline, for the crystals composing such stones are microscopically small. Nevertheless, the crystalline state is by far the most common among minerals and the few non-crystalline materials, such as opal and obsidian, among gemstones, merely solidified too rapidly to crystallize.

Some gem materials have not, however, been produced by the forces of inorganic (non-living) nature in the earth's crust and cannot therefore be counted as minerals. They are the products of living animals

Igneous rock (granite); the white crystals are feldspar, the black, mica and the grey, quartz.

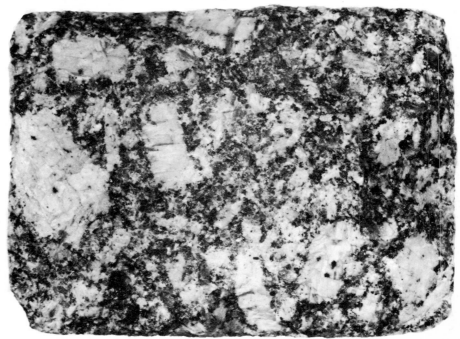

or plants, unaltered by geological processes; for this reason most of them are also quite recent. Chief of these, from the point of view of value and importance as gems, are pearls and allied materials such as mother-of-pearl and operculum, which are formed by various salt-water and freshwater molluscs. Similarly, coral consists of lime deposited by marine polyps. Ivory and tortoiseshell are also animal products. Amber and jet are less easy to classify, for though they were produced by trees, they have been buried in the earth for millions of years and have thereby undergone some structural changes. In addition, they are mined like minerals, and it is therefore usual to count them as such.

Another group of products which are certainly not minerals, though they may be composed of matter of mineral origin, are the man-made gem imitations, usually of glass, and the synthetic gemstones. True synthetics have almost the same composition and structure as their natural counterparts but nature has had no part in their formation. They are very recent in origin and have never been mined. They are made in factories by methods which are described in chapter three.

The formation and deposition of gemstones – and, of course, other minerals as well – are the result of natural processes. In geology it is usual to classify rocks into three broad groups: igneous, sedimentary and metamorphic.

**Igneous** rocks are those that have solidified from a molten state or from the residual very hot solutions. Their name is derived from the Latin word for fire, *ignis*, though most of the processes covered take place at temperatures both above and below those of, say, a coal fire.

**Sedimentary** rocks are formed by the deposition of rocky material broken up by erosion, solution and similar processes.

**Metamorphic** (altered in shape) rocks are those changed more or less profoundly by the influence of high pressure and/or temperature.

This classification, however, refers to the formation of rocks rather than to the origin of minerals. Few gem species owe their origin to sedimentary action, though very many are found and mined from sedimentary deposits into which they were carried after being eroded from their original environment.

Sedimentary rock (sandstone), illustrating its composition of compacted sand grains.

Metamorphic rock (gneiss), illustrating the banded, light and dark structure typical of this type of rock.

The time scale over which these processes have operated is inconceivably long. Mountain chains have been built up and then worn down by wind, ice and water to flat plains; the material of which they were composed has been carried away into the oceans. The tilting, raising and submerging of land has led to a succession of dry land and water over the same areas. Whole continents have moved across the surface of the earth like icebergs on the sea at speeds of a few centimetres a year. They have broken apart and joined up again in new places several times over. H. G. Wells uses a telling illustration of the geological time scale: if the history of the formation of the earth's surface were recorded in a book, twice the length of this present one and keeping the narrative strictly in proportion to the time taken, then the whole of recorded human history from ancient Egypt, Sumer or China to the present day would barely be represented by the final full stop at the end of such a book! During all this time the igneous, sedimentary and metamorphic processes have operated unceasingly, making and remaking rocks and minerals.

Igneous rocks, as already described, are formed from a molten state. At varying distances below the surface of the earth, and in areas where the crust is under stress, for example, through the impact of the continents against each other, rock material occurs in a molten and highly viscous state. This is the magma. It contains some solids with a high melting point (those that only melt at high temperatures) and among these may be some gemstones such as olivine and spinel. The magma also contains liquids and gases at a high temperature and pressure.

Where the earth's crust cracks under the strain, the magma penetrates the overlying rocks or forces its way out through weak places. There it cools and solidifies, forming rocks that now infiltrate into those above and around them. In this process minerals with a high melting point crystallize out first, leaving the remainder of the magma rich in fluxes and gases from which further minerals form as pressure and temperature fall further.

The consolidation of this more liquid phase forms the so-called

16

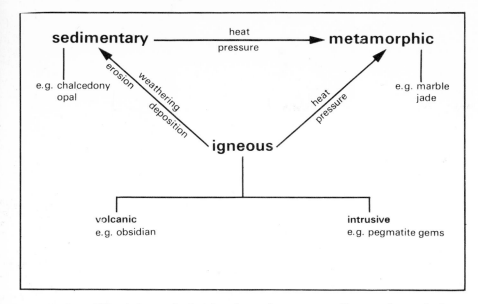

All rocks and minerals ultimately derive from the solidification of liquid, igneous material. Some of this was subsequently transformed into sedimentary and metamorphic rocks.

pegmatites. These intrude further into the surrounding rocks and since they tend to be very hard they often remain exposed after the rocks which they have penetrated have been weathered away. They are sometimes rich in well-crystallized gemstones and are indeed one of their richest original sources. The gaseous components of the magma consolidate in the pneumatolytic phase (mainly temperatures around 400–600°C) leaving the last residues of the magma dissolved in water which may still be at a very high pressure and at temperatures ranging from 100–450°C. These watery solutions are the last to yield up their mineral content in the hydrothermal stage of consolidation. All these stages overlap, each predominating at its appropriate temperature and pressure.

While the same gem species may be produced at different stages, certain species tend to be formed at one stage rather than at another. The type of gems produced in any igneous rock depends largely on the constituents present in the original magma.

The intrusion of the magma may not reach the surface and the rocks formed may only be revealed much later by erosion or upheavals of the crust. Rocks which have consolidated at depths below the surface are called plutonic or intrusive, as distinct from the volcanic or extrusive rocks which have reached the surface and emerged, as lava flows, for example.

The release of temperature and pressure is slow and gradual in intrusive rocks since they are blanketed by the pre-existent rocks surrounding and overlaying them. Their minerals crystallize slowly and have time to grow to appreciable sizes. By contrast, the temperature and pressure of extrusive rocks fall suddenly and markedly on extrusion, so that only small crystals, and sometimes even non-crystalline, glassy materials are formed. According to the temperature/pressure gradient, the same kind of gemstone may therefore occur in all sizes, from the very large to the ultramicroscopic.

Minerals with a high melting point crystallize out first and have a chance to grow to a larger size than those which melt at a lower temperature. For this reason many gemstones occur as larger crystals (phenocrysts) embedded in a groundmass of rock of a much finer texture. The same process also leads to their frequent appearance in undistorted, regular shapes, 'euhedral' crystals, since they were able to grow freely in all directions without interference from adjacent crystals. Where

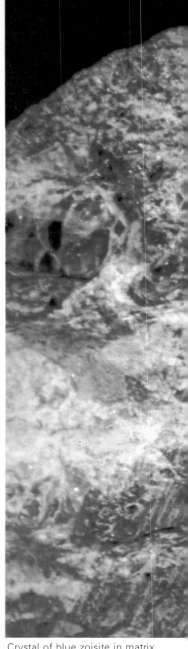

*Top* Alexandrite lit by a
tungsten lamp.

*Above* Alexandrite in daylight.

Crystal of blue zoisite in matrix,
with two faceted stones.

19

Some well-formed (euhedral)
gem crystals of
1  albite
2  corundum
3  beryl
4  tourmaline
5  fluorite
6  topaz
7  vesuvianite
8  garnet
Badly formed (anhedral) crystals
of topaz and garnet are also
shown.

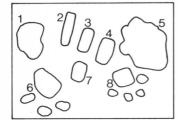

such interference does take place, oddly shaped 'anhedral' crystals
result. Since small crystals form a friable mass and can normally be
separated from each other more readily than large crystals can be ground
down, and since resistance to abrasion is one of the essential characteristics of gemstones anyway, they tend to survive subsequent erosion
intact while the fine groundmass of rock enveloping them is weathered
away.

The gases present in the magma expand as pressure is released, sometimes forming oblong bubbles and cavities of all sizes. These cavities
may subsequently be lined or filled entirely by other consolidated
minerals, so forming almond-shaped bodies called amygdales. Agates
and other forms of quartz are typically found in this form. Where the
centre of the cavity remains empty, usually with the tips of crystals
protruding into it, the formation is called a druse or geode. Geodes
are sometimes lined with amethyst. Both geodes and amygdales may
weather out to lie as loose pebbles or boulders on the surface, quite
inconspicuous in appearance. Only when they are sliced or broken open
is their beauty revealed.

Unless they are laid bare by erosion, access to the deeper plutonic
gem-bearing rocks is only possible by mining, the profitability of
which depends entirely on the density and the quality of gems present.
Frequently, however, pegmatites have been exposed by erosion, forming
wall-like structures called dykes where they formerly penetrated vertical
fissures in rocks which have since weathered away. Where intrusive
rocks forced their way between more or less horizontal layers of rocks,
they now appear as sills. Both may show up over considerable distances
and the extraction of gems from such structures at and near the surface,
is, of course, much easier and cheaper.

The diamond-bearing igneous pipes which are so important in South
Africa are somewhat similar features – intrusions of roughly circular
outline reaching from the surface to unknown depths. At some stage
carbon must have become trapped within the minerals filling these pipes.
Under the enormous pressure and temperature created as the intrusion
worked its way upwards, the carbon crystallized out as diamonds. The
pipes were probably capped with volcanic mounds originally but these

Successive layers of minute, differently coloured crystals of silica have been deposited in a cavity, nearly filling it. At the centre some larger crystals have been able to form.

had weathered away by the time the pipes were discovered, leaving a flat surface. By this process the constituent minerals, including the diamonds, were distributed over a wide area around. This kind of distribution is typical of the process which ultimately leads to the formation of the next main class of rocks: sedimentary rocks.

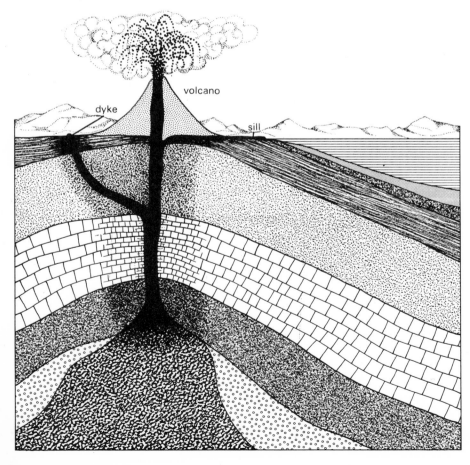

Igneous magma has broken through layers of sedimentary rocks, forming a volcano and intrusive dykes and sills. The heat and pressure of the intrusion has metamorphosed the adjacent rocks.

21

*Right* Two facets of the same cube of cordierite, a strongly dichroic gem.

*Below* The strong dispersion or 'fire' of synthetic strontium titanate, lithium niobate and rutile (bottom row) is here contrasted with the weak dispersion of rock crystal, scapolite and fluorite (top row).

*Far right* The star stones and cat's-eyes of Burma: pink, yellow and purple scapolite cat's-eyes, white and blue moonstones, ruby and sapphire stars, brown star diopside, pink star rose quartz, green star enstatite, blue apatite and tourmaline cat's-eyes.

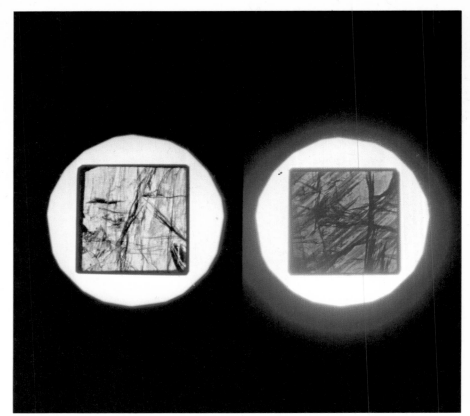

*Right* A dyke of intrusive igneous rock.

*Far right* Stalactites and stalagmites formed by the deposition of lime from water in the Campanet Caves, Spain.

All rocks, whatever their origin, are constantly being worn down. Rain, river currents and sea waves cut into them; frost splits them and glaciers gouge them out; wind abrades them with the particles it carries; the biosphere of living matter above them produces chemicals by which they are dissolved or altered. The broken-down particles are then carried away by gravity, wind, water and ice, to be deposited in rivers, valleys, estuaries, the sea and other new environments.

Often the distribution is in the form of liquid solutions that percolate into cracks or porous rocks where the dissolved matter may be left behind, as it is, for example, in stalagmite caves, which are full of grotesque limestone columns formed by endless drips of water carrying lime in solution. Or sea water, rich in salts, may dry out and leave behind its salts in layers that are ultimately mined, as rock salt, for instance.

Finally, the shells of molluscs, the coral formed by certain marine

*Below* Amber, ruby, ivory, fluorite and opal, in daylight.

*Below right* The same, displaying their fluorescence in ultraviolet light.

*Right* On entering a highly dispersive gemstone, white light is broken up into its constituent colours. These are totally reflected within the stone in such a way that they emerge through the crown as a 'rainbow', giving the stone its 'fire'.

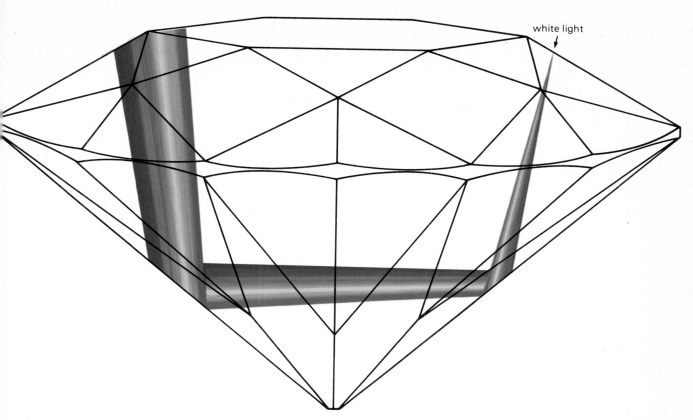

white light

polyps, and the skeletons of great masses of microscopic animals may, in the course of geological epochs, accumulate to form limestone layers hundreds of feet thick. Other sedimentary rocks formed by the action of living plants are the coal measures or beds and, among gem materials, the jet and amber deposits already mentioned.

As sedimentary rock layers gradually build up, their enormous weight compacts them and binds together the mineral particles of which they are composed, forming solid rock from what was previously an agglomerate of loose grains. The deeper the rocks are buried, the greater the pressure on them and the more solid they become.

Another means by which sedimentary rocks are composed is by cementation. Watery solutions containing lime, silica and other minerals in solution percolate through the loose rock particles. The lime and other substances gradually coat them all over and finally cement them together. In both these ways sand carried down by rivers is compacted into sandstone and the crushed shells of marine animals into limestone or chalk. Gem material is sometimes trapped in these compacted layers.

If the original rocks, now weathered away, contained gemstones, these are likely to survive more or less intact because of their superior hardness. They are carried away with the other material and may become embedded or cemented into an entirely new environment, a process which may be repeated several times.

The washing away of the softer debris often leads to a concentration of the gemstones which may be aided by their higher density. The heavier material, including the gemstones, remains in pockets or hollows in the river beds, so-called 'placer' deposits, while the lighter, valueless material is carried away. River and beach gravels in which gems have become concentrated in this manner are by far the most prolific and important source of gems. It is estimated that at least half of the world's gem production is now derived from such sources.

Gem-bearing gravels are sedimentary deposits – rocks in the making. Sometimes such deposits can be scraped together from the beds and banks of existing rivers and brooks; frequently, however, the water course has disappeared or taken another direction, leaving the gem gravel behind under a cover of silt or clay. In either case the extraction of the gemstones is relatively simple and can often be carried out by primitive methods, such as picking them by hand from gravel that may or may not have been concentrated first by swirling it in a pan of water.

Water, under heat and pressure, will dissolve many minerals or leach out some of the chemicals contained in them. Even at normal pressure and temperature water always contains traces of the minerals with which it has been in contact, as is only too obvious in areas where the water is 'hard'. The furring of domestic water pipes and kettles illustrates one method of sedimentary formation which is paralleled in nature. Occasionally the deposition of chemicals from solution results in the creation of gemstones and ornamental stones.

The gemstones most commonly formed in this way are many varieties of the silica gem family – the agates, chalcedonies and notably also opal. Water percolating through sandstone absorbs minute quantities of silica, the material composing sand and sandstone. The higher the temperature of the water, the more readily will it dissolve silica and other minerals. This silica is then deposited at lower levels or in adjacent cavities at lower temperatures. In the course of time it forms ever-thickening crusts, ultimately filling veins and cavities in the rock. Depending on environmental conditions, the silica usually crystallizes out in the form of microscopic or larger crystals (chalcedony or quartz); if conditions do not favour crystallization, opal may be deposited. Pure silica forms white or greyish deposits but if other mineral matter is also present a wide range of colours can result.

Solutions can carry materials other than silica. Alumina and copper in solution from volcanic rocks may lead to the formation of turquoise, malachite or azurite; iron may form marcasite.

All the gemstones mentioned can also arise at the hydrothermal stage of the deposition of igneous rocks; in fact the line of demarcation between these two processes is rather blurred.

Metamorphic rocks and the minerals comprising them can be changed by stresses other than the compacting of sedimentary rocks. These other stresses arise largely from movements of parts of the earth's crust relative to each other or from the intrusion of igneous rock masses. The extensive changes in pressure and temperature accompanying these events may transform the pre-existing rocks either slightly in shape only (low-rank metamorphism – limestone changed to marble, for example) or they may lead to the creation of quite different minerals, including many gem species (high-rank metamorphism). Metamorphic changes may be purely local, confined to an area where intrusive igneous rocks and the gases carried in them have been in contact with existing rocks (contact metamorphism); part of the crust may have slipped down or sideways producing colossal friction and heat (dynamic metamorphism); stresses may have altered rocks over a very wide area, for example, when rocks are folded and mountains built through the collision of continental plates (regional metamorphism).

Some minerals, including quartz, remain largely unaffected by these upheavals while others are reconstituted and re-crystallized. Even some forms of quartz may be changed, however, and produce ornamental amethystine quartz, for instance, if conditions are favourable. Other gemstones formed by metamorphism include various garnets, jade and lapis lazuli. As in igneous rocks, heat and pressure may also cause the production of the same gems as a result of metamorphic processes.

While the stones are still in their original environment it is possible to tell how they were formed. With sedimentary deposits it may be more difficult to trace the gems back to their origin, though this can often be inferred with some assurance. Once gemstones have been mined and their original location has been lost it is no longer easily possible to distinguish an igneous spinel, for example, from a metamorphic one.

An attempt is made in the list below to set out the more usual mode of formation of the main gemstones mentioned in chapter four. It will be seen that some occur under two of the headings; this means that both modes of formation are common. No clear distinction can be made between the different stages of igneous formation since gems may be formed at more than one stage. They have therefore been listed roughly in order of descending temperature of formation.

## IGNEOUS
*High temperature :* olivine, pyrope garnet, zircon, spinel, diamond (by eruptive action); *Pegmatitic :* chrysoberyl, quartz, spessartine garnet, apatite, corundum, beryl, feldspar; *Pneumatolytic :* tourmaline, topaz, euclase; *Hydrothermal :* chalcedony, pyrite, marcasite, opal.

## SEDIMENTARY
chalcedony, turquoise, malachite, azurite, opal, jet (fossil wood), amber (fossil resin).

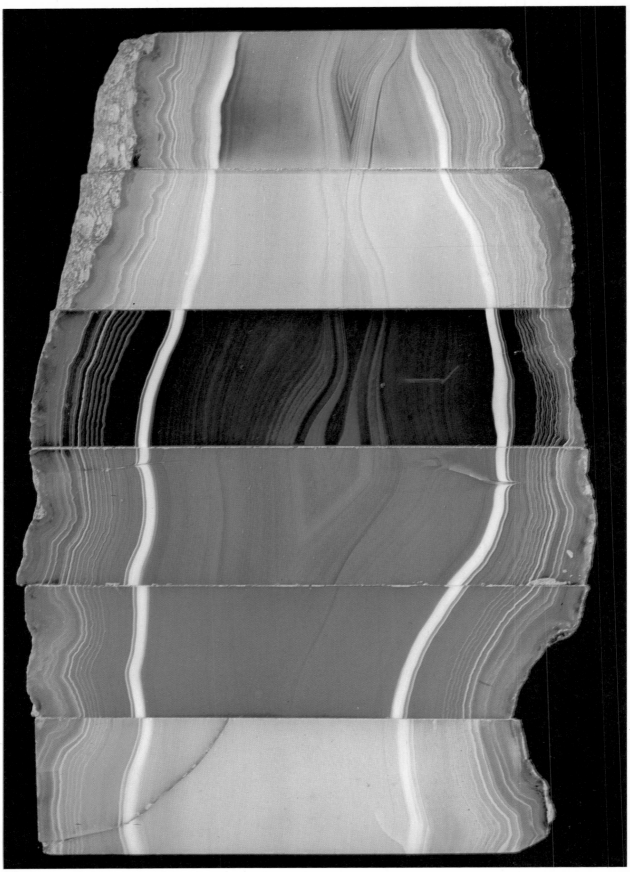

*Left* A banded agate showing its
natural colour and some tints
produced by staining.

*Top* A natural black diamond and
two diamonds coloured by
irradiation in an atomic pile.

*Above* Various imitation gems
made of glass or plastic.

## METAMORPHIC

olivine, grossular, almandine and andradite garnets, corundum, beryl, spinel, andalusite, kyanite, sillimanite, cordierite, epidote, nephrite, jadeite, lapis lazuli.

It should be borne in mind that this classification relates to the method by which the gems named were originally formed and not necessarily to the environment from which they are now recovered. Most of the minerals named can be found in the alluvium (the mud and gravel) recently deposited by rivers, but none were ever formed in it. The rivers merely brought them from another, rarely far distant, environment.

It is of course the present environment and not the original mode of formation that matters from the practical point of view of winning or recovering the gems. From the commercial aspect, great importance is attached to the ease with which a maximum of good quality gemstones can be won. The richest sources are at present in countries where the yield per ton of material mined is high, the gems occur in accessible places, labour is cheap and plentiful, economic stability and security is adequate, and a recognized marketing procedure for the gems mined has developed.

Gem sites of one kind or another have a fairly wide distribution over the face of the earth but, in consideration of the factors just mentioned, relatively few localities have won fame and importance for the quality of gems they produce. For instance, cornelians and jaspers of fair quality can be picked up on many beaches but it is not worth exploiting them commercially except where they are both abundant and exceptionally fine. Even with rare stones there may be prohibitive obstacles to commercial production. Many formerly productive sites have now become exhausted, which means that though gems can still be found in the area a great deal of labour would now yield only a small return. A list of all localities at which gems are known to exist would be very long indeed, but most of them are of scientific interest only.

On the other hand, there are several areas scattered over the world which have produced a rich harvest of gemstones. Occasionally they yield only one kind of gem but from what has been said earlier in this chapter it will be clear that conditions which favour the formation of one gem species often also favour the formation of others. Pegmatites may contain several gem species and these may be collected and concentrated in nearby gravels. In listing the main commercially productive localities of different gemstones, the same names tend to occur again and again.

The oldest, and still very productive, gem localities lie in the Orient, mainly in southern Asia. To this day the prefix 'oriental' is applied to several gemstones – sometimes quite misleadingly – and the lustre of pearls is known as their 'orient'. In the past India was the classical source of gems. Though a big producer herself, she has also drawn on neighbouring countries and acted as a market for gems from other parts of Asia. Famous are the diamonds of Golconda, the sapphires of Kashmir, the emeralds of Ajmer and Udaipur as well as the garnets, moonstones and agates from other sites in India. Indian sapphires and emeralds are pegmatitic in origin and garnets metamorphic.

An even wider and more prolific output of gemstones is derived from the neighbouring island of Ceylon, the 'Serendipe' of Haroun al Rashid's Arab sailors. Ratnapura, the 'City of Jewels', is the centre of an area from which comes an amazing variety of gems – practically every well-known stone occurs, with the exception of diamond and good-quality emerald. It is the only known source of the rare gem ekanite, first described as recently as 1954, and it produces several other rarities as well. Gems have come from Ceylon for well over 2 000 years. They originated in pegmatites but have now been concentrated in river gravels.

Slightly less prominent in quantity, but on the whole superior in quality, are the gems from Burma. It produces the choicest rubies from metamorphic deposits and is the main source of the more precious jade species, jadeite, and of a great variety of other gems mainly of pegmatitic origin, but now found in gravels. Neighbouring Thailand (Siam) shares some of its fame for rubies and sapphires though the Thai rubies have a more yellowish tint. They come from volcanic rocks.

Other Asian and Far Eastern sources that are of importance include the pearls of the Persian Gulf, the Afghan deposits of lapis lazuli, Iranian (Persian) turquoise, and the important new diamond finds of Siberia in addition to the older and much smaller diamond deposits of Borneo and Australia.

Australia is most famous for its superb opals and for sapphires of less prominent quality. Exploration is revealing further gem deposits and the north coast has an important pearl fishing industry. So has Japan, but here the pearls are mainly cultured. New Zealand has its 'greenstone'—nephrite jade of a rich colour. Such jade comes, too, from the vicinity of Lake Baikal in Siberia where other gem species are also found. All jades are formed by metamorphism.

Africa, too, has long and historic associations with gemstones. Emerald, turquoise, and peridot have been mined to the east of the Nile Valley for 4 000 years or more, but the emerald mines, in particular, are now exhausted. Today Africa's main importance rests on the fact that it is the largest producer of diamonds and gold. These are of special importance in South and South-West Africa, but many diamonds also come from the Congo, Ghana, Sierra Leone and Tanzania. In the latter country there have recently been several discoveries of other gemstones, including rubies and sapphires of metamorphic origin, which should guarantee Tanzania a prominent place among the gem countries of the world in the future; at present Tanzania is the only producer of gem-quality blue zoisite. Important finds have also been made in Rhodesia, particularly of emeralds in pegmatites.

Another area of great importance in the gem world is Malagasy (Madagascar). It produces garnets, pegmatite and quartz gems of fine quality together with a wide range of rarer stones, gem hambergite and rhodizite being amongst the rarest of these.

Although the gem production of Europe is not of great importance, it should be mentioned to complete the picture of the Old World. Perhaps its outstanding gem material is the amber from the southern coasts of the Baltic. This has been mined and traded for thousands of years all over the world. Very old opal mines still exist in eastern Czechoslovakia and Bohemian garnets were extensively used in the nineteenth century. Mention must also be made of the agates from the Palatinate of Western Germany and of jet from Whitby in Yorkshire, which are reputed to have been worked in Roman times. The mining and working of jade from Silesia and southern France may go back even earlier, but supplies are now exhausted.

Some exciting gems come from the Ural Mountains, the border between Europe and Asia; they mostly occur in pegmatites. This area is the original home of alexandrite, but topaz, aquamarine, emerald, malachite, zircon, and diamonds are also recovered from this region.

In the New World, South America, and Brazil in particular, claims pride of place. A vast range of gemstones originates there, from diamonds through all the rarer pegmatite minerals to a great variety of quartz gems. Brazil is the home of tourmaline and topaz, aquamarine, chrysoberyl, garnet, and fine amethyst, which also occurs in Uruguay. The recently discovered and unusual brazilianite has been named after that country – its main, if not only, source of supply. South American gems occur partly in pegmatites or their detritus and partly in decomposed volcanic rocks.

Colombia is famous as the producer of the world's finest emeralds. They occur in veins and have been mined for centuries, even before the arrival of the Spaniards. Central Chile has some lapis lazuli of mediocre quality.

In Central America the opal of Mexico is noteworthy and also perhaps the jadeite which was prized more highly than gold by the Incas.

In spite of thorough exploration, the gem wealth of North America is not comparable with that of its sister continent. Many finds have been made but few localities are of more than minor importance. Pegmatites produce interesting gems in the San Diego district of California and in Maine and Connecticut. New Mexico has the oldest mine in North America – one for turquoise, worked by Indians long before the advent of Europeans. Montana has some sapphires; quartz and agates, as well as petrified wood, are found in several localities.

In this chapter the origins of gemstones have been considered briefly from three aspects: the manner in which they have been formed, the geological environment in which they are found and the main localities that produce them. An uncut gemstone in its matrix (the mother rock in which it occurs) can often be traced back to its origin by a knowledgeable mineralogist. With gem gravel and with cut and polished stones the origin can still be inferred in many cases. Some stones have a peculiar hue or a characteristic distribution of colour. Most carry at least a trace of their associated minerals within them in the form of microscopic inclusions. These have been studied extensively in recent years and some give reliable clues as to the origin of the stone. Further means of determining the genesis and origins of gems may come from analytical methods now being evolved which use X-rays and other radiations. At present these may be laborious and involve costly apparatus. In the East it is common to require a 'pedigree' from the seller of an important stone, specifying its history from the point at which it was found. In the West there appears to be little interest in origins and even historic stones are not always well documented.

# The Structure of Gemstones and their Imitations

Before setting out on a description of individual gemstone species in the next chapter, it is necessary to be clear about the meaning of the terms used in defining the intriguing and characteristic properties that gems possess. Without going fully into the details that a study of gemmology would involve, it is helpful to have some familiarity with its concepts and definitions, with the methods used in classifying, identifying and describing gemstones unambiguously and in distinguishing them from one another and from their imitations.

For example, most gemstones, as already noted, are crystalline, but what is a crystal? The word conjures up a vision of a sparkling, limpid object, hard, pure and angular. Transparency also seems to be important, for we speak of making things 'crystal clear'. Most gemstones are like this, but to a mineralogist none of these attributes is fundamental. A crystal can be dull and opaque; it need not be particularly hard; it may contain many impurities and even flat angular surfaces are not a necessity. The one essential requisite that distinguishes a crystal from a non-crystalline, amorphous solid such as glass, is that the atoms of which it is composed should be arranged in a regular, symmetrical, three-dimensional pattern or *lattice* throughout the crystal. Amorphous bodies, by contrast, have an irregular internal structure. To use a very crude analogy, a crystal is like a stack of bricks built in an orderly manner, leaving no gaps. The same number of oblong, square or lozenge-shaped building blocks would form stacks of different shapes and different stability each bounded by flat surfaces meeting at well-defined angles if completed. An amorphous body could then be likened to the same bricks tipped out haphazardly into separate piles. Such tips would have no shape, there would be gaps between the bricks, and whatever the shape of individual bricks, all heaps would look much the same; they would mould themselves to whatever shape their environment prescribed.

In some crystalline materials the crystals are so small that they can only be seen through a microscope. Each of these tiny crystals, however, still has its appropriate shape and contains many millions of atoms in orderly array. Such materials – agate, turquoise and jade, for example – are called micro-crystalline or cypto-crystalline.

An important effect of this regular arrangement of atoms is that crystals are thereby endowed with properties which are constant for each mineral species but which can vary within defined limits according to direction. For example, each gem species has its own degree of hardness, but it may be easier to scratch a crystal lengthwise than across; some crystals will cleave, showing flat surfaces, but they will do this in certain directions only; light will pass through a gem crystal at a speed peculiar to that species, but this speed may vary according to the direction in which the light travels. No such directional properties can ever be found in glass.

These distinctions are most important, for glass has long been used to imitate gems and the methods used to differentiate between glass and crystals with absolute certainty depend on them. Shape alone is the least useful guide, for glass does not become a crystal by being cut and polished to a crystalline shape, nor does a gem become any less crystalline by having its crystal faces polished away to form a dome-topped cabochon. It still retains its regular atomic structure and the characteristic properties peculiar to it. These properties can be measured, and provide important criteria for identification.

Directional forces also influence the growth and form of crystals. The electrical bonds which bind atoms together operate in such a way that crystal growth proceeds in certain preferred directions only, resulting in crystal shapes that are peculiar to each mineral species. These shapes are the outward manifestation of the regular internal pattern of atoms in a crystal. Such patterns can be seen to be built up of groups of atoms, the so-called unit cells, just like the pattern of a wall-paper is made up of ever-repeating units containing different elements, only the unit cells are much smaller, millions being required to measure a millimetre. Although the size and shape of these unit cells varies from one mineral species to another, there are only thirty-two different ways in which the cells can be linked together. Crystals can therefore be grouped into thirty-two classes which can in turn be more broadly assigned to seven crystal systems in accordance with certain similarities

The crystal systems.
Simplified forms indicating the axes of reference are shown together with some actual crystal forms.

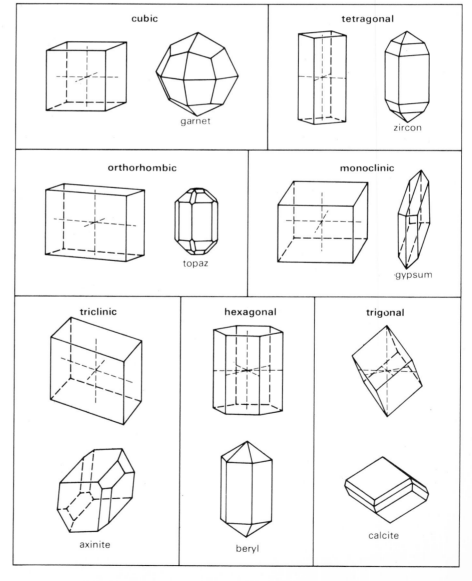

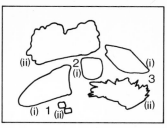

Some polymorphs, which are minerals of the same chemical composition but different crystal structure:
1  (i) graphite and (ii) diamond, both pure carbon;
2  (i) pyrite and (ii) marcasite, both iron sulphide;
3  (i) calcite and (ii) aragonite, both calcium carbonate.

in the arrangement of their unit cells. The crystal system to which a gem species belongs has a profound influence on its physical properties and so forms an important frame of reference for the classification and identification of gemstones. The crystal system can be determined by observation of a well-formed crystal or much more accurately by X-ray measurement.

The differences between the seven crystal systems can here be indicated only broadly and therefore somewhat less than precisely. The differences can be thought of as the relation of an ideal crystal's height to its length and breadth and as any inclinations of these parameters to each other. The relevant facts can best be measured along imaginary lines running through the centre of the crystal, called the *axes of reference*. They are imagined as running (a) from front to back (length), (b) from right to left (breadth), and (c) from top to bottom (height).

In crystals of the *cubic* system these axes run at right angles to each other and are equally long; height = length = breadth. Typical shapes are the cube (pyrite), the octahedron (diamond) and the dodecahedron (garnet).

In the *tetragonal* system the two lateral axes (length and breadth) are equal but the vertical axis (height) is either longer or shorter than these. A typical shape is the prism, as in zircon.

In the *orthorhombic* system all three axes are unequal in length. The simplest shape would resemble a matchbox, though no actual crystals have quite such a simple shape. Peridot and topaz form orthorhombic crystals.

In the *monoclinic* system all axes differ in length and in addition the axis that runs from the front to the back of the crystal is inclined in relation to the vertical axis. The third axis, from right to left, meets the other two at right angles. The effect produced is that of a matchbox leaning backwards. Sphene and spodumene crystallize in this system.

In the *triclinic* system all the axes, unequal in length, are inclined towards each other; the matchbox now leans sideways as well as backwards. Axinite and kyanite belong to this system.

Crystals of the remaining two systems are broadly hexagonal or triangular in section so that they can no longer be defined by two

*Right* Some pseudomorphs, which are minerals that have replaced and taken the shape of quite different minerals: left, galena after pyromorphite; middle, haematite after calcite; right, marcasite after polybasite.

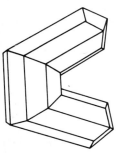

Cyclic twinning, a 'trilling' of chrysoberyl.

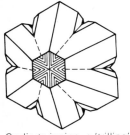

Genicular twinning of rutile.

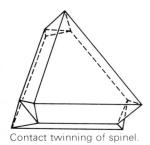

Contact twinning of spinel.

lateral measurements. Ambiguities would arise if one tried to measure from front to back and right to left. Instead, three lateral axes are needed. These always run at 120° to each other—12 o'clock, 4 o'clock and 8 o'clock. They are equal in length and lie in one plane, at right-angles to the vertical axis. Crystals of both the *hexagonal* and *trigonal* systems are defined by such axes, the main difference between them being that the trigonal system has less symmetry: its crystals cannot be bisected to give exactly equal halves in as many ways as hexagonal crystals. Among common shapes are six-sided and three-sided prisms. Important gemstones crystallizing in these systems include rubies and sapphires; all quartzes are trigonal, beryl is hexagonal.

The influence of its crystal structure on the nature of a gemstone cannot be exaggerated. It sometimes happens that exactly the same chemical compound crystallizes in more than one crystal class because the atoms align themselves in different ways, forming unit cells of different shapes. The resulting crystals (called polymorphs) then differ in appearance and in all their properties. An extreme example is presented by diamond and its hexagonal polymorph, graphite, which forms the 'lead' in pencils. Both consist of carbon but graphite is opaque and so soft that it is used as a lubricant, while diamond can possess unrivalled clarity and is the hardest substance known.

Even this brief account of crystallography would not be complete without mentioning the *twinning* of crystals. This occurs in the course of the growth of some crystals and results in the appearance of two or more crystals of the same kind which look as if they had grown into or through one another. Twinning sometimes produces remarkable shapes, at other times it is not obvious except on close inspection. Some gemstones such as quartz, chrysoberyl and members of the feldspar family are particularly prone to twinning. Its effects are usually undesirable;

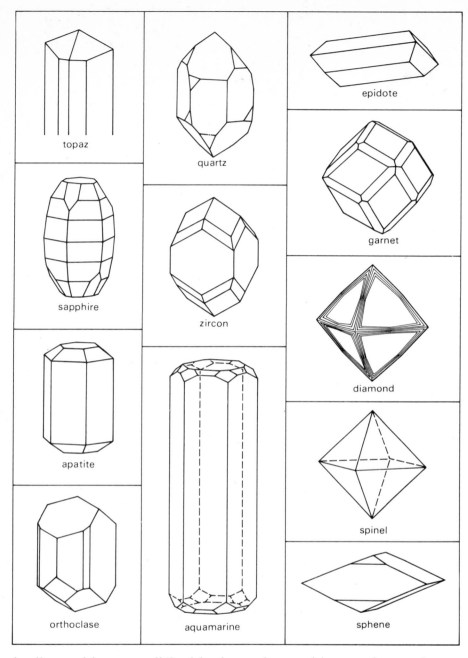

topaz

quartz

epidote

sapphire

zircon

garnet

apatite

diamond

orthoclase

aquamarine

spinel

sphene

The shapes of some gem crystals.

in diamond it causes difficulties in cutting, and it may also produce a certain patchiness in colour, as in some amethysts.

The crystals of minerals found 'in situ', that is in their original environment, usually occur in distinctive shapes. For example, rubies are often squat with a flat top and base, while sapphires tend to be barrel-shaped; tourmalines are like triangular pencils and diamonds occur as octahedra scored along the edges. These typical forms are known as the *habit* of the mineral concerned. Although the shapes of individual crystals vary, they have a certain underlying similarity by which the mineral can be recognized instantly. Some minerals, including many gems, occur in more than one habit, according to their mode of formation and the locality.

Each habit, of course, reflects the crystal structure of each mineral and each crystal system has its own range of habits; for example, cubic,

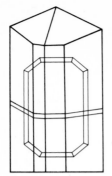

The cleavage plane in topaz runs parallel to the base of the crystal.

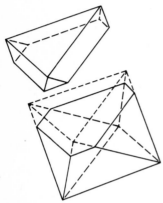

A diamond crystal cleaves parallel to any of its octahedral faces.

octahedral and dodecahedral habits can only occur in the cubic system which cannot, however, produce the long rod-shaped crystals known as prisms. These are typical of the tetragonal, trigonal and hexagonal systems, each of which has its own shapes of prism peculiar to it. There are also habit names that describe the shapes which can occur in several crystal systems, such as 'tabular' (flat), 'acicular' (needle-like) and 'botryoidal' (like a bunch of grapes). Minerals without a clearly visible crystalline structure are often designated 'massive'. The shape in which gemstones are cut is influenced by their habit; since emeralds, topazes, and tourmalines occur in long prisms, they are usually cut into oblong shapes to make the best use of the material.

An unwelcome directional property possessed by a few gemstones is a tendency to *cleave*. This happens when the bonds linking the unit cells are notably weaker in one or more directions than in all others. A sharp blow may then result in the stone coming apart in that direction with perfectly smooth, flat surfaces. This can occur, for instance, in topaz (usually across its narrow dimension) or, in two possible directions, in moonstone. Diamonds will cleave in four directions and this fact is turned to good account by diamond cutters, who can thereby reduce awkwardly shaped stones to a more acceptable form or remove blemishes with little labour. A diamond will not cleave in ordinary wear, however; some preparation and a very hard blow are needed to bring this about.

The term *fracture* is used when minerals are broken in ways other than by cleavage. The form which a fracture takes is often peculiar to a mineral and is described by such epithets as 'splintery', 'smooth' or 'conchoidal' (like the ridges on a shell). Tiny conchoidal fractures are sometimes taken to indicate glass imitations, but quartz and certain other gems also fracture conchoidally. Stones that are brittle by nature or contain flaws or large inclusions are prone to fracture. Opals and cloudy emeralds are particularly at risk when used carelessly. On the other hand, jade is notably tough and fractures less easily than minerals of similar hardness.

On the whole, far less damage is done to gemstones in personal use by cleavage and fracture than by abrasion. As explained in chapter one, the daily wear of stones and even the rubbing of unprotected stones against each other in a drawer or jewel box spoils their polish and wears down the sharp facet edges, impairing the lustre of the gems over the years. The degree of damage done depends in part on how much and where a stone is worn, but stones also differ greatly in their structural resistance to abrasion, often termed their 'scratch hardness'. As in the case of graphite and diamond described above, this hardness depends on the crystallization of the stone – the bonding of its atoms – and not on the type of atom bonded.

Hardness is measured on a somewhat rough-and-ready scale conceived by the German mineralogist Friedrich Mohs in about 1820. Knowing that minerals of the same species have the same hardness the world over, he numbered ten standard mineral species in such a way that each lower number could always be scratched by one of a higher number. The ten standard minerals are known as Mohs' scale. They are:

| | |
|---|---|
| 1 Talc | 6 Orthoclase feldspar |
| 2 Gypsum | 7 Quartz |
| 3 Calcite | 8 Topaz |
| 4 Fluorite | 9 Corundum |
| 5 Apatite | 10 Diamond |

Hardness does not increase between the standards by regular amounts;

there is a greater difference, say, between 7 and 8 than between 6 and 7, while the difference between 9 and 10 is greater than that between 1 and 9 owing to the incomparable hardness of diamond. Intermediate hardnesses are indicated by fractions, such as pyrope garnet $7\frac{1}{4}$. Mohs' scale is still useful as a broad indication of the wearing quality of a gem, as is witnessed by its continued use over a century and a half.

From the tables at the end of this book it will be seen that most gemstones have a hardness of 7 or more. This is hard enough to scratch glass and to prevent a stone being scratched by a steel file. Hardness 7 is accepted as a desirable minimum for gemstones that are to be worn in rings and, *a fortiori*, in other jewellery; a higher hardness is desirable for rings which are worn constantly such as engagement rings.

To test hardness, it is best to draw the stone firmly but not violently across a piece of one of the standard minerals. Stones of the same hardness do not scratch each other, so if a scar is left, it will prove that the stone being tested is the harder of the two. 'Hardness pencils' are also available. They incorporate a small pointed fragment of standard hardness with which a stone can be tested in an inconspicuous place, using the pencils in ascending order till a small scratch is made. At one time hardness tests were widely used to tell gems from glass but they are now frowned upon since they are very likely to damage a stone and better tests are available. Yet the scratch test still remains a useful quick test for jade carvings, which will not be scored by a steel needle or knife point, while most of the numerous jade imitations are soft enough to be so marked. Many gems besides diamond will scratch glass, but of all minerals it alone will scratch corundum readily.

Another quality peculiar to each gemstone species is its *density or specific gravity*. This is the ratio of the weight to the volume of a stone and it is constant within well-defined limits for each gem species. Stones of the same size but belonging to different species differ appreciably in their weight; the density of a stone therefore determines how large a stone can be obtained at a given weight. For example, a ruby would be only about half the volume of an opal of the same weight and the difference between the lightest gem material, amber, and the densest, zircon, is greater than 1 to 4.

Some gemmological equipment:
1 spectroscope and slide,
2 refractometer with sodium light source and contact liquid,
3 light source employing fibre optics,
4 hardness pencils,
5 colour filter,
6 dichroscope,
7 polariscope,
8 low power polarizing binocular microscope with built-in light source.

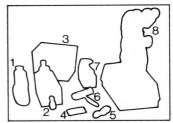

*Above* In a liquid of exactly the same density the beryl at the centre would remain suspended wherever it is placed. The denser tourmaline sinks to the bottom while the less dense amethyst floats at the top.

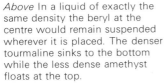

*Right* Determining specific gravity by hydrostatic weighing. The stone is first weighed dry in the balance pan, then again fully immersed in water (preferably distilled). The dry weight divided by the dry minus wet weight gives the specific gravity.

Density depends both on the chemical composition of a stone and on its crystal structure. It is expressed as the ratio of the weight of a stone to the weight of the same volume of distilled water (at 4 °C to be precise). Opal weighs about twice as much as the same volume of water, nephrite jade about three times and ruby about four times as much. Their densities are therefore approximately 2, 3 and 4 respectively.

The density of a stone can be readily determined by weighing it normally first and then re-weighing it suspended, completely immersed, in pure water. This second weight will be less, the difference representing the weight of water displaced. The density is then found by dividing the weight of the stone by this difference. This provides a most important aid in identifying gemstones. Sometimes even simpler tests may be helpful. These employ liquids heavier than water. For example, honey-coloured cat's-eyes occur both in quartz and in the much rarer and more costly chrysoberyl; on immersion in, say, bromoform (density 2·88) the quartz (density 2·65) would float while the chrysoberyl (density 3·71) would sink. Similar tests quickly distinguish yellow citrine from the somewhat similar yellow topaz. There are numerous other applications.

Density also has some bearing on the appearance of necklaces. Small amber beads and plastic imitations of pearls, for instance, are light and therefore do not 'hang' well. Large beads of these materials are more appropriate.

The density of gemstones may be affected by the *inclusions* contained within them. These are found in a vast variety of forms but most are so typical of the gem species in which they occur that it is often possible to identify a stone by means of its inclusions alone and to tell from which source or even from which particular site it has come. Its pedigree is thus for ever enshrined within it, unalterable even by the cutting and polishing processes it undergoes. An important stone is sometimes sold together with a photomicrograph of its inclusions so that it can be identified after loss or theft, even after it has been re-cut. Under suitable magnification, inclusions can be found in every gemstone.

Gemmology owes a great debt to Dr Edward J. Gübelin of Lucerne, Switzerland; his extensive research has led to a detailed classification and interpretation of gem inclusions which has greatly improved the techniques of identification. Further work is in process all over the world and no description of a species or important gem is now considered complete without a mention of its inclusions. These can consist of tiny crystals of pre-existing associated minerals, in a very great variety of forms, round which the gemstone crystallized. They can be irregularities in the growth pattern of a gem, forming cavities which sometimes enclose liquids, gases or solid crystals, occasionally all three being seen within the same cavity. Associated minerals, such as rutile, may crystallize within the gem when it is formed or soon after; cat's-eyes and star stones owe their peculiar structure to this cause. Sometimes the material colouring a gem may be concentrated in distinctive patterns, perhaps indicating the crystal system to which the gem belongs. Cracks often form in a gem during or after crystallization and these may become filled with solutions from which other minerals later crystallize out. Most inclusions have now been identified, often by the use of advanced techniques such as the electron probe microanalyser which can analyse objects of less than one thousandth of a millimetre in diameter.

In most stones of good quality inclusions are not obvious to the naked eye. In diamonds they are ignored as invisible and immaterial if they do not show up under a loupe (magnifying glass) enlarging ten times. In other stones still larger inclusions are not considered a blemish unless they spoil the appearance of the stone. Even a low-powered microscope will, however, reveal them clearly. They can then be regarded as a useful feature, guaranteeing that the stone is genuine, for the inclusions of imitations and synthetic stones always differ from those of their natural counterparts. Glass often contains rounded bubbles and swirl marks indicating an uneven mixture of the melt; in synthetics there are curved bands, flask-shaped bubbles and relics of the materials or solutions from which they were created. Some inclusions form beautiful patterns, amply rewarding their study. The microscope which reveals them is the gemmologist's most useful tool, for only by its aid can he distinguish between some natural and synthetic stones.

Some of the other attributes by which gems may be identified deserve mention at this stage. Chief among them is their *refractive index*, the degree to which a gem retards light passing through it. This differs from species to species and can therefore be used as a means of identification, as well as some indication of the lustre of a stone.

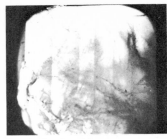
Synthetic emerald

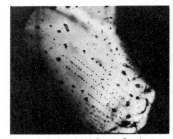
Octahedral spinel from Ceylon

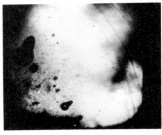
Synthetic ruby

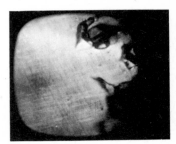
Star garnet showing intersecting needles
Photomicrographs of inclusions typical of some gemstones

In space, light travels at 186 000 miles (300 000 kilometres) per second. In rock crystal this is reduced to some 120 000 miles per second, in diamond to a mere 77 000 miles per second. By means of a refractometer, a small instrument employing refraction and reflection, the refractive index of a stone can be measured both quickly and accurately; the higher the index, the slower light travels through a stone. To say that diamond has a refractive index of 2.42 means that light travels 2.42 times faster in a vacuum than in the stone. Gems like diamond which crystallize in the cubic system, and all amorphous materials, have one index only but those of the six other crystal systems

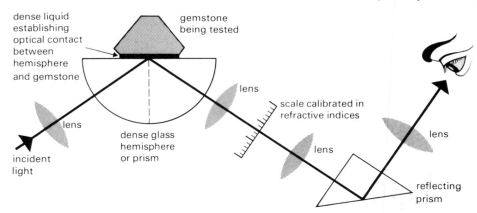

Schematic diagram of a refractometer.

dense liquid establishing optical contact between hemisphere and gemstone

gemstone being tested

lens

scale calibrated in refractive indices

lens

incident light

lens

dense glass hemisphere or prism

lens

reflecting prism

have two. Like all stones of the tetragonal, hexagonal and trigonal systems, quartz has one constant or 'ordinary' index and one 'extra-ordinary' index that varies. Stones of the orthorhombic, monoclinic and triclinic systems have two variable indices. These indices and the maximum difference between them (the birefringence) are invaluable aids to the speedy identification of a gem. They are usually quoted to two decimal places and are listed in the reference tables at the end of this book.

The refractive index must not be confused with opacity. No light can pass through more than the merest surface layers of an opaque stone

Light passing through anisotropic crystals is split into two rays. The Iceland spar variety of calcite is strongly doubly refractive.

like lapis lazuli; (RI 1.50), while a stone like diamond can be perfectly transparent though it has a much higher refractive index. The structure of lapis lazuli is such that all light that is not reflected from the surface layer of the stone is absorbed within it. In diamond very little of the transmitted light is absorbed; it is merely slowed down. It is usual to distinguish five degrees of transparency and to describe gemstones accordingly:

1 A *transparent* stone must allow the outlines of an object seen through it (for instance, print) to appear sharp and clear (example: rock cystal).

2 Objects can be recognized through a *semi-transparent* stone, but their outlines are blurred (example: moonstone).

3 No objects are visible through a *translucent* stone, but light can pass through all of it (example: agate).

4 In a *semi-translucent* stone, light will only pass through the thin edges (example: turquoise).

5 An *opaque* stone transmits no light at all (example: lapis lazuli).

Even opaque materials, such as metals, can, however, be made translucent if they are cut thinly enough. Light always penetrates at least an infinitesimal distance into any object before it is reflected or absorbed, otherwise we should see no colour or texture.

The importance of a good, clean colour has already been stressed as a desirable quality in most gemstones. Colour is an attribute of light. Coloured gemstones merely alter the light reflected from them or transmitted through them in such a way that an impression of colour is produced. White light, from the sun or any other source, is in fact made up of a mixture of colours ranging from red through orange, yellow, green and blue to violet. These are electromagnetic vibrations that differ from each other in wavelength and that together produce the visible spectrum. To produce the impression of 'white' they must be present in certain definite proportions and intensities, otherwise the light appears 'coloured'. A stone may look yellow because the light coming from it is deficient in blue vibrations; the shining red of a fine ruby is caused by the fact that it absorbs colours of various wave-

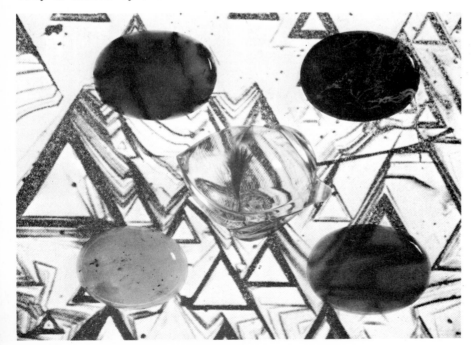

Different degrees of transparency found in quartz gems:
centre, transparent (rock crystal);
bottom right, semi-transparent;
bottom left, translucent;
top left, semi-translucent;
top right, opaque.

lengths and then emits some of the energy so gained as red light.

Gemstones owe their colour mainly to the presence of a few chemical elements in their structure which have the capacity to absorb some of the colours from white light; the remaining, unabsorbed colours then combine to give a gemstone its body colour. One of the commonest of these colouring elements (the chromophores) is iron. In various combinations it can produce a wide range of colours, often brown and green but also the red of almandine garnet and the blue of sapphire. Perhaps the richest and most luminous colours are caused by chromium (*chromos* is the Greek for 'colour'); the best emeralds and rubies owe their colour to its presence. Other chromophores of some importance in gemstones are manganese (in red spessartine garnet and rhodonite, for example), copper (as in turquoise and malachite), nickel (in some chrysoprases) and vanadium (in some emeralds and tourmalines), while a lesser role is played by titanium and cobalt. Rare earth elements and uranium also affect colour as do the defects in the crystal structure of some gemstones.

Unlike most organic dyes, the colours produced by these elements are very permanent and not subject to fading even after centuries of exposure to light. There are a few exceptions to this rule, however. Some zircons are known to fade in strong sunlight. Formerly, they were left in the strong Indochinese sun for long periods before being cut and marketed but this precaution does not now seem to be taken. Pink tourmalines and brown topazes have been known to grow paler in the course of decades. The author was once shown a zircon of a rich golden colour. The stone was taken from a safe and put in the sunlight. After ten minutes it had faded to a pale straw colour but the owner was undismayed, for he knew that the colour would be restored after a few hours in the dark safe. Such behaviour is most unusual, even in zircons!

The colouring elements can be present in a gemstone either as an essential part of its chemical composition or as an accidental impurity. Stones of the first kind are called 'idiochromatic', those of the second, 'allochromatic'. Both the green of peridot and the red of almandine are caused by iron, which is an integral constituent of these two gems. Such idiochromatic stones only have a limited range of colours; almandine is always red, peridot is green and, very rarely, brown. In contrast, allochromatic stones, which are rather more numerous, vary widely in the variety and depth of their colours. If perfectly pure, they are usually colourless. They acquire colour either by the replacement of a few of their atoms by one of the chromophores or by the insertion of chromophores into gaps in their crystal structure.

It is not always realized how many gemstones are merely allochromatic varieties of the same species. For example, beryl, corundum and quartz are perfectly colourless when pure. With the addition of chromium, beryl becomes emerald; with iron, blue aquamarine or brown heliodor; and with lithium, pink morganite. In corundum, chromium produces ruby but iron gives rise to blue, green or yellow sapphire. Pure quartz is colourless rock crystal but a little iron may turn it to purple amethyst or yellow citrine. Numerous instances of such variations will be encountered in the next chapter. The term 'colourless' is used for 'white' transparent stones because, although they absorb some light, it is absorbed in such a way as not to disturb appreciably the proportions of the colours present in white light. Such stones are in effect tinged with an exceedingly pale tint of some colour, often grey or brown, but ideally such tints should not be noticeable.

The appeal of colourless stones rests in part on their brilliance (produced by skilful cutting and polishing to magnify the light reflected from the back facets) but their main attraction is their 'fire'. This in turn depends on the power of the stone to separate the spectral colours present in white light. This power, known as *dispersion*, can then be used to facet a stone in such a way that a beam of white light entering the stone at one spot will emerge through different facets as beams of many different colours, as shown in the illustration on page 27. A few stones, notably diamond and some of its recent imitations, possess high dispersive powers.

The dispersion of light is used in an important gem-testing technique, first mentioned by Sir James Church in 1866 but fully developed only during the last fifty years by the distinguished British gemmologist, B. W. Anderson. If light that has passed through a gemstone is examined through a spectroscope, an instrument for dispersing light into its constituent colours, any colours absorbed by the stone can be identified as dark lines or bands where the light is missing from the spectrum. Anderson examined the spectra of many thousands of gemstones and showed that stones of some gem varieties consistently produced the same characteristic absorption patterns by which each could be identified; also that the spectra of certain elements possessed some similar features. The spectroscope has now become a universal tool in identifying gems.

A somewhat simpler technique employs colour filters that transmit only a narrow range of colours. The most successful of these pass only some red and some yellowish-green light. Their main use is as a quick, preliminary test for emeralds, which reflect some red but not any green of the kind passed by the filter. Consequently emeralds appear red or pink when viewed through the filter while other stones looking similar to emeralds remain green. From a mixed parcel of green stones the emeralds can therefore be picked out at sight. Rubies look brighter under the filter than other red stones. Several other gemstones can be identified in the same way, but it is advisable to confirm the filter result with other tests.

The reason for the bright appearance of fine rubies was mentioned briefly on page 45. Several other gemstones and minerals have the power to transform the energy imparted to them by friction, heat or invisible radiations into visible light. This phenomenon is called luminescence and there are several kinds. One that is widely used with gemstones is the fluorescence produced under invisible ultraviolet light or under X-rays. Ultraviolet light can be produced easily and cheaply; the equipment is portable and the light it produces gives rise to some spectacular effects. It will make most rubies and red spinels glow a bright red in the dark; many diamonds fluoresce sky-blue, as do pearls, opal and amber; some zircons and sapphires shine with a brownish-yellow and some emeralds with a red light. A few of the more unusual gemstones also fluoresce brightly in various colours. The effect varies in strength and can sometimes be seen only in complete darkness but many owners of gems have been pleasantly surprised to find how ultraviolet light can transform their treasures.

Another remarkable colour quality of gemstones, dichroism, has already been described briefly in chapter one. This occurs in coloured crystals except for those formed in the cubic crystal system. Light entering such a crystal is immediately separated into two distinct sets of light waves; the crystal has two refractive indices. The stone may then absorb different colours from each of the two sets of waves so that they emerge coloured differently, but the two colours overlap and intermingle so that the eye cannot tell them apart. They can, however, be clearly demonstrated side by side in a simple instrument called a dichroscope. This shows that the colour of a ruby is in fact made up of a bluish-red and a yellowish-red component, and that tourmalines, for example, transmit dark and light shades of their body colour. Each coloured variety of gem has its own distinctive type of dichroism which often helps greatly in its identification. In stones of the orthorhombic, monoclinic and triclinic systems a third, intermediate colour can often be seen in a certain direction, that is, they are trichroic. One of the most strongly trichroic stones, alexandrite, will show shades of red and green in one direction and either of these colours together with a pale brown when viewed from a direction at right angles to the former viewpoint. Dichroism may be strong or barely observable, but when present it proves that the stone is *anisotropic*, that is, it is neither amorphous nor cubic crystalline. The gemmologist therefore possesses a ready means of distinguishing, say, a ruby from a spinel or paste, or a tourmaline from a garnet.

The Dichroscope. The powerful double refraction of the calcite prism converts light from the small window into two contiguous polarized images of that window. If a coloured anisotropic gemstone is rotated in front of the window so that its polarization coincides with that of the calcite, the pleochroic colours of the gemstone will be seen side by side.

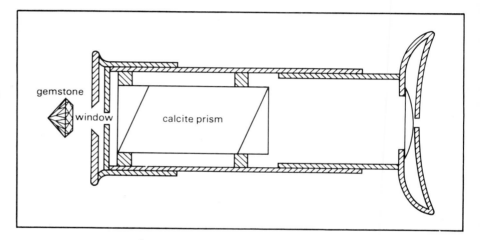

The colours of some gemstones can be altered or improved by a variety of treatments and colour can be imparted to colourless stones. The ethics of this procedure have often come under discussion, especially where the aim has been to give to a stone artificially a more desirable colour that also occurs in nature, so that it becomes difficult if not impossible to tell whether the fine colour is natural or not. Normally there is no motive in colouring a stone, beyond an endeavour to produce a more satisfactory article; there is no intention to deceive and the practice is recognized by the trade and often also by the public as admissible. There have, however, been some exceptions to this rule.

The most common procedure is the staining of porous stones such as agates. This practice was current in ancient Rome and provoked bitter comment even then. Most crypto-crystalline stones can be stained because there are minute gaps between the tiny crystals of which they are composed. Colour can be introduced into the gaps by various solutions and then precipitated. The oldest 'recipe', found in all textbooks, is to heat an agate in a solution of honey or sugar for several days and then either to heat the stone further by itself or treat it with sulphuric acid. In either case a jet black residue of carbon remains in the top layers of the stone, but any layers where the crystals are more closely packed and the sugar has not penetrated will remain white. Most banded onyx is coloured in this way. Brown colours can be created by greater subsequent heating. By using different chemicals a large variety of colours can be produced. Until fairly recently the chemicals used were closely guarded trade secrets but nowadays the knowledge of the fairly elementary chemistry involved is widespread. Metallic salts are always used since organic dyes would not be permanent, but these appear to have been used, nevertheless, in some 'improved' green jades from China.

The most commonly stained material is chalcedony in all its forms. Like agate it is usually grey in its natural state; it can be made red (cornelian), green (chrysoprase) and most other colours. The deep blue variety, often derived from a kind of jasper, is sold as 'Swiss lapis', an imitation of lapis lazuli. More convincing imitations are, however, now on the market and this also applies to turquoise, another stone that is often improved by staining.

A more pernicious form of staining consists of applying a trace of blue dye to a diamond that has a yellowish tint. This undesirable tint is thereby temporarily concealed, enhancing the apparent value of the stone. Recently fine coatings of metallic fluorides have been used for the same purpose. The fraud is easily detectable, but may deceive the unwary.

Careful heating will alter the colour of some stones by altering the structure of the colouring agent. In most cases the result is to make the gems paler in colour, which may be desirable with very dark stones, but aquamarines are given a richer blue tint by heating and they lose their green cast. Brown topazes become colourless with this treatment but on cooling assume a pleasant shade of pink, provided that exactly the right amount of heat has been imparted. All pink topazes owe their colour to heat treatment. Zircon is another species often heated; all blue, colourless and golden-yellow stones can be assumed to have been so improved. Amethyst turns yellow or brown on heating and a large proportion of citrines are produced in this way. There is also a green quartz, prasiolite, which derives from amethyst of Brazilian origin. Heat treatment appears to have been practised in the East for centuries and goes back well over 200 years in Europe.

A more modern method of imparting a desirable colour to colourless crystals is to irradiate them with sub-atomic particles. This procedure goes back to the turn of the present century when Sir William Crookes first put diamonds in contact with radium salts. These diamonds turned green – a very unusual colour in diamonds – but the coloration was superficial; it could be polished off or largely dispersed by heating and the stones were found to be slightly radioactive. Various forms of particle accelerators and atomic piles now present more effective methods of colouring stones. Colour is induced by a more or less profound disarrangement of the crystal lattice. The treatment is not cheap and is therefore mostly confined to cut diamonds, turning those with a slightly yellowish or brownish cast into attractively coloured green or blue stones, which on subsequent heating can be turned into a rich and permanent golden colour. They are not noticeably radioactive. Pink tints have also been produced. The distinction between natural and artificial colours is easy to determine in blue stones but not always so simple with yellow ones, where the assessment depends on accurate spectral analysis. There can be a big price difference between naturally and artificially coloured stones, though the latter will well repay the cost of treatment. Colourless topaz and rock crystal can be turned brown by radiation and smoky quartz is being produced by the same method in Japan.

This chapter has so far been concerned largely with the physical nature of gems. It has been shown how atoms link themselves together to form gems and how each species differs, for example, in its hardness and optical properties. The reader may now also wish to know something about the chemical composition of gems, as it is this, together with the crystal structure, that determines to which mineral species a gem belongs.

A diamond consists of pure carbon. It is the only gemstone made up throughout of a single kind of atom or chemical element. All other gems are compounds of various elements found in the earth's crust. The commonest of these crystal elements are oxygen, silicon, aluminium and iron, followed by a number of common metals. In various combinations, the four elements named make up nearly ninety per cent of the weight of the crust. All of them are well represented among gem minerals. For example, the silica gems – quartz, chalcedony and opal – are a simple compound of silicon and oxygen, silicon dioxide, which also occurs in vast quantities in impure, non-gem forms such as sand and sandstone. Corundum (ruby and sapphire) is essentially aluminium oxide; with the addition of magnesium it becomes spinel. Their scarcity derives from the rarity of the circumstances which caused them to crystallize in pure and transparent crystals of workable size with just the right admixture of chromophores, not from a lack of their basic constituents.

Silicon and oxygen are also a partial component of the largest group of gem minerals, the silicates. These vary from simple combinations as in zircon, which is made up of the metal zirconium (named after the gemstone) plus silicon and oxygen, to rather more complex compounds containing several metals in a more elaborate structure. Even so, the chemical structure of gemstones is simple compared with most organic compounds.

Most oxides and silicates are hard and resistant to attack by chemical agents. The same cannot be said of the relatively few gemstones that are sulphides, carbonates or phosphates. These tend to be relatively soft and are prone to deteriorate in contact with acids and alkalis. A peculiarity of the carbonates is their high birefringence. The chemical composition of gem minerals is given in the tables at the back of the book.

The chemical composition of stones belonging to the same gem species may vary through isomorphous replacement. This occurs when atoms of approximately the same size and with similar electrical capacities for combining with other atoms replace each other. For instance, chromium can replace aluminium in corundum, thus forming ruby; while in garnets and feldspars, in particular, several metals can replace each other so that an 'isomorphous series' of minerals is formed. This may range, for example, from magnesium-aluminium garnets (pyrope) to iron-aluminium garnets (almandine) with many intermediate forms which contain both magnesium and iron in varying proportions. The crystal structure and the general arrangement of atoms remains the same for all garnets but many of their properties, such as colour, density, refractive index and hardness, vary from one form to the next.

Having considered the structure and properties of natural gemstones, it will be useful to have some knowledge of the common attributes by which their main substitutes can be recognized. The distinction between gem *imitations* and *synthetic* gemstones must first be made quite clear. Imitations merely look like the genuine article without having the same crystal structure and chemical composition, whereas synthetic stones have a crystal structure and chemical composition which matches that of their natural counterparts exactly or very closely, differing from the natural stones only in the fact that they are man-made and not products of nature. While some gems have been imitated for thousands of years, science has only advanced during the last ninety years or so to a stage enabling it to synthesize gems.

The material most commonly used to imitate gems is glass or paste. Its distinction from gemstones is its amorphous nature, which precludes it from having such properties as birefringence, dichroism, cleavage and a hardness varying with direction. It is also rather softer and so wears less well than most gems. 'Paste' is merely another name for glass, derived from the Italian *pasta* meaning dough. In the ancient world it could not be produced in a transparent form and was therefore used to imitate turquoise and lapis lazuli; as technology improved, so transparent stones were imitated more widely.

Glass is essentially made from sand or flint, thus its basic material is silica. The addition of a vast range of metals and metallic oxides gives it widely varying properties to suit an equally wide variety of uses. Ordinary window or bottle glass (crown glass) made of silica, potash or soda, and lime is sometimes used to imitate gemstones but a more attractive imitation results if the lime is replaced by lead oxide. This gives the paste a higher refractive index and density – makes it heavier and more lustrous – and also greatly enhances its 'fire'. On the other hand, lead makes the glass much softer and subject to a gradual deterioration in appearance. Lead oxide may form well over half the composition of glass used for the imitation of diamonds. To enhance the brilliance of a paste stone, the base is sometimes coated with a metal mirror or metal foil. Colour is imparted to an imitation gem by the oxides of the chromophores already mentioned, but many other admixtures are used, including uranium to make it fluoresce or colloidal (minutely divided) gold to give it a rich red colour.

Gem imitations made of paste are usually merely moulded, to avoid the cost of cutting and polishing. In consequence the facet edges tend to be rounded, even in new stones. Old paste with cut and polished facets is, however, still sometimes encountered. The inclusions distinguishing paste such as rounded bubbles and swirl marks have already been pointed out on page 43. Scratches, loss of polish and conchoidal fractures are other features which arouse suspicion that a stone is paste.

More recently, clear plastics have also been used as gem imitations, mainly in such items as beads, pendants, and earrings. They can be moulded to give sharper facet edges but can easily be distinguished from crystal gems by their very low weight and refractive index and by their extreme softness. Their distinction from amber and tortoise-shell, which are somewhat similar in these respects, is also straight-forward. Plastics can be cut cleanly with a knife while amber chips; they will sink in a saturated salt solution (ten level teaspoonfuls of salt in a tumbler of water) while amber will float. The pigment in tortoiseshell shows up as separate spots under a microscope; in plastics it is like brush marks.

Other imitations which should be mentioned are porcelain for less transparent stones such as turquoise, lapis lazuli, jade and coral, and bone and vegetable nuts for ivory. There is also a whole range of common and inexpensive natural minerals which, to the uninitiated, may look like gem minerals or which may be artificially made to look like them. No mineral is more subject to this form of imitation than

Verneuil Flame Fusion Furnace.

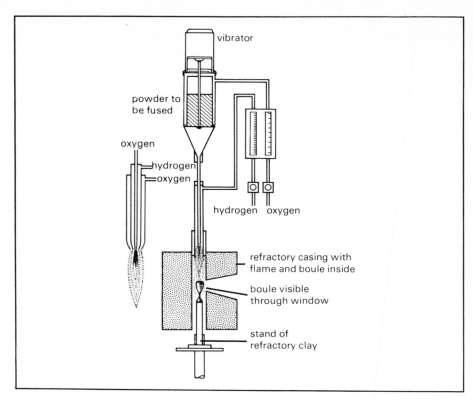

A modern boule of a synthetic corundum gemstone formed by the Verneuil flame fusion method.

jade but this is discussed in some detail later in chapter four.

Attempts to manufacture synthetic gems go back several centuries, to the days of the alchemists and earlier, but they were frustrated by two factors. Until the development of the physical sciences from the seventeenth century onwards the true nature and composition of gemstones was completely unknown; no true synthesis could therefore succeed. Even when scientists had finally discovered and analysed their structure, it took a long time before technology advanced to the stage where production could begin. Some scientists realized that pressures and temperatures similar to those involved in geological processes would have to be employed but the ability to reproduce such conditions was not achieved until the present century.

As was to be expected, the attempts at synthesis were first directed towards the most valuable gemstones: diamonds, rubies, sapphires and emeralds. F. H. H. Moissan in France, and J. B. Hannay in England claimed to have produced synthetic diamonds towards the end of the last century, but these claims could only be verified in part and the methods used were not commercially viable. Two other Frenchmen, however, E. Frémy and A. V. L. Verneuil, succeeded in producing 'reconstructed' rubies by fusing together small pieces of natural ruby and adding chromium salts to improve the colour. These stones were uneven and cloudy in colour and liable to crack. Verneuil went on to develop the process until in 1904 he could announce and describe fully the production of the first truly synthetic rubies. With some modifications his process is still widely used today to produce quite a range of synthetic stones.

The basic material in the process is finely powdered aluminium oxide made by burning pure aluminium. This is mixed with whatever colouring substance may be required and fed from a container through a sieve and a tube into an oxyhydrogen furnace. When mixed, oxygen and hydrogen burn with a heat sufficient to melt the alumina powder so that it forms a blob on a refractory clay stand at the bottom of the furnace. This stand can be lowered gradually so that the molten mass is able to grow upward. Although the consolidation of this molten mass is relatively rapid, not a glass, but a crystal is formed. Corundum is one of the materials amenable to the Verneuil process because it crystallizes very readily. The growth of the melt is so adjusted that a single cylindrical crystal, a boule, is formed. This is made to grow by regular increments as more powder is sent down into the furnace by the regular tapping of a small hammer on the container. This incremental growth can be seen through a microscope as fine curved layers within the boule or within any stone cut from it and is the means by which Verneuil synthetic rubies and sapphires can be recognized. Such stones usually contain oddly shaped bubbles and particles of unmelted powder. In all other respects, such as crystal structure, hardness, refractive index and physical density, dichroism and fluorescence, they are like natural corundum. Blue and yellow synthetic sapphires show some peculiar features in their absorption spectra, otherwise the microscope is the only means of distinguishing these synthetics with certainty.

A pupil of Verneuil's, J. Paris, soon discovered that a gemstone closely akin to natural spinel could be produced by the same process. It differs slightly from the natural stone in chemical composition and hence in some of its properties, so that it can be recognized by means other than its internal structure. At the beginning of the century spinel was not—and still is not—a particularly well-known stone and though it occurs in several attractive colours, it was not worth synthesizing in its own right. Like corundum it could be produced in a very wide range of colours and was therefore used to imitate other gemstones such as emerald, blue zircon, sapphire and tourmaline (from all of which it differed greatly in its properties). It was also manufactured

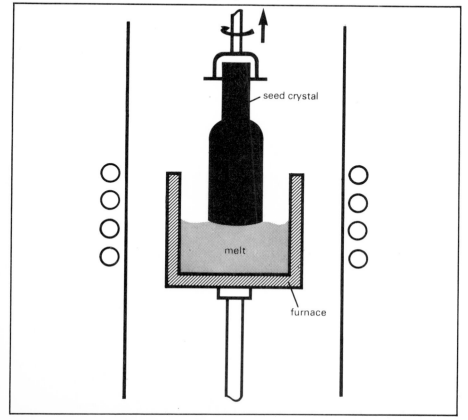

seed crystal

melt

furnace

The Czochralski method of producing synthetic crystals from a melt. A seed crystal is dipped into the melt contained in the furnace and slowly withdrawn under rotation. The melt crystallizes in conformity with the seed.

in various fancy colours not found in natural stones. In addition it could be made completely colourless and for a time was much advertised as a diamond substitute. As in the case of more modern imitations, excessive claims were made on its behalf.

These two Verneuil synthetics were produced in many countries and were the only true synthetics generally available until shortly before the advent of the Second World War. By that time, experiments which had been in progress over many years finally resulted in a fairly convincing synthesis of emerald. This stone will not crystallize in a Verneuil furnace. Researchers therefore turned to the so-called 'flux-melt' method in which the constituent oxides were dissolved under pressure and at a temperature of 800°C in a flux of lithium dimolybdate. Under these conditions it was found possible to grow emerald crystals which could afterwards be dissolved out from the cooled mass. The stones were marketed by the German chemical combine I. G. Farbenindustrie, under the name of 'Igmerald'. At about the same time Carrol F. Chatham succeeded in crystallizing emeralds hydrothermally by dissolving beryl in water at high temperature and pressure and then allowing it to re-crystallize on a small piece of beryl suspended at the cooler (upper) end of the apparatus. Both these early synthetics differed slightly from natural stones in their properties and had peculiar inclusions by which they could be recognized readily. More recent syntheses have produced stones which are much closer to natural crystals though the distinguishing internal features still remain. Synthetic emerald is now made by several producers in the USA as well as in France and Germany.

Synthetic diamonds, mainly cubic octahedral crystals, which are free cutting and long lasting. They are ideal for sawing stone, concrete, masonry and refractory materials.

A successful synthesis of diamond was first announced by the General Electric Company of Schenectady, New York, in 1955. Variants of the process evolved by this company are now employed in several parts of the world. They involve subjecting carbon to a pressure of 1 500 000 to 2 000 000 pounds per square inch (equivalent to the weight of a Saturn rocket on a fingertip), at temperatures above 2 700°C. Given these conditions the presses designed for the process will produce small diamonds in a matter of minutes, but the stones made by this method are for industrial use only; they supplement and in part replace tiny natural stones used mainly as abrasives. Just to prove that it was possible, six gem-quality diamond crystals of about one carat weight each were made in 1970. It is understood that the presses had to be kept at their phenomenal pressure and temperature for about a week so that the stones cost many times more than the market price of natural diamonds of the same size to manufacture. So far as is known these are the only synthetic gem diamonds produced; three of them are exhibited at the Smithsonian Institution in Washington.

The synthesis of gemstones has been stimulated greatly by the development of lasers from about 1960 onward. Several gemstones consist of crystalline material highly suitable for the production of laser beams; ruby in particular is widely used in this way.

Research into the production of crystals of high purity has progressed rapidly and there is now scarcely any gem mineral that cannot be produced synthetically, but few have appeared on the gem market. Of those that also occur naturally, synthetic rutile (titanium dioxide, also used as a pigment) has been crystallized in various colours for

Ten thousand ton presses used by De Beers creating pressures of one million pounds per square inch and temperatures approaching 2000°C.

55

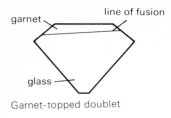

garnet — line of fusion

glass —

Garnet-topped doublet

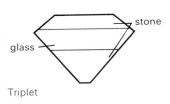

— stone

glass —

Triplet

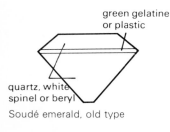

green gelatine or plastic

quartz, white spinel or beryl

Soudé emerald, old type

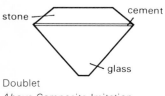

stone — — cement

— glass

Doublet

*Above* Composite Imitation Stones

*Right* Graphite and approximately one carat of synthetic gem diamonds, only slightly polished.

the sake of its phenomenal fire, and synthetic quartz (with many important industrial and scientific applications) has appeared as cut gemstones in various fancy colours from Russia. Other attractive synthetic materials are marketed from time to time. At least three of these are unlike any natural mineral: strontium titanate, sold under the trade name of 'Fabulite', lithium niobate, and various forms of aluminate with a garnet-like crystal structure. All these are mainly used as diamond imitations and sold under a variety of names. They are described in more detail in chapter four.

One more kind of substitute remains to be described: the composite stone. As its name implies, it is made up of two or three parts, usually cemented together at the girdle, where the upper part (the crown) and the lower part (the pavilion) of a cut stone meet; such imitations are called doublets and triplets respectively. The parts may be natural stones, synthetics or glass in any combination and the aim is to produce as natural-looking an imitation as possible, cheaply. Very rarely two small natural stones are joined together to produce one larger one. If any natural constituent is incorporated, it is only to bestow an appearance of verisimilitude. Thus a very pale emerald top may be cemented on a rich green base to give the effect of a stone of excellent colour, the natural top at the same time disguising the softness of the paste underneath and perhaps even providing some authentic inclusions. Or the softness of a glass base may be concealed beneath a thin slice of garnet fused to the crown of the stone. Garnet-topped doublets were used fairly widely in cheap jewellery of the nineteenth and early twentieth centuries but they have now been superseded by synthetics. They may still be found in older jewellery or where a lost stone has been replaced. The garnet top is so thin that it has almost no effect on the colour of the paste beneath. Doublets of all colours, and even 'colourless' ones can be found.

When jewellers became wary of doublets and tested them on the pavilion for hardness, triplets were manufactured which consisted of a hard layer in the crown and pavilion with a substantial body of strongly

This crystal of synthetic quartz has been grown round a seed plate, clearly visible down its middle.

coloured base in between. Such triplets are now rare, but another type, the 'soudé emerald' and its variants, is common. In this imitation a highly coloured layer of gelatine, plastic or other material is cemented between the crown and the pavilion, which in turn can be of almost any natural or artificial material, usually colourless or of a pale colour.

Composite stones are easy to recognize if one is alert to their existence. Where the setting allows it, the join between the parts can be seen with a loupe. When the stone is put in a white dish containing carbon tetrachloride (which must not be inhaled) or even water, the differences between the two parts become obvious. Garnet-topped doublets show a red rim round the girdle when laid on a white paper. Through a microscope, flat bubbles can often be seen in the joining plane. Ease of recognition is probably one of the reasons why composite gems are now less common.

This completes our brief general account of gemstone imitations. An accurate diagnosis is usually a matter for experts but all admirers of gems ought to be aware of the products that exist. As for the rest of this chapter, it was necessary to go into some technicalities without which the strange properties exhibited by some stones might not be understood and appreciated. It is hoped that the reader will be stimulated to find out more for himself and that he will derive greater pleasure from the next chapter in the light of the explanations given.

# The Gem Species

Gemstones can be allotted to three broad groups according to their commercial importance. First are those which are familiar, at least by name, to most gem lovers and which form the regular or occasional stock-in-trade of the larger jewellers. These have been given fairly full treatment in the present chapter without entering on too many technicalities.

Secondly, there are minerals which are suitable for use as gems to a greater or lesser extent but which are either not widely known or rare and not normally handled by jewellers. Brief references to these have been included in the second part of this chapter. Some of the salient physical and chemical data on the stones in these first two groups are summarized in the tables at the end of this book.

Finally, there are minerals which are not suitable for wear as gemstones but which are cut as such nevertheless, mainly to please collectors of rarities and oddments. One never knows what may turn up next in this group but usually these stones are freaks of nature that occur in one small deposit only. Some are the transparent or coloured sports of common rock-forming minerals such as dolomite and barite – much too soft to wear, difficult to polish and rarely exhibiting particularly attractive features. They are therefore not described in this chapter.

A few words need to be said about the naming of gemstones. The names of many gems known in antiquity have been carried forward, with modifications, to the present day but it is by no means the case that the modern and the ancient names necessarily apply to the same stone.

It is certain that in ancient times the same name was applied to quite a variety of different species. This practice was widely prevalent in the trade even recently and to a lesser extent persists today. Old and misleading trade names die hard. Such names often err in giving an inferior stone the name of a superior one. Thus Madeira topaz is only a dark citrine; Matara diamond is zircon; water sapphire is cordierite – there are scores of such misnomers.

Another misleading practice is the use of the term 'oriental' as in oriental topaz or amethyst; these are merely colour varieties of sapphire, totally unrelated to the stones named. Gemmologists and the more responsible trade associations have set up international bodies to reduce such ambiguities and to agree on nomenclature. They have evolved clear-cut definitions which enable one to know exactly which particular gemstone is referred to by which particular name. Some old names, such as hyacinth and carbuncle, have proved to be too non-specific and have been dropped. A good many new names have been introduced, largely following the rulings of scientific mineralogy, either to accommodate gemstones formerly known under a non-specific name or to designate newly discovered species. These new names may refer to the discoverer (zoisite, for example), to a locality (benitoite), to a component (sodalite), or to a structural peculiarity (euclase, meaning 'well cleaving') or some other aspect of the new gem. The ending 'ite' is derived from the Greek *lithos*, a stone, and has been in common use to denote a mineral species since early in the last century. Some minor ambiguities still exist; for instance, two or more mineralogists may independently analyse and name minerals which later turn out to be the same. Two or more names may then persist side by side. Thus cordierite is also known as iolite and as dichroite, but since these names have no other connotation they cannot mislead.

The position regarding the naming of colour varieties is somewhat less happy. Names like 'ruby' for red corundum or 'emerald' for certain green beryls are venerably old and generally accepted, but there has been a proliferation of contrived variety names, the need for which could be questioned. Mineralogical practice is to avoid variety names unless they indicate a more significant variation than allochromatic coloration. 'Red tourmaline' and 'blue tourmaline' are both more specific and easier to remember than 'rubellite' and 'indicolite', which are contrived names of recent origin.

Colour is not a simple criterion to apply in the classification of gemstones in any case. For example, ruby is always red and a pink stone of the same species is a pink sapphire; but who is to draw the line between a pale ruby and a dark pink sapphire? Since rubies are worth more than sapphires, the name may depend on whether one is buying or selling the stone! There are many similar borderline cases and such descriptions as 'cornflower-blue' for sapphire or 'pigeon's-blood red', a rather silly term purporting to describe the finest ruby colour, do not help much. Scientific work on an objective evaluation of gem colour is well advanced and it may be only a matter of time before new machines, simple to operate, will produce exact and acceptable colour assessments. The use of such machines (photometers) is gradually spreading in the diamond trade; it might simplify the buying and selling of other gemstones as well. Let us now consider these individually.

**AMBER** has been held in high esteem for thousands of years on account of its warm, golden transparency and the soft lustre it acquires on being polished. It has been used for ornament longer than most materials taken from the earth and so merits special mention here, though its claim to be a gem mineral may be disputed on various grounds.

Unlike other minerals, amber is formed from the resin of a (now extinct) species of pine tree and not from the inorganic constituents of the earth's crust. Against this it can be argued that amber has been dated back to the Oligocene geological epoch, some thirty million years ago or more. Since then it has been transported, buried in the earth, hardened and fossilized by soil acids and compression. Although a little amber is still found on seashores and land surfaces, most has to be won by open-cast mining like many other minerals. The claim that it is not a gemstone of great value is true; it is more appropriately classed among ornamental materials and sold by the piece, not by the carat weight. But no account of gemstones would be complete without its inclusion, if only because of its popularity and long history.

Amber varies in colour from a pale yellow to a dark brown, depending partly on its origin; some is naturally red, but many other colours can be imparted to it by staining, particularly green. Attractive spangled effects can also be obtained by 'hammering' the material, a skilful process of applying pressure to be attempted by experts only.

By far the most prolific source of amber is the Baltic seacoast to the north and west of a town now known as Kaliningrad in the USSR (formerly Königsberg in East Prussia). Amber from this source is sometimes called succinite (Latin *succus*, juice) to distinguish it from material derived, for example, from Rumania (rumanite), Burma (burmite), and

Sicily (simetite, strongly fluorescent). Small deposits occur elsewhere, notably in the Dominican Republic (retinite). On the Baltic coasts mentioned, amber has been dredged in nets from the sea bottom for centuries, the collection being strictly regulated; in bygone ages poaching was punished by hanging. Nowadays hardly any amber is won there by surface collection and mechanized open-cast mining is used instead.

The trees that exuded the resin grew in what is now central and south-eastern Sweden, from where the amber was carried by rivers and the sea to the present site. There are some placer deposits of amber further inland and it may also be picked up occasionally along all the Baltic coasts; sometimes it can be found even as far away as the east coast of England. Its surface has a peculiar 'goose-pimple' texture, perhaps caused by the imprint of the soil in which it was deposited. This soil, locally called the 'blue earth' – although really a greenish-grey – is also the layer from which amber is excavated in massive, irregular lumps.

Specialists distinguish many qualities of amber according to colour and cloudiness. This cloudiness is caused by minute air bubbles trapped within the stone. Amber is famous for containing insects and small animals of various kinds as well as leaves, bark and other contemporary detritus which became stuck and enclosed in the resin while it was still liquid. These objects have been preserved in minute detail to the benefit of palaeontologists and the delighted wonder of the lucky finders. Even Pliny mentions them in the first century AD. Beware, however, of imitations! Many a modern insect is now ensconced in an equally recent resin to be sold as a genuine 'fly in amber'. The identification of the insects is a matter for entomologists and many museums may be able to help. Modern resins such as dammar, copal and shellac are partly soluble in ether, which renders them sticky, while amber is hardly affected.

By heating small chips of amber under pressure they can be made to fuse together, forming 'ambroid' or 'pressed amber'. This is quite difficult to distinguish from the untreated material; elongated bubbles and a flowing structure are the most usual indications. Amber is also widely imitated by synthetic plastics such as Bakelite in which elaborate and artistic 'amber' carvings of Chinese origin have been executed. These plastics can be cut cleanly with a sharp knife whereas amber

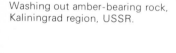
Washing out amber-bearing rock, Kaliningrad region, USSR.

comes off in splinters. They have a higher density than amber and if a small fragment is burnt it gives off an unpleasant odour while amber has such a distinctively pungent aroma that it is used as incense in the East. Ambergris, which is much used in perfumery, is totally different in appearance and is not even distantly related to amber.

Amber has been used for beads and pendants from remote antiquity. The beads may be fashioned quite roughly (baroque) or they may be formed as spheres, graded in size or faceted in many shapes. Most elaborate amber carvings are made in the East, particularly in China and Japan. In the Victoria and Albert Museum in London there is an exquisite small altar of seventeenth-century North German workmanship entirely inlaid with carved amber of different tints.

The name 'amber' is derived from the Arabic and has reached our language by way of Latin and French. The ancient Greeks called it *elektron*. They were the first to remark on its power to attract small particles of ash and other matter after it had been rubbed on cloth. When scientists came to study this phenomenon in the eighteenth century, they therefore named it 'electricity'. An 'electron' now means a small sub-atomic particle; the name 'electrum' was applied by the ancients to a yellowish alloy of gold and silver and this name is still used in the same way today.

BERYL comprises a whole range of attractive varieties, two of which are more familiar under their specific names. These are the rich green emerald and the paler green or blue aquamarine. There are in addition golden heliodor, pink morganite and colourless goshenite. Beryl is allochromatic and may therefore be found in almost any colour. It is a silicate of the metals beryllium and aluminium with small admixtures of colouring compounds which give rise to small variations in its physical and optical properties. It is one of the lighter gemstones, usually with good transparency, fairly widely distributed but by no means common since beryllium is a rare element. Its lustre is vitreous and it takes an excellent polish. A considerable hardness of $7\frac{3}{4}$ helps it to withstand wear.

The name comes from the Greek *beryllos,* applied apparently to aquamarine, though even as early as the first century AD Pliny surmised that emerald and *beryllos* had much in common. The emeralds of his day

Amber from Oligocene sands on the Baltic coast, showing animals and other matter trapped in it.

were from Egypt and rather paler than the magnificent stones from South America now available.

A clear **emerald** of a fine grass-green colour (with a slight bluish rather than a yellowish cast) and several carats in weight is the most highly valued of all gemstones. It will fetch a higher price than an equivalent ruby or diamond, largely on account of its rarity. A few clear stones of fair size were on offer at £5 000 a *carat* some years ago in London. Paler, small emeralds with inclusions visible to the naked eye can be bought for a tiny fraction of the price of really fine stones. The intense colour of fine emeralds is given to them by chromic oxide; strictly speaking, the yellowish-green stones coloured

Emerald crystal from Colombia embedded in limestone matrix.

by iron and not chromium should be called 'green beryl'. The name 'emerald' derives from the Latin *smaragdus* via the French *esmeraude*; the name does not seem to have been used in England until the sixteenth century.

The best emeralds come from South America – from Muzo and Chivor in Colombia – and are of metamorphic origin. They are found in thin veins, mainly in limestone marls. Both in their formation and subsequently, they have been subjected to collossal stresses, often resulting in numerous fractures and cracks, so that emeralds must be treated with some care lest they break apart. Perhaps this is the reason why some people regard them as unlucky, though this belief may be partly founded on the ill-luck that the superstitious associate with the colour green. Emeralds occur in long prismatic crystals and are therefore usually cut into oblong stones. To stop the points of cut stones being broken off accidentally they are often cut with bevelled points; so typical is this practice that this shape is commonly known as the 'emerald cut'. Similar considerations may explain why emeralds are often cut as cabochons – a very reasonable procedure if the stone has a good colour but lacks full transparency. The colour of emeralds blends beautifully with a gold setting and is not impaired when viewed in artificial light which tends to darken some green stones. Indeed, very few green stones can rival the rich tones of a fine emerald, though a few rarities coloured by chromium – hiddenite, diopside and kornerupine, for example – may come near.

Of all the emeralds mined, even at the famous Colombian mines, less than one per cent are of outstanding quality. Most of the other stones found are not even worth cutting, but a few remarkably large crystals have been recovered. The most famous and one of the largest of these is the Duke of Devonshire's emerald, fine of colour and weighing nearly ten ounces but full of flaws. Even larger stones have been found. A crystal half the size of the Devonshire stone is mentioned by Professor H. Bank; it was found in 1921 and most appropriately named Patrick, after the patron saint of Ireland, the Emerald Isle.

Production continues intermittently in Colombia and in a few other localities. Emeralds of very good colour but small in size and rather flawed were found in the late 1950s in Rhodesia, at Sandawana and elsewhere. Recent finds are also reported from Suwat, Pakistan and Australia. India is a historic source and some stones, mostly of indifferent quality, still come from there as well as from Brazil and the Transvaal. European sources are near Mursinka in the Urals and in the Habach Valley of Austria, but few stones now appear to come from these localities.

Reference has been made to the recent increase in the production of synthetic and imitation emeralds. The latter present few problems of identification but synthesis has now achieved such perfection that some care is required in distinguishing between natural and artificial stones. The inclusions within the stones are the surest guide. They often enable one to determine the origin of natural stones from different localities and always enable one to distinguish these from synthetic stones. There are also differences in their transparency and fluorescence under ultraviolet light and some synthetics have a lower density and refractive index.

The other important beryl gemstone, **aquamarine**, depends for its colour on iron, not on the much rarer chromium. It is therefore distributed more widely and does not approach anywhere near the value of fine emerald. Unlike emerald, it chiefly occurs in primary deposits in pegmatites and for this reason is often found in large, clear crystals that may weigh many pounds. The largest appears to have come from Marambaia in Brazil in 1910. It weighed 243 pounds and was perfectly transparent throughout its length.

The value of aquamarines depends on the depth of their blue colour and most stones are now in fact heat-treated. This is not necessary in the case of the best-quality stones, which come from the Santa Maria mine and from Espirito Santo in the state of Minas Gerais in Brazil. Even darker stones, of a deep sapphire-blue, are sometimes found in Malagasy but these are rarely 'clean'. Dark aquamarines show good dichroism which has to be taken into account when the stones are cut. Large crystals have also come from various parts of Siberia and these, together with stones from the Ural mountains, account for a fine collection at the Institute of Mining in Leningrad. Another splendid assembly is in the Morgan Collection in New York. Lesser sources of aquamarine are in India and New South Wales, Australia; in the United States aquamarines of varying tints are found at Stoneham in Maine, Haddam in Connecticut and in San Diego County, California. Cloudy stones, unsuitable for cutting, come from the Mourne Mountains, Ireland.

Among natural stones, aquamarine is most easily confused with blue topaz, which is, however, much paler as a rule, or with blue tourmaline. It differs from both of these in its refractive index, density and birefringence. Aquamarine is not synthesized but is imitated by blue synthetic spinel from which it differs markedly in the constants just mentioned. Synthetic blue spinel is also usually coloured with cobalt which gives it a different tint of blue from natural aquamarine and makes it appear red under the emerald filter while aquamarine looks green.

The yellow or pale brown variety of beryl is usually called **heliodor**, Greek for 'gift of the sun'. In spite of its antique appearance, this name is of recent origin since it was bestowed by the Germans on a slightly radioactive, and hence fluorescent, form found early in the present century at Klein Spitzkopje in South-West Africa, which was then a German colony. The name should strictly be reserved for stones of this provenance only. Yellow and brown beryls from other localities are not radioactive. They come, like aquamarines, from pegmatites and form clean hexagonal prisms that can be cut into brightly coloured stones, usually in the step-cut style. Other localities for these stones are in Malagasy, Brazil and Ceylon. Heliodor is one of the less valuable varieties of beryl and for this reason is not often imitated.

Another recently named variety of beryl is the pink **morganite**, so called in honour of the famous gem collector and banker, Pierpont Morgan. Morganite owes its colour to lithium, a rare element, and is therefore quite rare and valuable when of good colour. It usually comes in squat crystals from pegmatites and may be quite clear or cloudy, but in many stones sold as morganite the colour is barely perceptible. Its content of alkaline metals varies, which gives rise to variations in its density but in any case raises it above that of other beryls. The best quality stones come from Malagasy and these may considerably exceed the value of good aquamarines. Another source is Pala, San Diego County, California.

Colourless beryl is known as **goshenite** from the town in Massachusetts where it is found in very pure crystals. It is of no commercial importance but collectors buy it for the sake of having a complete colour range of beryls.

**CORUNDUM** is the mineralogical name for a species that comprises two of the best-known gems: **ruby** and **sapphire**. They are essentially the same substance, aluminium oxide, but traces of colouring elements,

Calcite crystals and silk in Burma ruby.

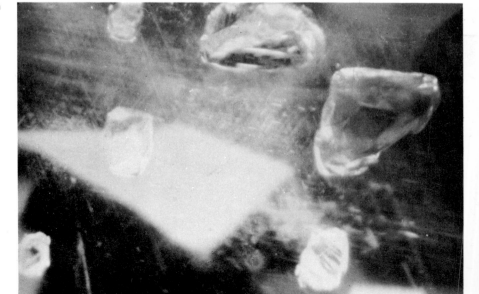

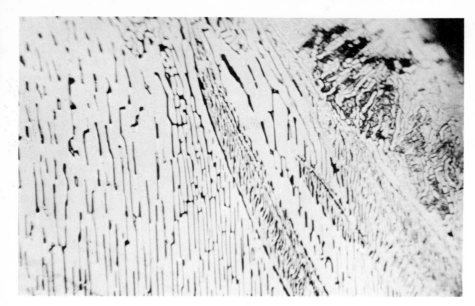

*Left* Liquid-filled, net-like inclusions in Burma sapphire.

usually present by isomorphous replacement, suffice to produce more or less intense colours in a material that is colourless when pure. A great many fancy names were current for the various colours – oriental amethyst for the purple variety, for instance – but these are now happily less in evidence and the modern tendency is to call all gem colours except red by the unequivocal name of sapphire with a suitable colour prefix. The name 'padparadscha' is still sometimes applied to orange sapphire, particularly in Germany, but it has not achieved wide currency, perhaps because of its lack of euphony. The name is said to be derived from the Sinhalese *padma ragaya*, lotus-coloured. 'Ruby' comes from the Latin *ruber*, red, while 'sapphire' can be traced via Greek to Hebrew and Persian or even to Sanskrit sources.

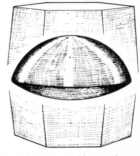

*Above* In some rubies and sapphires, fine acicular crystals enclosed parallel to the three lateral crystal axes of the sapphire cause a star to appear in reflected light if a cabochon is cut in the manner illustrated.

Sapphires can be of all possible colours, including pink, and can also be colourless; parti-coloured sapphires are quite common. There are also natural sapphires which change colour: they are purple in daylight and red in electric light. Traces of chromic oxide produce the best red rubies while sapphires can be coloured blue by titanium and ferrous iron, yellow by ferric iron and many other colours by these and other chromophores in combination. Impure corundum yields emery.

Though it is formed of the soft metal aluminium and the gas oxygen, corundum is very hard indeed – 9 on Mohs' scale. Rubies and sapphires can therefore be worn in any form of jewellery and have long been most popular as ring stones. Owing to their high density (about 4.00) they are smaller than most other gemstones of the same weight. They vary in transparency from complete clarity, through various degrees of cloudiness to sub-translucency, but some slight inclusions are not necessarily regarded as a defect. The shimmering whitish sheen produced by microscopic needles of rutile and known as 'silk' is accepted as an attractive attribute within reason and as a proof that a stone is genuine.

These acicular crystals of rutile sometimes crystallize out parallel to the trigonal crystal symmetry of the corundums to form the greatly prized star rubies and star sapphires ('asterias'). It is important that these should be cut so that the star is exactly in the middle of the round cabochon stone. Most star stones are a pale grey, but they can also be found in the richest colours. Occasionally one of the three rays of the star greatly predominates and stones are then cut as oval cat's-eyes. Twelve-rayed stars are extremely rare.

*Above* A natural emerald crystal in matrix, a cluster of synthetic emerald crystals of early manufacture and some cut synthetic emeralds made by different producers.

*Above right* Three synthetic gem diamonds made by General Electric. Each weighs about a third of a carat and was cut from a crystal weighing about one carat. These diamonds were much more costly to produce than equivalent natural gems.

*Below right* Diamond (centre) and its simulants: clockwise from the left are rutile (s), lithium niobate (s), zircon, scheelite (s), glass, spinel (s), rock crystal, yttrium aluminate (s), sapphire and strontium titanate (s). Synthetic stones = (s).

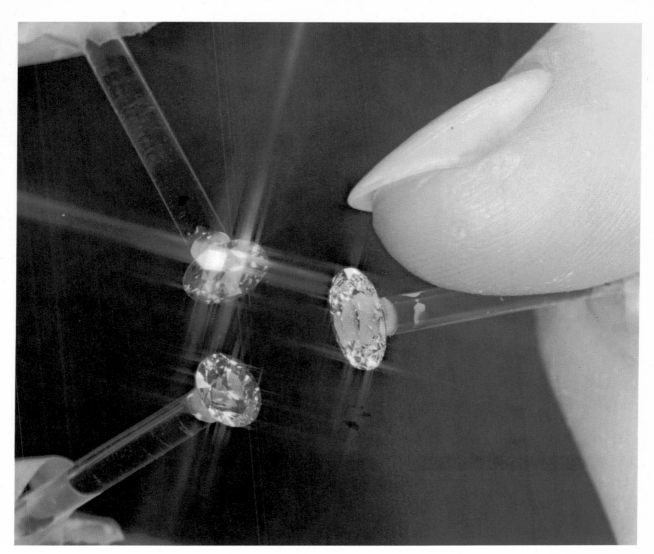

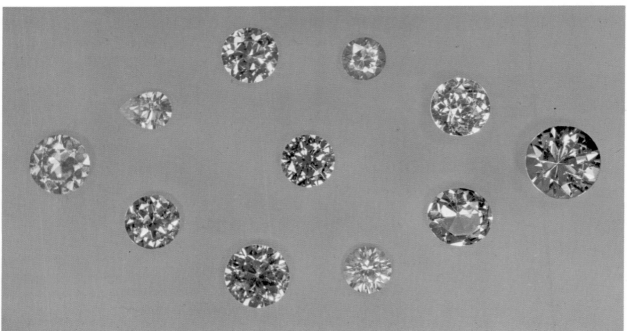

As already explained, the brightness of the red colour of the chrome-rich rubies from Burma (and of synthetics) is caused by their fluorescence. The effect can be spectacular when the stones are exposed to ultra-violet radiation in the dark. For the same reason rubies appear much brighter than other red stones (except red spinels) under a colour filter. The presence of iron in the stones, as in some from Thailand (Siam), for example, inhibits their fluorescence. Corundums have strong dichroism which has to be allowed for in their fashioning; the deepest colours are produced and dichroism is minimized when the table facet of the stone is placed exactly at right angles to the vertical axis of the original crystal.

Burma rubies are mined in situ from limestone in the area round Mogok. Elsewhere both rubies and sapphires tend to come from secondary deposits. Other important countries of origin for both are Thailand and Ceylon. Some of the finest blue sapphires come from pegmatites in Kashmir. In the USA corundum of many colours is found near Helena and at Yogo Creek, both in Montana, and at other sites. In Australia there are several deposits in Queensland and New South Wales. More recently Tanzania has joined the producers of ruby and sapphire in a major way. Fine rubies and sapphires can, however, come from various localities and the appellations 'Burma ruby' or 'Kashmir sapphire' often denote the quality of colour rather than necessarily the provenance of the stone. Even the unjustly maligned deposits of Montana and Australia have produced magnificent gems.

Production in Burma and Thailand is at present reduced by political troubles and elsewhere the production of fine stones cannot reach the levels that the market could absorb, so prices are high. They have always been a great deal higher for rubies than for sapphires of equivalent size and quality, even in antiquity. As usual with gemstones, there is a vast difference in value between really fine specimens and those of lesser quality. Among sapphires, those with a rich, but not too deep, blue colour are prized most highly. The other colours are less in demand, perhaps because it is not generally realized that sapphires exist in all possible colours (except of course red). Padparadschas of a rich colour, a reddish-orange, are rare and fetch high prices among collectors.

In jewellery settings rubies and sapphires are often combined with diamonds which set off their colour to perfection. Larger stones are often surrounded with small diamonds, smaller stones may be set alternately with diamonds of a matching size as in the traditional three-stone or five-stone rings. In such cases it is important that the stones should match exactly in colour and that they should conform to the design in size. If one stone is lost, it may be quite difficult to match it. For large corundums the step cut is usually appropriate; smaller stones are often fashioned in the mixed cut or, if round and clear, in the brilliant cut.

Every conceivable method of imitation and synthesis has been employed to produce artificial rubies and blue sapphires, from glass and synthetic spinel, through doublets to Verneuil, flux-melt and hydro-thermal substitutes. In addition, natural red spinels have in the past been sold as 'Balas rubies' or 'ruby spinels'. There is little difficulty in distinguishing the earlier imitations and synthetics, but recent flux-melt rubies call for great care. There has been no adverse effect on the value of natural stones from this proliferation of artificial products. Scientific gem testing began to evolve at about the same time as the marketing of the first synthetics and may have been greatly stimulated by it. Recognition depended then, and still mainly depends now, on the inclusions within each type of stone. Verneuil synthetics contain curved lines looking somewhat like the grooves on a gramophone record and peculiarly-shaped bubbles, while natural rubies contain associated crystals, flat flaws partly filled with liquids and hexagonal colour patterns.

Synthetic corundum can now be produced in almost any shape and is widely used in industry. The 'jewels' used as bearings in watches are made of synthetic ruby, as are laser crystals. Colourless synthetic sapphire has long been used as a diamond substitute on account of its hardness and purity. Pick-up styli for gramophones and a host of industrial components possessing great hardness are also made from it. Colourless synthetic sapphire is used as a component in heat-proof ceramics and the heat shields of space vehicles. It is a most versatile material for which new uses are still being discovered.

**CHRYSOBERYL** is not just a golden beryl as its name implies. It is a completely different mineral species which deserves to be known much better than it is. Like beryl it consists in part of the metals beryllium and aluminium, but it is an oxide, not a silicate, and it crystallizes in the orthorhombic, not the hexagonal, system, often as cyclic twins. Its properties are therefore totally unlike those of beryl. Its density and refractive index are much higher and its hardness ($8\frac{1}{2}$) makes it even more resistant to wear. On the other hand, though it is allochromatic like beryl, it does not occur in such a wide variety of lovely colours as its namesake. There are, however, two varieties that are most attractive, rare and much sought after: alexandrite and cat's-eye.

The colour change of **alexandrite** has been mentioned. The finest specimens change their colour from a deep grass-green in daylight to a strawberry-red in electric light, or better still, candlelight. Less pronounced changes, say from green to a reddish-mauve, are more common. Fluorescent light usually produces intermediate colours and is not a form of lighting that shows gemstones to their advantage. The colour change is caused by the nature of the light used; daylight is more blue and electric light more yellow. In an alexandrite red and green are so evenly balanced that either predominates in the appropriate light. The most striking colour change can be seen in stones emanating from pegmatites near the Takovaya river in the Ural mountains, but these stones are cloudy and the gems that it is possible to cut from the rough crystals only rarely exceed three carats. Much larger and clearer stones come from the gem gravels of Ceylon but their colour change tends to be less pronounced. A few fine alexandrites have come from Burma and, more recently, from Rhodesia.

Alexandrite was first discovered in the Urals in 1831 and named later after the crown prince who became Tsar Alexander II. Appropriately enough, red, white and green, the trichroic colours of alexandrite, were also the Russian national colours at that time. The stone obtains its colour from traces of iron and chromium present in its composition as accidental impurities, the chromium producing the richer colour and the more striking colour change. Alexandrite is now being made synthetically but at the time of writing the products had not been tested on the market. Imitations in synthetic corundum are very common. These are a very bright red in artificial light but a purplish-blue in daylight. They are coloured with vanadium and can be readily distinguished by their absorption spectrum as well as by their different refractive index and physical density.

*Right* Altar piece inlaid with amber of various shades, seventeenth century, north German.

*Far right, above* Beryl group: emerald, aquamarine, heliodor, morganite and goshenite.

*Far right, below* Corundum group: ruby and sapphire. The sapphire crystal (top centre) displays the hexagonal colour zoning so typical of natural corundum.

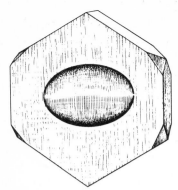

In some chrysoberyls, extremely fine tubes run through the crystal in one direction. These produce chatoyance in cabochons cut parallel to the tubes. Stones cut in this way are called chatoyant stones or cat's-eyes.

Alexandrite is usually step cut and looks well in a gold setting. Demand for it has increased greatly and made it one of the most expensive of gemstones.

Chrysoberyl **cat's-eye** or **cymophane** is also much sought after, on account of the luminous line that bisects it from top to bottom and moves from side to side as the stone is turned. Several other gem species also produce cat's-eyes, but none shows a line with such delicate yet sharp silky splendour as chrysoberyl. It is caused by extremely fine hollow channels traversing the stone at right angles to the line. In most other species the 'eye' is caused by solid fibrous crystals and is therefore coarser and more diffuse. Accurate cutting is required to place the line exactly in the middle of the stone; oddly, the half that is *nearer* the light looks darker than that further away. As extreme rarities nature produces alexandrite cat's-eyes, stones which show both a change of colour and a moving line. Normally the stones are honey-yellow to greenish in colour and translucent. They must be cut as round or oval cabochons. The other name, cymophane, means 'making a wave appear' in Greek. It is restricted to chrysoberyl cat's-eyes, as is indeed the name 'cat's-eye' without a prefix; cat's-eyes of other species are always qualified as in 'quartz cat's-eyes' and 'tourmaline cat's-eyes', for example.

Cat's-eyes come mainly from Ceylon's gem gravels and, unlike alexandrite, they have been much prized for thousands of years, particularly in India. Brazil has also produced some cat's-eyes fairly recently. The stones are simulated most closely by yellow quartz cat's-eyes but all applicable tests will clearly distinguish between the two species. No synthetic chrysoberyl cat's-eyes are marketed.

The more common variety of chrysoberyl consists of bright yellow stones, clear, transparent and with a good lustre. They are facet cut in all traditional styles and were widely used in Spanish and Portuguese jewellery of the eighteenth century. These stones were not large and were therefore often pavé-set, that is, touching each other and with the setting hardly visible, so that a large area was covered by the stones without an apparent break. Green stones without a colour change also exist; in fact all intermediate tints between yellow and green and, more rarely, colourless and even some parti-coloured stones can be encountered. No red or blue stones are known. Apart from Ceylon, the main sources are in Minas Gerais, Brazil; in Malagasy and Rhodesia; and in the USA at Haddam, Connecticut and Greenfield, New York.

**DIAMOND**, throughout history, has held a pre-eminent place among gemstones. In antiquity no means of polishing it was known and its fame rested mainly on its incomparable hardness. The way to cut diamond was probably first discovered in India in the Middle Ages but the knowledge soon spread to Europe. The lustre of diamond was then appreciated more widely but it was not until the seventeenth century, when the brilliant cut was evolved, that its full beauty was realized. Eventually, when the rich diamond fields of South Africa were exploited in the last quarter of the nineteenth century, it became far and away the most popular gemstone. Today it is estimated that some nineteen-twentieths of the value of all gemstones mined is represented by diamonds. Tradition, fashion, skilful marketing by which the value of diamonds has been more than maintained in a world of rampant inflation, have all contributed to this outcome.

The latest theory about the formation of diamonds is that in a few exceptional areas carbon was compressed at pressures of 500 000 to 1 500 000 pounds per square inch and heated to 1 000–2 500°C by movements of the molten magma in the earth's mantle at depths exceeding 100 miles from the surface. This pressure and temperature must have been maintained for a very long period during or after which the magma containing the diamonds was forced up to the surface, picking up other minerals on the way and forming the 'kimberlite pipes' from which all diamonds ultimately come. Some ten per cent of the world's production (or rather more if the Russian output is included) still comes directly from such pipes. They reach the surface in clusters, hence a number of mines often operate in the same area. The Big Hole at Kimberly was such a pipe; it is now exhausted but its associated mines (De Beers, Wesselton, Dutoitspan, etc.) are still productive.

Diamonds are only found within a pipe, never so much as a foot beyond it in the surrounding rock. They are embedded in the 'blue ground', as the old miners called the kimberlite; on weathering this would crumble into much softer 'yellow ground' nearer the surface. By far the largest recovery of diamonds is, however, from secondary deposits formed by rivers and the sea. The diamonds may have been carried to these from the volcanic hills that must once have topped the pipes. Both utterly primitive and the most highly mechanized methods of recovery from such deposits are in use.

The oldest source of diamonds is India, where they were known centuries before the Christian era. All the famous historic stones had their origin there. Mining was carried on until the new discoveries in Brazil and the exhaustion of the mines led to a great reduction in output in the eighteenth and nineteenth centuries. Golconda, now part of Hyderabad, came into great prominence in the sixteenth century, though the town of Golconda itself was only the trading centre. Mining has recently been resumed and expanded in India. Brazil was the main producer during the nineteenth century but the mines were exploited so fast that their yield decreased even before the 1880s brought South Africa to the fore. As the rest of Africa was opened up, many more diamond deposits were found. Most gem diamonds now come from the South-West African coastal strip running north from the Orange River, but by far the largest quantity of stones is recovered in an area that runs from Zaire (the Congo) to Angola, though these diamonds are almost wholly of industrial quality only. Other important African producers include Ghana, Guinea and the large Williamson mine in Tanzania. Outside Africa, Brazil still produces stones as do Venezuela and Guyana in South America. Borneo, Indonesia, the Ural Mountains and Australia provide small quantities but the most important recent discoveries have been in the area of the Vilyui River in Yakutia, in northern Siberia, and other places even further north beyond the Arctic Circle. A large number of pipes were found, but only a small proportion contain diamonds. These are, however, very rich and the Russians claim that production from them exceeds that of South Africa. About one-third of the total is said to be of gem quality and these stones have so far been marketed through western channels. Mining presents great problems as the ground is permanently frozen. Towns have been built to accommodate the workers and power is derived from atomic plants. The strategic importance of industrial diamonds no doubt led to the intensive prospecting and development which have taken place in this region.

Europe has no diamonds but a small number of stones have been found in widely scattered localities in the USA. The most productive area is near Murfreesboro, Arkansas, where several thousand stones have been found. No pipes have been discovered. The most bizarre occurrence consists of small crystals of an unusual type included in some meteorites.

*Above* Crystals and cut stones of peridot, spinel and chrysoberyl.

*Above right* A carved ewer of lapis lazuli, crystals of scapolite and feldspar, with cut stones of the same species.

*Below right* Photomicrograph of sunstone showing the flakes of haematite that produce its sheen.

It has already been noted that the hardness of diamond varies with direction. A diamond can be up to 100 times as hard to abrade in the hardest direction compared with the softest, though even the latter is incomparably harder than the next hardest gemstones of the corundum group. There are also differences in the hardness of diamonds from different localities, stones from Borneo and New South Wales tending to be harder than others.

Diamond is pure carbon and crystallizes in the cubic crystal system, usually as octahedra but also in other forms. Diamonds often fluoresce under X-rays and ultraviolet radiation, blue being the most common colour; orange, yellow or green fluorescence may also be seen. This fluorescence, which may change to yellow phosphorescence when the ultraviolet light is withdrawn, is one means of distinguishing diamonds from their many imitations; another is their complete transparency to X-rays. Other distinguishing features are the high single refraction (2.417), the distinctive absorption spectrum and the inclusions.

Most of the diamonds mined are translucent to opaque and vary in colour from grey to brown. Such stones are useless as gems but they are of the utmost importance in industry. They are used as tips for metal-shaping tools, as dies for drawing wire, as abrasives for truing grinding wheels and for drill bits, as styli for gramophone pick-ups, as glass cutters and stone saws and for countless other uses. The smallest industrial stones, known as boart, are crushed to various degrees of fineness and used extensively as abrasive powder.

Gem diamonds, however, must be clearly transparent to be worth cutting. Even small inclusions or imperfections in the cutting of the

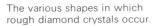

The various shapes in which rough diamond crystals occur.

stone, invisible to the naked eye but visible through a loupe magnifying ten times, detract from the value of a stone and this value plummets when these imperfections become clearly visible. The grades used in the United Kingdom are: F (flawless), VVS (very very slightly imperfect), VS, SI (slightly imperfect), 1st, 2nd and 3rd Piqué (visible to naked eye) and Spotted (easily visible to the naked eye). These grades are sometimes subdivided further, particularly in American and Continental usage into $VVS_1$, $VVS_2$, etc. In the USA the term 'Imperfect' ($I_1$, $I_2$, $I_3$) is used instead of 'Piqué'. Blemishes visible under the table facet are penalized more heavily than others.

Diamonds should be completely colourless, but if coloured, the colour must be definite and attractive. Brown and grey colours are not esteemed highly, nor is black, which, contrary to popular belief, is not very rare. More highly valued colours are green, canary yellow, blue or pink. Well-coloured stones are rare; they tend to be associated with certain mines.

Most colourless diamonds have in fact a faint tinge of yellow or brown, discernible only to the practised eye. Some fluoresce blue so strongly, even in daylight, that any yellow tinge is compensated. Completely colourless 'blue-white' diamonds are very rare; this description tends to be applied somewhat indiscriminately. Diamond dealers recognize eight to twelve grades in a colour scale which ranges from the finest white to the palest yellow. The first five grades would appear quite colourless to the untrained eye. Only an expert, working in a neutral north light and with the aid of standard stones for comparison, can come to a reliable assessment. The new diamond photometers are even more sensitive and objective in their measurement. Colour grades have not yet been fully agreed internationally. A system of names such as 'River', 'Wesselton', 'Crystal' and 'Cape' is used in the Scandanavian Diamond Nomenclature (Scan. D.N.) which has wide currency on the Continent and many adherents in the United Kingdom also. In the USA a system of letters is used by the Gemological Institute of America. Like clarity, colour has a great effect on value.

The value of a diamond is also influenced by its 'make'. In cutting a stone it is essential not only that the facets should be placed symmetrically and be of the same size and well polished, but also that the general shape of the stone should conform to certain proportions. To save labour or material, stones are sometimes made too deep or too shallow with a consequent loss of brilliance. The ideal proportions have been calculated theoretically and assessed in practice. The latest

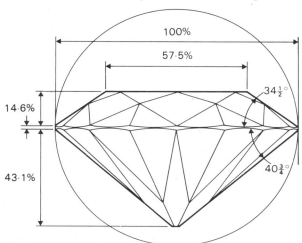

Ideal proportions of a brilliant according to the Scandinavian standard.

*Left* Garnet, jadeite and peridot.

*Above* Serpentine vase.

Diamond cuts including brilliants, a marquise and two step cuts.

calculations (Eulitz, 1972) indicate that maximum brilliance can be expected in a brilliant cut if the angle between the girdle and the pavilion and crown facets is 40.8° and 33.6° respectively, making the table facet 56½ per cent of the girdle diameter. Most modern brilliants come very close to these requirements, but those cut thirty years or more ago tend to be too deep. Unless deviations from the ideal are small, it is seldom advisable to have such stones re-cut as the loss in weight would depreciate them more than the improvement in quality would warrant; the value of a diamond increases roughly as the *square* of the weight, so that of two stones of the same quality but of different size, the one four times greater in weight would be worth approximately sixteen times as much. A loss in weight would therefore depreciate a stone more than proportionately. The greater rarity of larger stones, the greater care needed in fashioning them and the greater loss of rough diamond involved account for the difference in values. More than half the raw material is lost in cutting a diamond in any case, but in larger stones losses are often greater.

The value of a diamond therefore depends on the clarity, colour, cut and carat weight of the finished stone, the 'four Cs', but the importance allotted to each of these factors may well vary from stone to stone and valuation is not a matter of rule-of-thumb reckoning. Fashion and the condition of the market for stones of a particular kind at a particular time also have an important influence. More will be said on this subject when gemstones as an investment are discussed in chapter eight.

Although several references have already been made to diamond *imitations* a word needs to be said in clarification before enumerating them. Good jewellery set with clear and colourless stones of almost all types has at some time been mistaken for diamond jewellery but it was by no means always intended that this should happen. In past centuries, rock crystal, colourless topaz and even fine paste were often mounted in high-class jewellery in their own right, with no pretence that they were diamonds. On the other hand, paste has also been used as a diamond substitute for a long time and many a diamond has been replaced with it. Its main disadvantage is its softness; it can be made to look remarkably similar to the real stone when set in jewellery but it soon loses its sparkle. Rock crystal and topaz are harder but they lack the brilliance and fire of diamond. Zircon has both in fair degree but has also an unfortunate tendency to chip along the facet edges.

The newer *synthetics* were evolved with a view to overcoming these drawbacks, though some are a by-product of laser research. They have all been produced in the last twenty years or so, partly by the Verneuil process, partly from melts. The earliest, titanium dioxide or rutile – marketed as 'Titania' – has more than six times the dispersion of diamond. A dealer once described it to the author as 'an opal gone mad'. For this reason it could never be mistaken for a diamond. It is also soft and always shows a tinge of yellow or another colour – an attractive but 'flashy' stone. Strontium titanate, 'Fabulite', also has far more fire than diamond and is soft (6 on Mohs' scale) but is in many ways the most convincing imitation of a good diamond. A recent attempt at a closer approximation consists of a doublet with a fabulite pavilion and a crown of synthetic spinel, which because of its superior hardness protects the fabulite and also damps down the fire a little. Yttrium aluminium aluminate, YAG or Diamonair, often miscalled a garnet because it crystallizes in the same way, has considerable hardness (though even at $8\frac{1}{2}$ on Mohs' scale is still falls far short of that possessed by diamond), but it lacks fire. Synthetic scheelite and lithium niobate, 'Linobate', are both soft, but the latter has excellent fire.

The artificial coloration of diamond by irradiation has already been mentioned. By exposing diamonds of poor colour to high energy radiations from particle accelerators or atomic piles, the stones are coloured blue or green, rarely also pink. Further heating can then give them a permanent rich golden colour. Though such treatment enhances their value, there still remains a big difference in price between naturally and artificially coloured stones.

Diamond, the King of Gems, apparently so simple in its chemistry and crystal structure, has yielded some surprising secrets to recent research, with a profound bearing on our knowledge of crystallization processes. More discoveries will no doubt be made as scientific work on it proceeds.

**FELDSPARS** are among the most common rock-forming minerals of igneous formation. Their pale crystals, opaque to translucent, can be seen mixed with other minerals in granites and many other rocks, some of which form attractive cladding material for buildings. The feldspars form an isomorphous series. They are all aluminium silicates but in addition orthoclase contains potash, albite soda and anorthite lime. The gem materials of the feldspar group are relatively soft – orthoclase is the standard 6 on Mohs' scale – and they should therefore not be exposed to hard wear.

Four varieties of feldspar have found fairly wide application as gem and ornamental stones. Chief among them is **orthoclase**, the main constituent of **moonstone**. This owes its beautiful silvery to bluish sheen ('adularescence' or 'schiller') to its composition of extremely thin plates of orthoclase and albite. The thinner these plates are, the bluer is the sheen. There are also moonstones consisting mainly of albite. These are less translucent, but they can occur in a variety of colours: grey, blue, green, brown, yellow and white. There are also moonstone cat's-eyes. Moonstones are always cut as cabochons in such a way as to display the sheen to best advantage; they are set in necklaces, earrings or brooches, sometimes surrounding a coloured stone such as amethyst. They are also made into beads.

The main countries of origin are Ceylon, southern India (the district near Kangayam), Tanzania, and Malagasy which, together with Burma, produces some of the finest stones with a deep blue schiller. A fully transparent orthoclase of a fine golden colour comes from Malagasy; it is of little use for wear but has been cut for collectors. Orthoclase derives its name from the Greek *orthos*, right, and *klasis*, cleavage, because it has two cleavage directions at right angles to each other.

Closely akin to orthoclase is the microcline feldspar **amazonite** or **amazon stone**. It is semi-translucent and of a fine bluish-green colour which makes it suitable for beads and carved objets d'art. In spite of its name it is found mainly at Pike's Peak, Colorado; 'amazonite' was transferred to it quite erroneously from a totally different mineral found near the Amazon River.

The gem oligoclase feldspar, **sunstone** or **aventurine**, has a reddish-brown colour imparted by fine platelets of haematite, an iron oxide, which make it sparkle with innumerable flashes of colour – golden-yellow, red and many others – when the light strikes it at the right angle. Viewed under a microscope, sunstone is one of the most spectacular sights among gems. It is used in the same forms as amazonite and it comes from Norway; from near Lake Baikal in Siberia; and from Madoc County, California. Aventurine quartz is somewhat similar but is not so sparkling. It is also imitated by 'aventurine glass' or 'goldstone', an old artefact from which the name 'aventurine' derives. In the ancient glass factory at Murano near Venice molten copper was tipped by accident (*per avventura*) into a crucible of molten glass. The copper crystallized out in tiny bright triangular crystals forming a melt from which objects scintillating with countless points of coloured light could be formed.

The last member of the feldspar group widely used as an ornamental mineral is **labradorite**. It is dark grey in colour but suddenly flashes into bright spectral colours when it is viewed from the right angle. The usual colour of this sheen is a rich dark blue, but pale blue, green, orange, yellow, magenta and other colours occur, as well as combinations of colours. Labradorite is made into ashtrays and carved into various decorative objects. A translucent labradorite forms luscious black moonstones. As the name implies, the material comes mainly from Labrador, Canada.

Other members of the feldspar group occasionally provide transparent colourless gems but these are purely of interest to collectors.

**GARNET** has been extremely popular as a red gemstone from remote antiquity, perhaps largely because the red varieties are not particularly rare. Most of the stones called 'carbuncle' by the ancients – and by more recent sources also – must have been garnets, though the name was used somewhat indiscriminately for various red stones. What is not generally realized is that garnet can in fact occur in most colours except blue, including a magnificent green, and also in black and colourless forms. This wide variety of coloration occurs because garnet forms an isomorphous series. Each garnet usually contains at least traces of one or more of the other members of the family; some of the varieties are attractive in themselves and their combination produces still further interesting forms.

All garnets are silicates of two metals. They crystallize in the cubic system, usually as modified dodecahedra, and can be fully transparent to opaque. The name 'garnet' derives from the Latin *granatum*, a pomegranate, presumably by reference to the colour, but the root of the name goes back to Sanskrit. Six varieties of garnet are distinguished in accordance with their chemical composition and five of them are used as gemstones. They are called pyrope, almandine, spessartine, grossular, andradite and uvarovite. The latter is very rare and hardly ever occurs in forms which can be cut.

**Pyrope**, from the Greek *pyropos*, fire-like, displays the brightest red among garnets when pure. This is, however, rarely the case, for most pyropes contain an admixture of almandine molecules which darken them. Pyrope is one of the first minerals to crystallize out at a high temperature from a magma containing it and has been found in some very ancient igneous rocks. Good specimens have also come from the kimberlite pipes which carry diamonds, and minute pyropes even occur as inclusions within them. There are many localities in which pyrope is found – Australia, various parts of Africa and South America, and Arizona and Colorado in the USA – but by far the most prolific source of small stones was in Bohemia. Garnets from that country had a tremendous vogue in the last century. Small rose-cut stones were set in gold clusters to form every kind of jewellery. As time went on output increased but the quality of the gold used and the finish of the pieces declined. In the end garnet jewellery acquired a poor reputation from which it is only just recovering.

The closely related member of the garnet family, **almandine**, has an even wider distribution but fine stones are not very common. It is the traditional garnet of India, a darkish crimson in colour and widely used in oriental jewellery. It usually contains some pyrope; indeed every possible combination of the two varieties can occur. Never having been depreciated like pyrope, it is valued somewhat more highly and it is found in rather larger stones. It is often cut into cabochons, to which the name 'carbuncle' is still sometimes applied, and it occasionally displays a weak four-rayed star. The darker stones are not attractive, and in order to lighten the colour cabochons are sometimes hollowed out at the back and foiled to reflect more light.

**Spessartine** is a rather rare manganese garnet that occurs in a number of attractive colours, from yellow and orange to brownish-red. Having a high refractive index and density it forms lustrous stones which would be very popular if more became available. Slight admixtures of pyrope and almandine molecules are common; in fact, the three garnets so far described are grouped together in mineralogy under the designation 'pyralspite' from the first letters of the three varieties. The name spessartine comes from a district in Germany where the stone was first found but more recent sources are in the gravels of Ceylon and of Minas Gerais, Brazil; in Malagasy pegmatites; in a lode at Broken Hill, Australia; and in Virginia and Nevada in the USA.

The three other garnet varieties also tend to occur mixed with each other in isomorphous forms and are therefore collectively known as the 'ugrandite' garnets. The most common of them is **grossular** garnet, so named after *grossularia*, the Latin name for gooseberries, which the green translucent, crypto-crystalline variety resembles in colour. This comes mainly from the Transvaal, South Africa, and is used chiefly for ornamental carvings. It is sometimes miscalled 'Transvaal jade'. Unlike most jade simulants it is hard enough to withstand scratching with a steel knife, but it can be identified by its higher density and refractive index. Grossular of gem quality is yellow, orange or brownish in colour and is known as **hessonite** garnet. It is transparent though numerous inclusions often give it a treacly appearance. It is also known as 'cinnamon stone' and as 'jacinth', but the latter appellation is to be deprecated since it has also been applied to brown zircon. The Greek *hesson* from which the stone derives its name means 'less', in reference to hessonite's somewhat lower hardness compared with zircon.

The main source of hessonite is in the gem gravels of Ceylon where it occurs together with zircon. It also comes from Brazil and Siberia. Very recently perfectly clear crystals of green and colourless grossular garnet have been found in Tanzania and these are now reaching the market as rarities. There is also a pink translucent variety which is found at Xalostoc, Mexico. Grossular may therefore be regarded as the most versatile – although by no means the most valuable and beautiful – of garnets.

This distinction undoubtedly belongs to **andradite** or more especially to its green form, **demantoid**. This is coloured by chromium to an intense green in the best stones, in addition to which it possesses rather higher colour-dispersion or fire than diamond and a high refractive index; a truly splendid stone. Unfortunately, it rarely occurs in large crystals, so that gems cut from it very seldom reach three carats in size. It is also relatively soft, $6\frac{1}{2}$ on Mohs' scale. Tiny demantoids blend well with other gemstones and are sometimes used surrounding them. The finest specimens come from the Ural mountains, but green and yellow andradites also come from northern Italy and Switzerland. Demantoid was formerly known in the trade as 'olivene', a bad misnomer since olivine is the proper name for an entirely different gemstone. The name 'demantoid' refers to the diamond-like sparkle of the stone; 'andradite' celebrates the Portuguese mineralogist, d'Andrada, who first described it.

The last of the garnets, **uvarovite** – named after Count Uvarov, a distinguished Russian academician – is always an intense chromium green in colour but hardly ever occurs in sizes which can be cut. The few small stones cut for collectors tend to be rather cloudy. It was first found in the Urals but small isolated occurrences have been reported from several other areas.

**JADE** has been held in high esteem since neolithic times both for its pleasant colour and its toughness in use. A further reason for its popularity may be hinted at by its name, for the word 'jade' is derived from the Spanish *pietra d'ijada*, colic stone; it was once regarded as a potent medicine.

'Jade' is a trade name, however, and not used by mineralogists, for it refers to two quite distinct minerals of which only some varieties resemble each other. The more common of these minerals, **nephrite** (from the Greek *nephros*, kidney – another allusion to lithotherapy), is the stone with the long history. The other, **jadeite**, has a rather narrower geographical distribution and does not appear to have been used much before the eighteenth century, at any rate, in Asia and Europe. Both minerals owe their origin to metamorphic processes and both consist of felted fibrous crystals, which accounts for their toughness; they do not splinter as easily as their rival tool stones, the chalcedony minerals. Both have a hardness around 7 or below on Mohs' scale and, with one notable exception, both are translucent to semi-translucent. Contrary to general belief, both occur in a great variety of colours besides green. In China, where jade has been venerated for thousands of years, over a hundred different names are in use for different colour varieties, though some are no doubt applied to other stones as well. Both jades crystallize in the monoclinic system but no single crystals of any size exist. The simplest way to separate the minerals is by their density, jadeite being the denser; nephrite is also fractionally softer. Both materials occur in boulders of various sizes.

Nephrite ornaments and implements of great antiquity have been

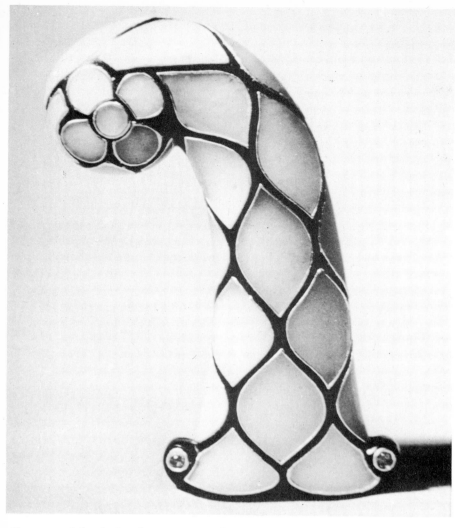

A Mogul dagger handle inlaid with nephrite jade.

discovered both in those parts of the world in which the mineral is found and in places far distant from these. It is the 'greenstone' so highly esteemed by the Maoris of New Zealand who carved it into pendants, sometimes representing their hero Tiki, and into chieftains' war clubs (*mere*). The classical land for artistic nephrite carvings is, however, China. Here it has been used in all colours, from brown through all shades of green and mottled colours to the purest white of coarse or fine grain. Some carvings can be dated to hundreds of years before Christ. Modern use in the western world is somewhat restricted since more colourful materials are now available, although beads, pendants and inlays are still being made.

Jadeite comes in many colours but is mostly of a much lighter green than nephrite; it often owes its colour, in part at least, to chromium. Pure chrome jadeite the Chinese *fei tsui*, is a rich emerald green. The extremely rare Imperial jade, so-called because its possession was the prerogative of the Chinese emperors, is transparent; it is prized by the Chinese above all other gemstones. It is so clear that it is possible to read print easily through a good specimen.

A necklace of thirty-one graduated beads of a fine green translucent colour was sold at an auction in Geneva for £156 250 in May, 1973. Jadeite also occurs in all other colours, purple, blue and red being most highly valued after emerald green. Pieces of the best colour are usually merely polished as cabochons or flats; only those of poorer colour are carved. Advantage is taken of mottling to form contrasting items in the design. A very dark green or black form of jadeite, rich in iron, is called **chloromelanite** and is also carved occasionally.

The most important occurrence of jadeite is in stream beds and hillsides in the Mogaung district of Upper Burma. From there it was formerly transported over a difficult mountain route to China, which absorbed the entire output. Nowadays it goes to Rangoon and then by ship to Hong Kong and other ports. Minor deposits exist in Mexico and California. It has been carved in Central America for well over a thousand years and the ancient Mayas prized it above gold. Chloromelanite adze heads found in France suggest that the mineral may also have been found in Europe in antiquity.

There are a great many green and other coloured minerals that have been mistaken for jade. The most common of these is serpentine. This is soft and, unlike jade, can be scratched with a steel pin or knife. The same holds for verdite, a deep green micaceous rock. Saussurite is harder but is rather a greyish-green. Imperial jade is imitated in glass; grey jadeite may be stained a fine green – caveat emptor!

**LAPIS LAZULI** is another stone that has been in high favour for ornamental purposes over thousands of years. The ancient civilizations of Sumer, India, Egypt and China all esteemed it greatly and archaeological finds have proved that its deposits, in a very remote part of Afghanistan, have been worked for more than 6 000 years.

It owes its popularity to its intense purplish-blue colour which is utterly resistant to fading in sunlight. It has been used to make inlays, figurines, seals of both cylindrical and flat shapes, scarabs, beads and pendants, but it is not wholly suitable as a ring stone since it only has a hardness of 6 and is subject to corrosion by chemicals. Its use as a pigment in the past is famous. Though apparently of even colour, it can be separated into particles which differ slightly in hue. These are then graded and ground to a fine powder which is the painters' colour ultramarine. Many ancient pictures owe their still luminous blues to it, but nowadays a synthetic pigment is used instead.

Lapis lazuli is a rock rather than a mineral. Its blue constituents are supplied by an isomorphous series of aluminium silicates, the chief of which is haüynite. This is partly replaced by three closely related minerals, lazurite, sodalite and nosean. In addition lapis lazuli contains white or grey calcite, yellow metallic specks of pyrite and minor admixtures of other minerals.

The name of this stone seems to have originated in the Middle Ages: 'lapis' means stone and 'lazuli' is derived from the Arabic word for blue. According to Pliny's description it is clear that lapis lazuli was the 'saphirus' of the Romans and Hebrews.

An imitation of long standing has been a porous jasper stained blue and marketed as 'Swiss lapis'. This does not show the yellow specks of pyrite and soon loses its colour in wear. A more recent imitation is in synthetic blue spinel in which the manufacturers have gone to the extraordinary lengths of counterfeiting the pyrite specks in pure gold! A poor quality of lapis lazuli, mottled grey and blue in colour, comes from Chile; minor deposits are on Lake Baikal in Siberia; in Upper Burma; in the Sawatch Range of Colorado and in San Bernardino County, California.

**MALACHITE**, with its bands of dark and bright green, is a most attractive ornamental material which takes quite a good polish in spite of its low hardness of 4. Being quite opaque, it is made into beads, eardrops, pendants, and a great variety of objets d'art, sometimes of large size. It is a copper carbonate, an important copper ore, and occurs in vast deposits in Siberia and the Shaba (Katanga) district of Zaire (Congo), but well-coloured and patterned pieces are not very common. Sometimes it occurs mixed with **azurite** a closely related blue mineral. Magnificent urns, bowls and other examples of the stone carver's art are in the Vatican and in Russian collections.

**MARCASITE** and **PYRITE** or 'fools' gold' are sulphides of iron. The tiny bright metallic stones much used as surrounds or designs in cheap jewellery ,and sold under the name marcasite are in fact usually made of pyrite, a much more common polymorph. Pyrite often occurs in well-formed and interesting cubic crystals while marcasite crystals are orthorhombic. Both have a wide distribution in Europe and North America; the chalk downs of Kent in England are a well-known source. Both minerals have a hardness of $6\frac{1}{2}$; they may tarnish or decompose after a time and, because they are cut in small thin pieces, they crack easily and fall out on impact. Pyrite means 'fire-like' in Greek; the origin of the name 'marcasite' is uncertain.

**PERIDOT** (pronounced peridow), a transparent green gemstone popular since antiquity, presents a problem in nomenclature. In America it goes by the name of chrysolite, but 'chrysolithos' meant a 'golden stone' to the ancients who used the term to describe what we now call yellow topaz; 'topazios', contrarily, referred to peridot. European mineralogists call the stone 'olivine' but this term (like chrysolite) includes both gem and non-gem qualities; moreover, it has been wrongly used for demantoid garnet. In the present book 'olivine' is used to cover all qualities of the mineral and 'peridot' refers unequivocally to this gemstone only; it is universally recognized to have this particular meaning, so perhaps it is the safest name to use. Although this form of the name is French in origin its ultimate derivation is uncertain.

Peridot is a member of an isomorphous series of minerals, halfway between a magnesium silicate, forsterite, and an iron silicate, fayalite. It therefore contains both iron and magnesium in proportions that vary a little from stone to stone. Since iron also gives the gem its idiochromatic colour the depth of that colour differs between specimens, but is nearly always green. Khaki and brownish stones occur as rarities but are not particularly attractive. Stones of lustrous brown and yellow shades, until 1951 taken to be peridots, were identified in that year as belonging to a new and completely different mineral species, sinhalite. Peridot crystallizes in the orthorhombic system but its properties may vary a little as the chemical composition of the stones varies. All peridots have a strong birefringence which gives them a peculiar oily lustre and is an important clue in their identification. Stones of the best quality usually have a hardness nearer 6 than 7 and such stones should therefore not be exposed to hard wear. Peridot does not fluoresce but displays a distinctive absorption spectrum.

Olivine forms at very high temperatures both in igneous and metamorphic rocks; it is therefore found in a variety of environments. Crystals up to the size of a pea have been found embedded in meteorites. It is the only gemstone so far reported to have been found in Antarctica. The most famous source of gem material, probably mined since the days of ancient Egypt and Rome, is the island of Zeberged (St John's) off the coast of Egypt in the Red Sea. This may well be the island mentioned by Pliny as the source of the green 'topazios', famous in antiquity and one of the stones of the Jewish High Priest's breast-plate. Peridot of good quality came from there until the mines were closed down in 1914. Stones of even better quality come from the Mogok district in Upper Burma, though the output is restricted at present because of bandit troubles. As may be inferred from the name, peridots are found in the diamondiferous periodotite pipes in South Africa, but these tend to be small. Gem-quality stones are mined in Minas Gerais, Brazil, while paler stones are found in Norway and darker stones in the gem gravels of Ceylon. Peridot is also found in Queensland, Australia and Arizona. There are several other sources in the USA, such as North Carolina, Vermont and New Mexico, but these are not commercially important.

Peridot is not particularly brilliant and the most appropriate cuts for it are the step cut or the scissors cut. It is set in necklaces, brooches, earrings and other jewels and looks charming surrounded by small amethysts, rubies or garnets. It has been widely used in regalia and reliquaries, where it often masquerades as emerald. Famous treasures in which peridots are incorporated are on display at the Cathedral of Cologne in Germany and in the Armoury of the Kremlin, Moscow. Imitations exist in glass doublets, synthetic spinel and synthetic corundum but these rarely attain the right colour and never the strong birefringence so characteristic of peridot.

**SILICA** gems, based on quartz, contain the two most common chemical elements in the earth's crust in combination: the gas oxygen and the non-metallic element silicon, somewhat akin to carbon in its properties. It is not, therefore, surprising that this family also forms the largest group of gemstones, both in the number of varieties and in the quantities mined (though they are not the greatest in value – that distinction belongs to diamond). It includes one truly precious species, opal, and a large number of less precious stones, down to the common varieties of jasper. For gemmological purposes it is usual to classify the family into varieties which provide transparent or sub-transparent gems cut from a single crystal, collectively referred to as 'quartz'; translucent crypto-crystalline varieties covered by the term 'chalcedony', if mainly pure, or 'jasper', if opaque and mixed with other minerals; and 'opal' and 'natural glass' for the amorphous varieties. The crystals of quartz and chalcedony are of exactly the same composition and structure. They differ only in size and there is a gradual transition between all these groups so that it is occasionally a matter of indifference to assign a stone to one group or the other.

The name **quartz** derives from the German *Querertz* meaning 'crossing ore' from its way of running across other mineral veins. When pure, it is absolutely colourless and is called **rock crystal**. Small allochromatic admixtures of colouring agents give it a wide range of colours but do not affect its properties such as hardness (it is the standard mineral of hardness 7 on Mohs' scale) or refractive index and density. The coloured quartzes are more highly esteemed as gems; rock crystal is now rarely cut and set as jewellery. One delightful form of art was to engrave it from the back of a flat cabochon and then to colour the engraved design. Some minute pictures of great delicacy were created in this way as well as a great range of more homely art. Well-made and artistically designed rock crystal jewellery of the seventeenth and eighteenth centuries can be seen in many jewel treasuries.

Quartz mainly occurs as an essential component of igneous rocks. It percolates into any cracks and lines any cavities that exist; it can then form euhedral crystals. A few years ago a climber found some well-formed rock crystals in a remote part of the Alps. They were several feet high and weighed from 200 to 1 300 pounds. The Austrian army mobilized a helicopter and some troops to bring them safely down to a museum in Salzburg. Excellent small rock crystals are found in many places: in the marble quarries at Carrara; in the French Dauphiné; near the St Gotthard pass in Switzerland; in Herkimer County, New York; in Cumberland and Cornwall, England; and elsewhere.

Rock crystal is now synthesized extensively for industrial and scientific use. During the last year or so such synthetic quartz, tinted in various colours, has been cut as gemstones in Russia.

Of the coloured varieties of quartz **amethyst** is pre-eminent. Until the eighteenth century it ranked among the most precious stones, an emblem of high rank and wealth, but its value fell with the discovery of a large South American deposit in about 1760. Even so, no other stone can match the rich deep purple of a well-coloured amethyst. Stones that show a distinct tendency towards a reddish-purple are preferred. *A-methystos* means 'not tipsy' in Greek and the name was given to the stone in the belief that it would preserve the wearer from drunkeness. The belief derives from a charming ancient legend about a most abstemious nymph; it was not always made clear that the protection from drunkeness only extended to those who eschewed alcoholic liquor!

The purple colour is thought to be caused by finely dispersed iron. As already mentioned, heat treatment changes this colour to brown or yellow, according to its intensity, and many citrines are in fact heat-treated amethysts. While amethyst and naturally coloured citrine display distinct dichroism, 'heated' citrine does not. Amethyst from one particular mine in Brazil can be made green by heat treatment; it is marketed under the name of prasiolite; an unfortunate choice since the name praseolite belongs to an entirely different mineral.

Amethysts of the finest colour come from Uruguay and the neighbouring part of Brazil. Fine stones are also found in the Ural mountains and in Japan, but stones of lesser colour have a fairly wide distribution.

**Citrine** is the correct name for all yellow and pale brown varieties of quartz, though it is still occasionally sold under the name of 'topaz', often with some prefix. Fortunately this once common pernicious practice is now being abandoned. There is, of course, a considerable difference in value between the two stones, though at first sight they may look very similar. Topaz is much rarer and harder, and has a much wider and subtler range of colours. Citrine is the most common yellow stone available. It comes mainly from various parts of Brazil and from Malagasy but it has a wide distribution. Darker brown stones are sometimes called 'cairngorm' from the Scottish mountains of that name where they were first found. The name 'morion' is sometimes applied to really dark brown stones and also to those that are cloudy and translucent, but the appellation 'smoky quartz' is preferable for the latter.

Another semi-transparent to translucent variety is **rose quartz**, coloured a subtle shade of pink by manganese. This is rather rarer than the varieties so far named; it comes from Minas Gerais, Brazil and from South-West Africa, sometimes in pieces large enough to be carved into quite large figurines. Curiously, it seldom occurs in well-shaped crystals. It is famous for producing translucent six-rayed star stones, the star being particularly bright in transmitted light (light which has passed through the stone). For this reason rose quartz stars

Synthetic star stone. In these early synthetics the star did not reach the girdle.

are usually polished on their base as distinct from star corundums which are left rough. The base then acts as a mirror reflecting the incident light and enhancing the star. Sometimes coloured varnishes are applied to the base to produce star stones of many colours. These can be distinguished from star corundums in that a reflection of the light source can be seen at the centre of the star.

At some sites quartz has crystallized round pre-existing minerals, completely enclosing and sometimes altering them. This process has produced some striking effects. Quartz enclosing the delicate fibres of amianthus, a kind of asbestos, gives rise to cat's-eyes that may approach cymophane in quality. **Quartz cat's-eyes** may be yellow, brown, green or even black. They are found in the Ceylon gem gravels, like cymophane, and also in Bavaria. The coarser, wavy fibres of crocidolite asbestos are enclosed in **tiger's eye**. This is a golden-brown variety often cut as brooch stones or larger ornamental objects since it occurs in substantial layers. Crocidolite is normally blue, only oxidation makes it brown. The blue **hawk's eye** formed round this unoxidized mineral is somewhat less common but is used in much the same way. There is also a mottled variety incorporating partly altered crocidolite. The main provenance of these stones is near Griquatown in South Africa.

A very attractive effect is produced when rock crystal encloses more widely spaced crystals of a fibrous texture, particularly rutile. This is a yellow to reddish-brown mineral possessing a very high lustre and forming shining hair-like or needle-like structures which make very spectacular inclusions. The trade names of such stones are 'Venus hair stone' and '*flèches d'amour*', but the mineralogical name is merely 'rutilated quartz'. It comes from Brazil, from North Carolina and from Lake Onega in Russia. Needles of black, brown or green tourmaline also occur. Quartz enclosing purple or brown dumortierite is found in Arizona and Nevada. Green crystals of quartz may be formed round chlorite or fuchsite mica; these sometimes present the ghostly outline of one crystal within another. Multi-crystalline varieties include translucent white **milky quartz** and purple **amethystine quartz**. They are occasionally carved as ornamental objects.

The quartz varieties made up of microscopic crystals, the crypto-crystalline forms, are grouped together as **chalcedony**, of which there are innumerable variants. Those most widely used in jewellery include red **cornelian**, named after a berry; light green **chrysoprase** and darker **prase** (leek in Greek) or **plasma** (meaning a carved figure); brown **sard** (named after the capital of ancient Lydia) and **sardonyx** where sard is layered with white **chalcedony**; black or black and white layered **onyx** (it means 'fingernail' in Greek)–the so-called 'Mexican' or 'Algerian' onyx, yellow, brown or green in colour and of a banded structure, is a completely different mineral, a form of calcite called alabaster in ancient times; **bloodstone** or **heliotrope**, an opaque green variety speckled with bright red spots; and the agates. In **banded agate** coloured layers alternate with white ones; in **fortification agate** these bands enclose an irregularly shaped design; **moss agate** consists of translucent grey chalcedony formed round green, black or red inclusions of crypto-crystalline manganese, iron and other oxides; in **mocha stone** these crystals form flat tree-like or fern-like designs within cracks in the chalcedony. Chalcedony also occurs in white, grey, brown and blue tints. Like all its varieties, it is porous and can be stained in many colours. Most onyx and banded agate is stained and much cornelian, blue chalcedony and chrysoprase has had its colour deepened.

Agates–both of these and of many other kinds–and chalcedonies are found in most countries but only in Brazil, Uruguay, parts of southern India and Malagasy do they occur in qualities and quantities sufficient to warrant mining on a commercial scale.

**Jasper**, a compound of silica with a great variety of other materials, is even more common and more various in colour and design than chalcedony. It also goes under a greater diversity of names, some of which properly belong to quite different mineral species. Thus 'Egyptian marble' is a jasper with beautiful light and dark brown markings; 'ruin marble' has designs reminiscent of ruined buildings in grey and brown; 'puddingstone' consists of coloured pebbles cemented together with silica; 'Oregon jade' is a rich green jasper; 'ribbon jasper' comes in layers of various colours. Many jaspers are called 'agates' to which they are indeed closely related. Handsome specimens can be picked up on many beaches and at other localities known to 'rock hounds'. They form fine subjects for amateur lapidaries.

**Opal**, the most famous and precious of the silica gems, owes its renown to the vivid flashes of coloured light that the stone reflects. These flashes can be evenly spread over a large part of the stone's surface or they can come from numerous irregular patches or points of light which cover it with a radiance made up of all the colours of the rainbow. No other precious stone can show such bright and pure colours because the 'play of colour' in opal is produced by quite different means from that which colours other gemstones: it is produced by the diffraction of light, not by its absorption. This is an effect similar to that which gives the bright metallic colours to the plumage of humming birds, for instance, but clearer and stronger, because the active principle in opal is even more delicate. It consists of an array of ultra-microscopic spherules forming layers within the stone and acting as a three-dimensional diffraction grating of the utmost fineness. This fact was only discovered in 1966 when Australian scientists examined opals under an electron microscope. Previously, other theories had been advanced to account for the play of colour.

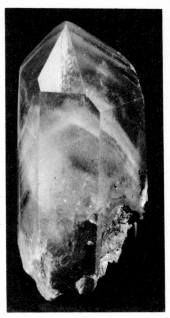

Ghost crystal of chlorite in quartz.

This difference in internal structure is the essential feature that distinguishes precious opal from common opal (amorphous silica), of which there are many varieties. Perhaps the best known of these is the **fossil wood** of petrified forests, where silica has replaced the fibres in ancient trees so exactly that their structure can still be seen in every detail. Another variety is **cachalong**, which is white and resembles porcelain; it is so porous that it will adhere to the tongue. Common opal is usually translucent and can occur in many colours.

Opal consists of amorphous silica of varying degrees of porosity, always holding some water. It is deposited at relatively low temperatures from watery solutions in rocky fissures or even in the gaps between grains of sand and pebbles. It is being precipitated from hot springs even now. Precious opal is classified by its body colour into four groups: black, white, fire and water opal.

**Black opal**, in which the jet black background sets off the play of colour to perfection, is the rarest and most valuable variety. Only a small proportion of gem material, all from Australia, is truly black.

**White opal** shows its colours against a milky or greyish background. This is the variety that has been known and prized since ancient times.

**Fire opal** is so named for its transparent or translucent orange to red colour, not necessarily for any fiery glints. Much of it shows no play of colour at all and is cut solely for its body colour. It is then the least costly of the gem opals and is often faceted while all other opals are cut with a flat or domed top.

**Water opal** is completely colourless and transparent, which gives the play of colour within it a curiously ethereal quality.

**Opal matrix** consists of specks or veins of precious opal contained in dark brown, opaque limonite from which it is not worth separating the opal.

Precious opal frequently fills quite thin fissures and is therefore often cut into thin flat stones. Sometimes these are so thin that they would soon break in wear and they are therefore cemented to thicker pieces of common opal, onyx or even black glass. These *opal doublets* are usually sold for what they are and the joint between their components is often visible. When it is hidden in a setting it may be very difficult to determine the true character of the stone without unsetting it.

Opal derives its name, via ancient Greece, from the Sanskrit word *upala* meaning a precious stone, but there are now no major sources of opal in the Orient. The main historic source seems to have been in what is now eastern Czechoslovakia and white opal of mediocre quality is still found there. This source is now completely superseded by Australia, where stones of superb quality have been gathered from the 1880s onwards. Some of these fields are now exhausted but others are still productive. Perhaps the largest stone ever found, one of 203 carats, was that presented to Queen Elizabeth II by the South Australian Government in 1954, the Andamooka opal. Mexico produces fire and water opals.

The stupid superstition that it is unlucky to wear opals dies hard but it has not depressed the value of stones of good quality. Until quite recently it has been impossible to imitate opal at all convincingly, but recent reports from Australia state that a synthesis has been successful and that commercial exploitation is feasible.

No account of the silica gems would be complete without mention of the amorphous impure **natural glasses** found on the earth's surface in a few areas. The most common of these is **obsidian**, a name derived from the Latin word for it, *obsio*. It is a translucent to opaque material, usually black but sometimes grey or brown, formed by the rapid cooling of volcanic lava. It often contains inclusions of gases and minerals which may give it a silvery sheen, a spangled effect, a chatoyance, or the semblance of white snowflakes on a black background. It usually contains bubbles. In jewellery it is formed into brooch cabochons, pendants or beads, its low hardness (5 to 6, the same as man-made glass) precluding it from exposure to hard wear. It occurs in many parts of the world and was a vitally important raw material from which neolithic peoples made knives, scrapers, arrowheads and other tools as well as objects and figurines for ceremonial use.

Complete mystery still surrounds the origin of another group of natural glasses, the **tektites** (from the Greek for 'molten'). Volcanic and meteoric provenance has been postulated for them but no satisfactory theory yet exists. They are named after the localities in which they are found, as australites, indochinites and billitonites, for example. The only variety that has found some use in jewellery is **moldavite**, named after a river in Bohemia. It is olive- to bottle-green, full of curious swirls and bubbles; it is usually cut with facets. Equally mysterious is the origin of the yellow, cloudily transparent **silica glass** found in the Libyan-Egyptian desert in 1932. In contrast to all other natural glasses it is almost pure silica and is found in fairly large pieces. Some faceted stones have been cut from it, mainly for collectors. None of the natural glasses are of much value since few are sufficiently attractive and rare – and none are hard enough – to make good gemstones.

Tektites from Australia and south-east Asia.

**SPINEL** deserves to be known and appreciated far more widely than it is, for it possesses most of the virtues which make a gemstone popular. It is bright and fully transparent, occurs in a wide range of handsome colours and with a hardness of 8 takes a good polish and wears well. Its misfortune may be that it is often found in the same places as the corundum gems which have all these virtues in even greater measure.

When quite pure, spinel is colourless, but it can show any colour except, curiously, a clear yellow. The reds and blues approximating to the colours of ruby and sapphire are valued most and they have been sold under such misleading names as 'balas ruby', 'spinel ruby' and 'sapphire spinel', but there are usually slight differences in colour which give spinel the less rich hue.

Spinel is an oxide of magnesium and aluminium, but both these metals may be replaced by others. This explains the wide range of colours and also accounts for some variations in its properties. Recognized varieties that are occasionally cut as gemstones include **ceylonite** (green), **pleonaste** (black), **chlorospinel** (green), all of which contain iron, and **gahnospinel** (blue), which contains zinc. All these have higher refractive indices and densities. Apart from these names, it is best merely to use a colour prefix when describing spinels. All spinels crystallize in the cubic system, typically as octahedra, and they therefore have a single refractive index only and no dichroism. Spinels are often found as twin crystals that look as if two octahedra had grown into each other. This form of twinning is so typical of the species that it is commonly known as 'spinel twinning'. Red spinels fluoresce under ultraviolet light and also appear bright red under the emerald filter – two more reasons why they might be confused with ruby. That such confusion was widely prevalent is shown by several instances of historic 'rubies' that are really spinels. Perhaps the most famous of such stones is the 'Black Prince's Ruby' in the front of the Imperial State Crown of the UK, an unfaceted gem of 352 carats, which is in fact a red spinel.

The origin of the name 'spinel' is uncertain except that it has been adopted from the French. The stones can be formed in both igneous and metamorphic processes and they crystallize at a high temperature.

The gem gravels of Ceylon and Burma which yield corundum gems, also produce some of the best spinels.

Spinel appears in almost any kind of jewellery. It is used both as a single stone and as small stones to surround others, but it is by no means in common use.

Much has already been said about the wide variety of colours available in **synthetic spinel**. Moonstones, lapis lazuli, alexandrite and every coloured gemstone has been so imitated, and several hues have been produced that are unlike any gemstone found in nature. Such stones are bright, cheap and wear well – what more can one expect?

**TOPAZ** crystals have been held in high regard as gemstones from classical times, though they then went under the name of 'chrysoprasios', the golden stone, and not 'topazios' (see under peridot). At that time the stone we call topaz was probably lumped together with other yellow gems, such as yellow sapphire, beryl and chrysoberyl. The wholly improper trade practice of applying the name 'topaz' to the much cheaper citrine quartz is now, fortunately, less prevalent than it used to be.

Most people know topaz as a yellow gemstone and in jewellery it is seen most commonly in a range of tints from pale yellow to a rich brown. The most desirable shade is a medium brown with a tint of red – a subtle colour not found in any other gemstone. Pink topazes are also much admired, the more so the deeper their colour. They are very rare in nature; practically all are produced by a carefully controlled heat treatment of brown stones. A topaz colour rarely seen in jewellery is blue, probably because few blue topazes have a sufficiently deep colour. Most are paler than aquamarines and like these can have a greenish tint. Most common and also least valuable is completely pure, colourless topaz.

Coloured topazes have been very popular from the sixteenth century onward, and have often been worn in exquisite settings as necklaces, earrings, brooches or entire suites. Being hard (they are the standard 8 on Mohs' scale), they take an excellent polish and display a fair lustre. Their depth of colour varies from stone to stone, so that it is no simple matter to match a number of stones exactly. For this reason, and also to deepen and brighten their colour, both pink and brown topazes were often backed with metal foil of an appropriate shade which largely compensated these inequalities. Such foiling, also used with other pale transparent stones, has to be contained in a closed setting (one that covers the entire back of the stone). An open setting, which leaves the pavilion largely uncovered, usually indicates that the stones have been more carefully matched for colour. This in turn implies that a wide selection of stones was available which was not the case until the nineteenth century. Foiling in old jewellery therefore carries no pejorative implications, even when the original foiling has faded and lost some of its virtue. It is often not practicable to refoil and reset the stones without damaging them, quite apart from the adverse effect on the historical value of the jewellery.

Topaz is a fluo-silicate of aluminium, mostly formed by pneumatolytic igneous processes, that is, by condensation from hot vapours carrying its constituents. Well-coloured specimens show fair pleochroism, one of the three colours visible usually being near-white. Its main drawback for use in jewellery is its readiness to cleave across its narrowest dimension, but this is only likely to occur on sharp impact with a hard object. It crystallizes in long orthorhombic prisms so that the gems cut from it also have an oblong shape. It is often seen in he mixed cut, particularly in older jewellery; the modern tendency is towards the step cut.

In antiquity topaz came from mines in Upper Egypt; during the Middle Ages and subsequently it was brought from the East (Ceylon) and from the eighteenth century onwards, from Minas Gerais, Brazil; from near Sverdlovsk in the Ural Mountains and from Kamchatka and elsewhere in eastern Siberia. There are several minor localities, including the Cairngorms in Scotland and the Mourne Mountains of Ireland. In the USA topaz is found in California, Colorado, New Hampshire and Utah. Very well-formed crystals have came from South-West Africa and Nigeria, but these are mainly colourless. Very large crystals are exhibited at several museums, some of which weigh over 100 pounds.

Topaz is not synthesized commercially, the usual substitute being citrine. Some synthetic spinel and, of course, paste, has been marketed imitating both pink and sherry-coloured topaz.

**TOURMALINE** shows the widest range of lovely colours of all gemstones. Every possible hue can be found in every degree of saturation in this most versatile of all gems; besides which there are parti-coloured stones where the colour changes sharply or gradually from one end to the other or where two or more colours are arranged concentrically or in a multitude of parallel stripes. There are also somewhat coarsely grained cat's-eyes in all colours.

The name 'tourmaline' comes from a Sinhalese root meaning 'a coloured stone' and least confusion is caused by using it with an appropriate prefix when referring to the various colours, as brown tourmaline and blue tourmaline, for example. It is not surprising, however, that so polychromatic a species should have become endowed with a large number of variety names. Thus we have **achroite** for the colourless variety (the word means 'colourless' in Greek); **dravite** (after a Russian river) for brown colours; **rubellite** (dangerously suggestive of ruby) for the pink and red varieties; **indicolite** for blue; **siberite** (after Siberia) for violet; and **schörl** (a German mining term pronounced 'shirl') for black, a stone formerly much used in mourning jewellery. There are also some wholly misleading names, such as 'Brazilian emerald' for green stones, which are best forgotten quickly.

The profusion of colours is caused by the somewhat complex chemical composition of the stone. It is a borosilicate compound of several different metals which can be present in varying proportions. In consequence the properties, particularly the density, can vary considerably. The only constant feature is the crystal structure. Tourmaline usually occurs in long striated trigonal prisms which have a roughly triangular section. These are found in both igneous and metamorphic rocks and commonly owe their origin to pneumatolysis, that is, they crystallize from very hot vapours, sometimes in association with topaz.

Tourmaline is a fairly hard gemstone (7 to $7\frac{1}{2}$) which can be worn in any form of jewellery. Fully transparent stones were formerly fashioned in the mixed cut (brilliant cut crown, step cut pavilion); now a simple step cut is more usual. Cloudy stones are made into cabochons or beads. The stone is very popular in many countries and in China was worn to indicate mandarin rank. It was also carved, sometimes quite elaborately, as pendants, buttons, tiny bowls, and 'fingering pieces' which were passed across the fingertips to soothe the nerves. Advantage was clearly taken of any parti-coloration present in a stone to introduce different colours into the carved design. In the western world the most valuable colours are a clear ruby red and a bright sapphire blue, followed by parti-coloured stones and bright greens. The duller greens and browns are rather more common.

Outstanding optical attributes of tourmaline are its marked birefringence and its strong dichroism. In most stones a light and a dark tint of the main body colour are present and the stones can accordingly be cut so as to present either a lighter or a darker shade.

Another characteristic property of tourmaline is its pyro-electricity. When heated, or even rubbed hard with a cloth, it acquires an electric charge, positive at one end and negative at the other, and will attract such items as ashes and small scraps of paper. As with quartz, specimens of high purity can be used to control oscillations.

Although tourmaline has been gathered in the East for centuries, in Burma, Thailand and particularly in Ceylon, it does not seem to have been imported into Europe much before the eighteenth century and there is no obvious mention of it in antiquity. Possibly it may have been grouped with other stones, but this is curious in a species as widely distributed as tourmaline. The gravels of Ceylon still contribute to world production but more is mined in Minas Gerais in Brazil. Excellent material also comes from San Diego County, California; other localities in the USA are in Maine and Connecticut. Malagasy has rich deposits of gem-quality tourmalines in every colour; fine green, pink and blue stones come from the Ural Mountains of Russia; Tanzania has recently increased its production. In Europe, a little tourmaline comes from Switzerland. The stone is not synthesized commercially.

**TURQUOISE** has been used as an ornament since the dawn of history. Rich necklets and plaques of gold set with turquoise have been found in Egyptian and Sumerian tombs of the fourth millennium BC as well as beads of even greater antiquity. It was widely used by ancient civilizations and in the Middle Ages and it retains great popularity to the present day. Pliny describes it under the name of 'callais'. Its present name, meaning 'Turkish' in French, is thought to derive from the circumstance that it reached Europe from Persian mines via Turkey. Its extensive use in antiquity may have been promoted by its relative softness (a little less than 6 on Mohs' scale) which made it possible to drill and polish it with the primitive means then available.

Turquoise is a phosphate of copper and aluminium containing some water. It is always found as crypto-crystalline aggregates and it fills fissures and cavities where rocks have weathered in the proximity of copper deposits. It is porous as well as soft and liable to discoloration by chemical agents. It should therefore be kept away from soap, sprays, detergents and any chemicals, as well as from dirt. Turquoise is usually impregnated with wax or resin after polishing to minimize the danger of loss of colour. Since the most valuable colour is a deep sky-blue, a dye is frequently added when treating material of mediocre quality to deepen natural tints and to overcome a tendency towards the less desirable greenish hues that many stones possess. The colour of untreated stones is apt to fade after long exposure to sunlight. Some stones are veined with black limonite; when this veining is substantial the material is called **turquoise matrix**.

The obvious style of cutting turquoise is as cabochons, but large pieces are polished flat. Gilt designs are sometimes incised into stones in the East. In Tibet and elsewhere, small but well-coloured fragments are sometimes set closely together, held by pitch in a hollow mount of silver. Turquoise often looks to best advantage in a surround of small rubies.

Tibet still produces a little turquoise but the most famous and productive locality is Khorassan in Iran. The Shah's treasury holds a wealth of beautiful turquoise objects, including some large urns assembled from translucent material. Other ancient mines are in Turkestan south of Samarkand, but the oldest of all may well be those in the Sinai peninsula from which the ancient Egyptians obtained their supplies. These mines were abandoned and the knowledge of their whereabouts lost for many centuries until their rediscovery in 1845; but little material has come from there for some time. The oldest mine of any kind in the USA is in New Mexico, near Santa Fé, from which the local Indians obtained turquoise long before the arrival of Europeans. Turquoise of a greenish tint is still obtained from that State.

Few gemstones have been imitated as widely as turquoise. Even in ancient Egypt beads were made from blue faience, a kind of glazed earthenware, which resemble turquoise closely. They were made, together with insets for jewellery and such small items as scarabs, for thousands of years and similar products based on glass and ceramics are produced to the present day. Other imitations are made from a variety of powders similar to turquoise in composition and either compressed or bonded with plastics. An exact synthesis of turquoise has recently been reported from Germany. Most of these artefacts can be distinguished by their lack of the characteristic absorption spectrum. This also applies to two natural minerals that somewhat resemble turquoise, namely **variscite** from Utah, which is green, often flecked with white, and **odontolite**, fossil bones stained blue or green by phosphate of iron which often show signs of a structure typical of bone.

**ZIRCON** was well known to ancient civilizations and its use as a gem extends back at least to Greek and Roman times. As usual, it went under different names according to its colour varieties and was often confused with other species. One of its names was 'hyacinth' (taken from Greek mythology), which later became 'jacinth', and normally applied to the magnificent reddish-brown varieties of zircon, but also to hessonite garnet. Another name, 'jargoon', probably of Persian or Arabic derivation, was applied to pale yellow zircons.

Zircon, a silicate of the metal zirconium, occurs quite commonly in igneous rocks such as granite. It crystallizes out at high temperatures but forms only tiny crystals. These rocks may then weather out to form sands and many gold-bearing sands carry small zircons. Larger, cuttable crystals are found in pegmatites and in gravels derived from these. There are only a few areas where zircons of gem quality are found. Ceylon, that treasure-house of gems, ranks high among these and produces stones of many colours but perhaps the finest zircons come from Cambodia from where they are taken to Bangkok in Thailand for processing and distribution.

The natural colours of zircon range from colourless (rare) through all shades of yellow and brown to a deep brownish-red or a brownish-green. The darker colours can be improved by heat treatment owing to a most unusual peculiarity of zircon.

Most zircons contain varying amounts of uranium as an impurity and, as is well known, uranium is so unstable that it undergoes spontaneous nuclear fission during which it emits neutrons with great force. These collide with and displace atoms in the surrounding zircon, impairing the strict order of its crystal lattice. Over many millions of years this internal bombardment partly or wholly destroys the crystallinity of the host zircon, greatly affecting its physical properties. It is therefore possible to divide zircon into three types: a 'high' type in which there is little or no damage to the crystal structure; an 'intermediate' type in which the crystal structure has been disorganized to a greater or lesser degree; and a 'low' type in which the crystal lattice has become completely destroyed and the stone is amorphous or very nearly so. The three types merge into each other. The less crystalline a zircon is, the lower its hardness, its refractive index and density, its birefringence, its dichroism (rarely great to start with) and the clarity of its very distinctive and interesting absorption spectrum. By heating an intermediate stone its atoms are made to vibrate more violently so that they may jump back and stay in their original positions, making the stone high or fully crystalline again. In most low stones the damage has gone so far as to be irreversible. Colour changes accompany the changes in crystal structure; low stones are green, or extremely rarely orange. Most stones when found are intermediate and may be of any of the colours named.

When an intermediate zircon is heated it begins to glow long before the stage of red heat is reached, a phenomeon known as thermoluminescence. If the heating is continued for ten minutes or more and the stone is allowed to cool gradually, it will emerge rather lighter in colour, denser and with a much improved sparkle. According to the shade of the original material and the degree of heat applied, golden, yellow or colourless stones are produced. If the heating is done in a reducing atmosphere, that is one deficient in oxygen, a blue colour is obtained. The mineralogist G. F. Kunz introduced the name 'starlite' for the blue variety thus produced.

High zircon has a hard, clear sparkle, an adamantine lustre and a high dispersion of colour. It has a hardness of $7\frac{1}{2}$ but is somewhat brittle, so that its facet edges are apt to show wear. Its birefringence is so strong that in a large stone the back facets appear double even to the naked eye. It has the highest density of any gemstone in common use and is normally perfectly clear and transparent with an extensive range of fine colours. These are surely qualities that should procure for the species an even wider popularity than it possesses. Perhaps it suffers from the same disability as spinel and many another choice gemstone, namely public ignorance and suspicion of the unknown.

The high lustre of zircon makes the brilliant cut easily the most appropriate style of cutting this gem. As a ring stone it should be worn with care but in all other settings it enhances jewellery with its brightness and fire. The most highly esteemed colours are a rich blue or red, followed by golden shades. Colourless zircons are favourite substitutes for diamond. Zircons of different colours, often grouped together in the same setting with less bright stones, do not always harmonize well with them.

Blue zircons are sometimes imitated in synthetic spinel or corundum, but no synthetic zircon is on the market. Some near-white zircons from Matara in Ceylon are marketed under the misleading name of 'Matara diamond'.

**PEARLS** have been treasured by civilizations in all parts of the world from the remotest ages. Their iridescent lustre, their mysterious origin and rare presence in the depths of the ocean have always appealed to the imagination and emotions. To this day, natural pearls are among the most precious of gemstones.

They are always included under that designation although they are not 'stones' or minerals at all. Everybody knows that they are produced by shell fish but few realize that almost any mollusc, including some snails, is capable of producing a 'pearl' of sorts and that, in addition to the truly precious pearls produced by oysters of the *Pinctada* genus, there are numerous other kinds of molluscs, both marine and freshwater, which produce quite attractive pearls of many colours.

They do this by building a shell in reverse round an irritant that has managed to enter the folds or tissues of their soft bodies. The irritant is not a grain of sand, but usually some parasitic larva or egg. This the mollusc first tries to smother with conchiolin, a substance that also forms the horny outer skin on most shells. It then proceeds to deposit a shell of minute crystals of lime (calcium carbonate) in smoothly concentric platelets over the intruder and goes on doing this until eventually a pearl is formed. The size of the pearl depends on the duration of growth and on the type of mollusc, its shape and the anatomical environment in which it originated. In the *Pinctada* oysters the platelets are exceedingly thin and translucent; together they form the *nacre* of the pearl and produce various optical effects that give rise to its lustre or *orient*. Other molluscs form coarser structures, creating pearls of less or no orient. While the smaller species of the *Pinctada* genus are fished mainly for their pearls, the larger species and the other genera of molluscs are fished for their shells, the lining of which is used for making mother-of-pearl buttons and ornaments; any pearls are a by-product.

The finest pearls come from the Persian Gulf and the straits between India and Ceylon. These pearls are not large but their lustre is exceptional and they are a fine white colour, sometimes with a rosy tinge. Larger white pearls are found in the waters north of Australia up to Burma and the Philippines. Yellow pearls come from Western Australia, black ones from the Gulf of California. The abalone which lives in the Pacific Ocean also produces some yellow pearls, but mainly green or even blue ones. The Giant Conch, a marine snail from the tropical Western Atlantic, produces beautiful pink or salmon-coloured pearls, but without any orient. Other important pearl fisheries are in the Red Sea, and on the coasts of Mexico and Venezuela.

Growing cultured pearls. Pearl oysters implanted with mother-of-pearl beads are kept in cages suspended from rafts until they have formed sufficient nacre round the beads.

Pearl fishing is now carried out with modern diving equipment but the most primitive methods were used in the Persian Gulf. A nose clip, stalls to protect the fingers from the sharp shells and a rope basket in which the shells were collected was all that the diver normally carried. He stood on a stone that was attached to a rope and by giving him additional weight helped his descent to the bottom. This was drawn up while he worked and a jerk on another rope tied round his waist then signalled that he was ready to be hauled up. The strong current carried him well astern of the ship. When the area under the ship had been cleared, the ship was hauled forward by its very long anchor rope. Long hours of work, the inability to eat while diving, the coldness of the water and danger from sharks attracted by blood from cut hands, all added up to make this one of the most unpleasant ways of earning a living. Only one oyster in forty contained a pearl. Fishing declined between the wars when discoveries of oil provided a much more lucrative livelihood; the industry is now almost wholly defunct in this area and no more do the loveliest pearls come from the Persian Gulf.

From antiquity fine pearls have also been found in mussels (mainly of the family Unionidae) living in rivers. Various Roman writers have praised the river pearls of Britain. Flourishing pearling industries were still operating in North Wales and in Scotland in the nineteenth century,

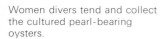

Women divers tend and collect the cultured pearl-bearing oysters.

Natural pearl consists of tiny crystals of nacreous calcium carbonate in a concentric and radial arrangement throughout.

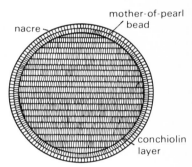

A cultured pearl consists of a mother-of-pearl bead coated by the oyster with conchiolin and then with a thin layer of nacre.

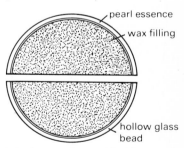

Imitation pearl coated inside.

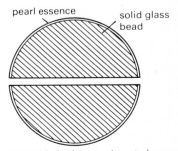

Normal imitation pearl coated on outside.

which exported their produce even to the Orient and left their mark in local placenames such as Pwll-y-crochan (the pool of the cauldron where mussels were boiled prior to extracting the pearls) in Wales. There is now only one pearl fisherman left in Scotland. A few rivers in North America, Austria and Bavaria are fished to the present day. Extensive mother-of-pearl fisheries existed along parts of the Mississippi; they also supplied most of the beads used in the Japanese cultured pearl industry.

*Cultured pearls* are made by inserting such a bead, together with a piece of the inner skin (mantle) of an oyster into the body of another oyster. The mantle is the organ that forms nacre and when the wound has healed, the oyster covers the bead as it would any irritant, first with conchiolin, then with nacre. The treated oysters are nursed for three years or more in cages suspended from rafts. This makes it possible to move them into the most favourable environment, where food is plentiful and parasites few. A constant supply of young oysters is reared at the same time.

A cultured pearl is therefore a bead, usually of mother-of-pearl, covered by a thin veneer of nacre. Apart from occasional marks on their surface and the dark conchiolin line visible below the drill holes, only X-rays and certain optical instruments can distinguish cultured from natural pearls with certainty. To the unaided eye they are often indistinguishable. Their value is, however, only a small fraction of that of natural pearls.

Very much cheaper still are *imitation pearls*. While cultured pearls have only been marketed since 1920, imitation pearls have been made for centuries. Queen Elizabeth I, who could never have enough pearls, did not disdain to wear them. They are merely glass beads coated with a varnish containing guanine, the silvery substance on the scales of herrings and other fish. Hollow beads coated on the inside were formerly made as well as imitations of high quality that had many coatings of extreme thinness. Modern methods give acceptable results with just one dipping in varnish. Imitation pearls look rather different from natural or cultured pearls. They can also be distinguished by the tendency of the varnish to peel away, especially near the drill holes.

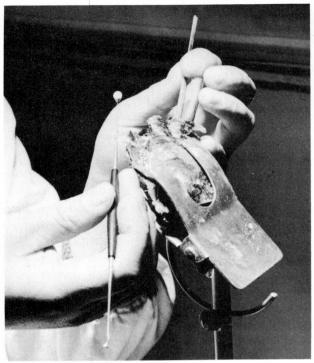

*Above left* Inserting a mother-of-pearl bead into an oyster.

*Above right* Grading and assembling imitation pearls.

An imitation pearl shows up strikingly in an X-ray picture.

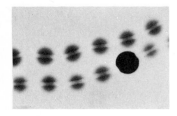

The most highly prized pearls are perfectly round. They are by no means the most common. Most pearls have more or less obvious deformities and are then called 'baroque'. They are found even among cultured pearls which start from a perfectly spherical bead. Some people prefer baroque pearls because they have more 'character', but a necklace of carefully graduated round pearls all matching in colour remains the most valuable. Drop-shaped pearls are much in demand; they are made to dangle from earrings and necklaces and flat 'button' pearls are made into ear-studs and collar-studs. Very tiny pearls, called 'seed pearls', may be strung into thin chains or formed into jewels on a backing of mother-of-pearl and metal, or used in embroidery. Small pearls may also be cut in half and cemented on to brooches and other pieces of jewellery as a surround for stones or to form a design. Larger half-pearls may originate as 'blister pearls' which are formed on the inner surface of a pearl oyster's shell.

In view of their softness ($3\frac{1}{2}$ on Mohs' scale) and porosity it is not advisable to wear pearls in a ring. Nor should they be exposed to sprays of any kind, cosmetics, soap or water. Some pearls, even if used only in a necklace, are liable to wear down to a barrel shape at the back of the neck after much wear, especially on an acid skin. For this reason it is important to have a valuable necklace restrung at regular intervals – every six to twelve months if it is worn frequently. The cleaning of pearls is best left to experts.

As many pearls are small and relatively light, a special unit of weight is used, the pearl grain. This is 0.05 (one twentieth) of a gram. As with some other precious stones, the value of a natural pearl increases as the square of its weight; a three-grain pearl would be nine times ($3 \times 3$) as valuable as a pearl of one grain, given the same quality. Value also varies according to whiteness, absence of surface blemishes and shape.

The name 'pearl' is thought to derive from the Latin *perula*, a small pear, which indicates that even then round pearls were not the rule. The Romans also used the names *unio* for large pearls and *margarita*, from the Greek, for smaller pearls. The name Margaret therefore means a pearl.

Other non-mineral materials hold a much more lowly place in jewellery.

**CORAL** is akin to pearl in that it is also formed by marine creatures – various kinds of polyp – and consists mainly of lime. The polyps build branching structures in many fantastic shapes but only the 'noble' coral is widely used for ornament. It comes from the Mediterranean shores of North Africa and is fashioned into beads and all kinds of pendants, mainly in Italy, where it was – and in some regions still is – regarded as a protection against the 'evil eye'. It can be carved easily as its hardness is less than 4. Its colours vary from a soft white through all shades of pink to a deep red, the most highly prized colour. Much valued in the last century, it has greatly declined in popularity. Lime-free black coral is found and carved in the Far East. Red coral was well known to all ancient cultures. The name comes from the Greek *korallion*. Coral has been imitated in glass, porcelain and celluloid.

**JET** (a name derived from the Greek *gagates*) is a compact variety of lignite, a coal-like fossil wood formed over 150 million years ago. Although it is soft ($3\frac{1}{2}$) it takes an attractive polish and was extensively used for mourning jewellery. The best quality is found at Whitby in Yorkshire; it was worked there in Roman times. Quite elaborate carvings were made, including cameos and floral ornaments, but the craft now appears to have died out. It has been imitated by black glass, sometimes known as 'French jet'.

**IVORY** (named from the Latin *ebur*) objects are carved from the tusks and teeth of large mammals such as the hippopotamus and walrus but elephant or mammoth ivory yields the largest and most workable pieces and is favoured most. Its hardness is only $2\frac{1}{2}$ but it is tough and has been carved from remote antiquity to form articles for daily use as well as objects of the highest artistic merit. In jewellery it is sometimes encountered as most delicately carved brooch pieces and earrings. Its main imitations are in bone, stag's horn, various vegetable nuts and, more recently, plastics. From all these it can be distinguished by examination under a microscope.

**TORTOISESHELL** is obtained from the carapace of the Hawksbill Turtle (*Chelone imbricata*). This carapace is composed of separate overlapping plates up to one foot in length. The central plates of the back show the familiar golden and brown mottling and are valued most but the 'blond' shell underneath is also used to give contrasting tints. Tortoiseshell becomes malleable on being heated and at a temperature of about 100°C it can be flattened and pressed together to form larger or thicker pieces. It is used for combs and hair ornaments, fans, inlay and veneer work, small boxes and many other ornamental objects. Like ivory, it is sometimes carved intricately, especially in China and Japan. It is widely imitated in plastics but can be distinguished by the fact that under a microscope the darkly coloured pigment is seen as separate flakes whereas the colour is in continuous swathes in the imitations.

This concludes our review of the gemstones and ornamental materials which are widely used in jewellery. A rather larger number of minerals are cut to form gemstones, but they are seldom seen set in jewellery,

A 'Bombay bunch' of natural pearls. Each silk thread holds pearls of the same size and colour. The bunch is embellished with fine silver wire.

103

either because they are rare or because they are not wholly suitable for normal use in jewels, or both. Some are stones of interest mainly to collectors and full details about them are contained in the more advanced gemmological literature. A brief description only of the less esoteric gemstones that have been cut for wear as jewels is given here; their physical constants are summarized in the table at the end of this book.

**ANDALUSITE** is found in various shades of green, but with striking reddish reflexes caused by its strong dichroism. It is eminently suitable as a gemstone but rather rare in gem quality. The opaque variety **chiastolite** shows white and dark cross-like markings. It comes mainly from Brazil, Ceylon and Malagasy.

**APATITE** forms clear and attractive yellow gems with a distinctive spectrum; more rarely blue, green, pink or violet stones are found, and occasionally cat's-eyes also. It is too soft for general wear. It comes mainly from Ceylon, Burma and Maine, USA.

**AXINITE** is also strongly dichroic; it is mainly brown but with red or violet reflexes. It is just about hard enough for general wear ($6\frac{1}{2}$ to 7) but cuttable crystals of gem quality are very rare. It comes mainly from France and Tasmania; minor localities are Cornwall, Ottawa, New York, Pennsylvania and California.

**BENITOITE** yields exceptionally bright blue gems with a dispersion equalling blue diamond. It was first discovered in 1907 at San Benito, California, and is still found only there. It has a hardness of only $6\frac{1}{2}$ and must be cut carefully owing to its dichroism. It is very rare; cut stones seldom exceed $1\frac{1}{2}$ carats.

**BERYLLONITE** is a rare mineral containing beryllium which forms colourless crystals. It is too soft and plain for general use. The only gem locality is at Stoneham, Maine.

**BRAZILIANITE**, discovered in eastern Minas Gerais as recently as 1945, has been cut into clear and bright yellow gems, sometimes exceeding 20 carats in weight, but with a hardness of only $5\frac{1}{2}$. It is rare, but becoming more common.

**CORDIERITE**, also known as **dichroite** and **iolite**, is one of the most dichroic minerals. It is deep purple when viewed in one direction and pale yellowish when viewed at a point at right angles to this. It is transparent with minor flaws and sometimes spangled with red spots of haematite. It has fair hardness and is often cut into cabochons or carvings that intrigue the viewer by their change of colour as they are turned. It comes mainly from southern India, Ceylon, Malagasy and Burma.

**DANBURITE** is fairly hard and clear but lacks attractive colours. At best, but very rarely, it is a rich yellow; mostly it is colourless to very pale yellow. Originally from Danbury in Connecticut, it now comes mainly from Japan, Upper Burma and Malagasy.

**DATOLITE** suffers from the same disadvantage as danburite and is in addition rather soft. It is cut into colourless gems for collectors and comes from Austria and from Michigan and Massachusetts, USA.

**DIOPSIDE** is coloured brown or green by iron but occasionally chromium gives it a luscious and bright green colour and good cat's-eyes of that colour exist as a rarity. Brown cat's-eyes and two- or three-rayed star stones are fairly common. The hardness is only $5\frac{1}{2}$. Green specimens have come from northern Italy, Austria, Burma and from Minas Gerais, Brazil. Brown stones come from southern India, Ceylon and Malagasy.

**ENSTATITE** found in the diamond pipes of South Africa sometimes comes in crystals large enough to be cut into pleasant green gemstones which may owe this colour in part to chromium. It is very rare in this form and it is comparatively soft. With increasing iron content it passes successively into **bronzite** and then **hypersthene** which are both dark brown and may contain inclusions that give them an almost metallic sheen. Cloudy enstatite is also found in Burma; hypersthene comes from Norway, Bavaria and the Isle St Paul off Labrador.

**EPIDOTE**, though often transparent, is usually of too dark a brown colour to make an attractive gem; interesting olive-green stones are found on rare occasions. It comes mainly from Austria, Alaska, Norway and Italy. It is related to zoisite and forms an intermediate member, **clino-zoisite**, which also, rarely, produces transparent material that is worth cutting.

**EUCLASE** is both rare and most difficult to cut because of its strong cleavage. Though hard and transparent it is therefore very rarely seen as a gemstone. It is mostly colourless but yellow and delicately green and blue forms exist. It comes from Brazil, Kashmir and Tanzania.

**HAEMATITE** is an exceedingly common iron ore, black and quite opaque, that is sometimes cut into cabochons or carved and even faceted on account of its metallic lustre. It derives its name from the Greek word for blood because it leaves a red streak when it is scratched on a hard white surface.

**HAMBERGITE** is an extremely rare colourless transparent gemstone from Malagasy.

**IDOCRASE**, also called **vesuvianite**, can be both yellow, brown to greenish transparent and green crypto-crystalline translucent. Its hardness is $6\frac{1}{2}$. The transparent varieties are occasionally clear enough to be cut but possess no great beauty. The translucent material sometimes imitates jadeite.

**KORNERUPINE**, though transparent, is mostly a nondescript dark brown or green in colour, but attractive varieties ranging from colourless through light shades of brown and green occur in the Ceylon gem gravels. Both rare and extremely beautiful are the chrome-green kornerupines from Burma. Its rarity and moderate hardness ($6\frac{1}{2}$) make it a stone for collectors rather than for wear.

**KYANITE**, also called **disthene**, is famous for its fine blue colour, for its extreme variation in hardness according to direction, and for its marked cleavage. This last attribute makes it most difficult to cut. The colour is sometimes uneven and merges into green. It is strongly dichroic which adds to the problems of cutting this stone. It comes from India, Burma, Kenya and Montana, USA.

**PETALITE**, a colourless to greenish-white mineral, is also known as **castorite** because it is found together with **pollucite** on the Isle of Elba. Both are named after the heavenly twins, Castor and Pollux, and both are rare. They have a moderate hardness of 6½ and are faceted as gemstones for collectors when transparent. Both are found in Maine, USA.

**PHENAKITE** is another colourless transparent collectors' gemstone of considerable hardness (up to 8). Since it is a beryllium mineral it is somewhat rare. It comes from the Ural Mountains, from Minas Gerais, Brazil and from Tanzania.

**PREHNITE**, a fairly common mineral occurring in translucent crypto-crystalline masses, is rarely of a colour attractive enough to warrant cutting as a cabochon, though this is sometimes done with stones of a pale yellowish-green colour. Prehnite is found in France, South Africa, New South Wales, Renfrewshire in Scotland and in the USA.

**RHODOCHROSITE** and **RHODONITE**, two crypto-crystalline manganese minerals, are sometimes cut to form cabochons of attractive pink to rose-red shades, but are more commonly used as materials for bowls, ashtrays and other ornamental objects. Rhodochrosite is the softer (hardness 4) but has the more pleasing colours and designs, being banded with white. Beautiful but small red transparent gems of both species have been faceted as great rarities. Rhodonite with a hardness of 6 is much more common; it is darker in tint and has black flecks.

**SCAPOLITE** is an isomorphous group of minerals but occurs in several beautiful colours – yellow, gold, pink, violet – as well as white. The hardness is, however, often below 6. Transparent yellow stones are faceted, the other colours are usually translucent and cut to produce handsome cat's-eyes. The deep purple cat's-eyes are rare and unparalleled by any other gemstone. Scapolite comes from Burma and also from Malagasy and Espirito Santo, Brazil.

**SCHEELITE** is beginning to establish itself as a collectors' gemstone in spite of its low hardness, because of its high lustre, fire and rarity. Its colours are mostly yellow to golden and it comes mainly from Mexico. It is synthesized for laser purposes.

**SERPENTINE** is a common and widely used ornamental material found as pendants and cabochons in cheaper jewellery. It is mostly green in colour and sold under names such as 'Iona stone' and 'Connemara marble'. The variety **bowenite** is often substituted for jade ('new jade', 'China jade') but can be distinguished by its low hardness (4). A pin will scratch it.

**SILLIMANITE**, also called **fibrolite**, is very rare as a cut stone, partly because transparent material of cuttable size is seldom found but more especially because the pronounced cleavage makes the material practically impossible to cut. It can, however, produce truly magnificent transparent gems of a subtle shade of blue and with remarkable fire. Very fine bluish-grey cat's-eyes also exist. The hardness is 7½ and the best material comes from Upper Burma. A massive variety was discovered by Professor Silliman in Idaho, USA.

**SINHALITE** was classed as brown peridot until 1951 when it was found to be chemically and crystallographically an entirely separate mineral, though most of its properties are close to those of peridot. It can form splendid yellow to brown gems. As its name implies, it comes mainly from Ceylon but has also been found in Burma.

**SMITHSONITE** has a rich bluish-green crypto-crystalline variety which is sometimes cut to form cabochons. It is sold under the trade name of **Bonamite**. Its hardness is only 5 and it comes from Mexico, though other sources now supply it also.

**SPHALERITE** or **zinc blende**, an ore of zinc, occurs rarely in transparent cuttable crystals of yellow or brown shades. Though it only ranks 4 on Mohs' scale, it is faceted to produce collectors' gems because of its wonderful fire which is three times as strong as that of diamond. The best material comes from Spain and Mexico.

**SPHENE** or **titanite** is another gemstone that shows dazzling fire. Its colours are yellow, gold, brown or green. Its hardness of $5\frac{1}{2}$ and the fact that it rarely yields cut gems exceeding 2 carats again means that it is found in collections rather than in worn jewellery. Splendid gem material has come from Austria, Switzerland, Mexico and, in the USA, from Maine and Pennsylvania.

**SPODUMENE** is a moderately rare gemstone, yellow, pink or green in colour, endowed with an adequate hardness of 7. The yellow variety has no particular advantage over other yellow gems but **kunzite** can have a lovely pink colour tinged with blue and **hiddenite** a rich emerald green. Unfortunately, many kunzites are so pale that deep stones have to be made to bring out the colour. The true hiddenite only occurred in a small deposit in North Carolina that is now exhausted and the pale green spodumenes from Brazil ought to be called 'green spodumene' since they are coloured by iron and not chromium as hiddenite is. The best kunzite comes from California and from Malagasy which, together with Minas Gerais, also produce yellow spodumene.

**ZOISITE** has long been known as an opaque ornamental mineral, pink or green in colour. Its discovery in the Usambara mountains of Tanzania in 1967 as a fully transparent gloriously blue gemstone tinged with purple caused a big stir in the gem world. The colour is strongly influenced by dichroism and varies as the gem is viewed from different aspects, but a more even blue can be ensured by heat treatment. Transparent green stones and other colours have since been found as well. These transparent varieties are marketed in the USA under the name of **tanzanite**. Export from Tanzania is restricted at present and the material is therefore rather rare, but in spite of its hardness of only $6\frac{1}{2}$ it bids well to becoming a very popular and distinguished gemstone in the future.

Zoisite completes the list of jewellers' and collectors' gems. It would have been possible to include more gemstones within this chapter but these are either so rare that they are never obtainable or so common that they are used for ornamental work only. The selection of the stones described may have been influenced by the author's subjective pre-dilections, but a sincere effort has been made to cover all those stones that enjoy a fairly wide reputation as gems.

# The Gemstone Industries

Many and diverse are the steps by which a gemstone progresses from its discovery in the earth to its ultimate setting in a jewel. The actual process starts with some form of mining but this is preceded by prospecting, exploration or the verification of an accidental find.

In ancient times the finding of a gem must have been largely the result of a happy accident, and it is only fitting that one of the ancient names of the gem isle of Ceylon was Serendipe, a word that has come to connote happy accidents. But ancient peoples also invoked their gods in the search for such stones as jade. The gods then answered their prayers by leading a chief or priest to the desired goal – perhaps such a man may have known more about the environment associated with jade than we may suppose.

A knowledge of rock formations, surface environment and minerals associated with the ores or gems sought is certainly one of the essential qualifications of a prospector. Such a man may have started as a miner and in this way have become familiar with the conditions in which a particular mineral occurs. He may have set out on a far from random search to find similar conditions. Tales or stray specimens may have reached him, narrowing down the area of search. He then went over the area methodically, examining each likely spot. In some places he may have dug down where the configuration of the soil suggested it until he found traces of the gravel bearing gems or the hard, silicious rock which covers opal. Looking for diamonds in South Africa, he may have examined antheaps or their residues. Some ants dig deeply into the soil to build their nests and in so doing bring grains of sand to the surface. Prospectors then look for traces of such minerals as garnet and ilmenite in the sand because they know that these minerals occur in association with diamonds. This may have been one of the techniques used by Dr J. T. Williamson, a geologist formerly employed by De Beers, when he set out to find diamonds known to exist in Tanzania. Though he knew a good deal about the geology of the area and could make sound scientific deductions from the lie of the land, he spent nine years in prospecting until he discovered his mine, one of the largest ever found, in 1942.

The first diamonds discovered in Africa were pebbles with which

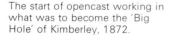

The start of opencast working in what was to become the 'Big Hole' of Kimberley, 1872.

children played. In Brazil, goldminers disregarded similar pebbles until a priest who had lived in India recognized them. All this is in complete contrast with modern prospecting for diamonds in which teams of specialist geologists use the latest scientific techniques. Such teams have discovered several new pipes in Africa; it is also reported that thousands of trained geologists collaborated in finding and developing the rich Siberian diamond fields.

Recent discoveries of other gemstones have also tended to owe more to science than to chance. Emeralds have been found in Rhodesia and elsewhere by geologists applying their science to survey data. Sapphires were found in Malawi as a by-product of an offically sponsored general geological survey. Serendipity – the happy accident – first drew attention to taaffeite, ekanite, painite and blue zoisite to name some recent discoveries, but they might easily have been passed over except for the curiosity and expertise of scientists; indeed, the first two named must have been mined for many years without being recognized for what they were. No doubt luck and science will find many more new gem deposits yet.

When gemstones are found, samples are usually sent to dealers in rough stones for marketing. These dealers may also help to arrange finance for a mining venture, for few of the small-scale prospectors have much money behind them. Opening up a mine may be a highly speculative matter since it is rarely simple to establish the extent of a deposit, both as regards quantity and quality. Test borings may define the amount and quality of a metal ore but no such assessment of the productivity of a gem deposit is feasible. The gems are usually distributed irregularly and the deposit or vein may cease suddenly. The quality of the stones will almost certainly vary, making a large proportion unusable. Deposits are frequently small, precluding the installation of more efficient but costly machinery. This is why, throughout the world, much gem extraction is in the hands of small-scale operators who often work in their spare time and have another source of livelihood to keep them going.

This was also the nature of the first diamond miners – men with little capital and much hope, working their small individual claims by hand. But diamond pipes and some alluvial deposits can only be exploited profitably by large-scale, highly mechanized methods. Only by buying out the individual miners, combining their surface claims into single,

Rock drilling at Finsch mine.

comprehensive units that could be worked systematically with heavy machinery and later with modern deep-mining procedures, was the present diamond empire established in South Africa. Only then did diamond extraction become the vast and profitable business it now is. Earlier, in Brazil, diamond mining had operated spasmodically, times of plenty giving way to periods of scarcity when low prices caused by the swamping of the market combined with inadequate capitalization, forced work to stop. The more provident planning of production and distribution made possible by large-scale enterprise has undoubtedly been beneficial in levelling out supply and maintaining work and prices at a steadier rate.

When a new diamond pipe is opened up, extraction of the diamondiferous 'yellow ground' first proceeds by opencast working. The rock is removed by powerful scrapers along a broad road that spirals down towards the central point of the pipe. It is loaded into enormous trucks that take it to the processing (concentrating) plant continuously, day and night. As the yellow ground is removed and the spiral road goes deeper, more and more of the unproductive rock surrounding the pipe has to be cleared away to provide access and ultimately a point is reached when it is cheaper to start underground mining. By then the weathered, softer yellow ground has also given way to the harder 'blue ground' or kimberlite, a peridotite rock that cannot be scraped off readily. Normally, opencast mining continues for several years.

Underground mining nowadays employs the 'block caving' method. Well below the floor left by opencast work, caves are blasted out above passages (drifts) connected ultimately with the mine shafts. The caves are connected with the drifts by funnel-shaped openings through which the excavated rock falls into the drifts and is then removed by stirrup-shaped scrapers towards openings (hoppers) beneath which are trucks attached to electric tramways that take the rock to be crushed. Crushing releases the diamonds from the matrix. The crushed rock is then sent up the mine shaft to be concentrated on the surface. As the caves are enlarged their roofs fall in under the pressure of the rocks above, so that a continuous supply of blue ground passes through the funnels without any need for further blasting. All material is handled mechanically. When it has all been mined, new caves are started further down.

In South-West Africa opencast mining is employed to collect the gem gravel deposited by rivers and built up in terraces by the sea. The gravels are covered by sand up to thirty feet in depth and this sand has first to be removed. Enormous scrapers and bulldozers are used and a

*Below left* General view of the Williamson mine.

*Below right* Aerial view of the Finsch diamond mine.

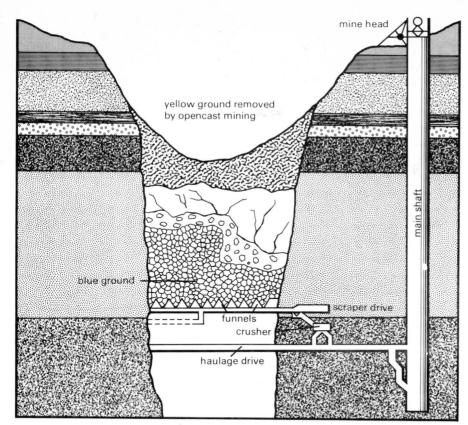

The block caving method of diamond mining. The blue ground containing the diamonds distintegrates under its own weight and falls through funnels into a drive from which it is scooped out with a mechanical scraper. It is then crushed, loaded into haulage trucks and brought to the surface via the main shaft.

mine head

yellow ground removed by opencast mining

blue ground

main shaft

scraper drive

funnels

crusher

haulage drive

Present-day aerial view of the Big Hole of Kimberley.

Removing sand overburden along the coast of south-west Africa.

huge kind of vacuum sucker extracts the gravel from potholes. Vacuum tubes are also used to dredge up diamond gravel from the sea bed by a specially designed ship on which most of the processing is done. The expense of these operations is rendered economically feasible by the fact that these South-West African alluvial gravels are rich in diamonds, up to ninety per cent of which are of gem quality. In the early years of this century diamonds were gathered by rows of men on their hands and knees picking up the stones from the surface! There were areas (strictly patrolled) where one could rely on picking up diamonds as one walked.

The product of the processes described, is either gravel or crushed kimberlite containing loose diamonds. The next step is to get rid of as much of the unwanted rock or gravel as possible without losing any diamonds, a process called concentration. It is not economic to pick out

Dredging and processing vessel *Pomona* recovering diamonds from the sea bed off south-west Africa.

the diamonds directly, for to recover diamonds totalling one carat rough weight, two cubic yards of rock must be examined; they represent only one part in ten million of the ore and only one fifth of this is of gem quality. The material is first washed to remove dusty fine matter, then passed through screens to separate large barren lumps and through separators using specific gravity. The most efficient of these is one where the rock is swirled round vigorously in a liquid of high density. The lighter material is drawn off as waste from the top of the liquid while the much denser diamonds and certain other minerals are drawn towards the sides and sink to the bottom. The concentrate is then washed over broad moving belts coated with grease. Neither clean diamonds nor grease can be wetted, so the diamonds stick to the grease while other stones are kept off the grease by the film of water coating them. Some diamonds from South-West Africa and a few other localities

A grease belt separator. Diamonds stick to the grease while other stones are flushed away by the water.

113

*Above* Malachite: botryoidal mass and a polished section.

*Above right* Small pyrite crystals encrusting calcite.

*Below right* Quartz crystal, quartz gems—rock crystal, amethyst, citrine, rose quartz and tiger's eye—and opals.

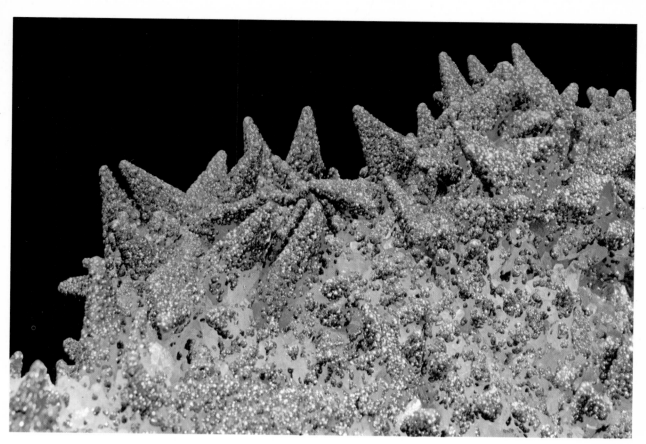

are, however, coated with exceedingly thin films of salts that make them wettable. In such cases the concentrate has first to be treated chemically, or other methods of separation have to be used. Another efficient way of separating the diamonds uses their fluorescence under X-rays. Washing and screening is also used in more primitive mining methods, the final separation then being by hand picking.

At all stages in he winning of gemstones the prevention of theft is a big problem. In the case of diamonds, strict laws against illicit dealing and smuggling are in force in all producing countries. The risk of theft is minimized where mining, concentration and separation are mechanized; even so, workers in the large concerns often live in compounds excluded from all outside contacts and have to pass through a rigorous search and spend some time in a kind of quarantine when their term of employment ends. All sorts of precautions are used. At the Williamson mine where hand picking had to be resorted to for a time because wettable diamonds are produced, the pickers were enveloped in a sack-like garb that only had openings for the head and one arm, and their movements were closely scrutinized. At some diamond fields and also at the Colombian emerald mines workers were allowed to keep chickens until it was found that the birds could be readily induced to swallow gemstones which remained in their crops.

Rough diamonds come in many shapes and sizes and in many degrees of whiteness and purity. Their use in jewellery is wider and more varied than that of other gemstones and unlike most of these, diamonds have very important industrial uses. They therefore undergo a much more elaborate sorting process than other gems, a process designed to provide for each cutter exactly the stones he requires. Sorting may be done at the mine or by the dealers but the Diamond Corporation maintains large sorting offices at Kimberley and London and practically all diamonds produced in South or South-West Africa, and some other countries as well, pass through them. Here sorting is carried out on large tables covered with the whitest paper and facing away from the sun – north in London, south in Kimberley – so that the light is neutral. The stones are sorted in heaps, by size in the vertical direction and in decreasing quality from left to right. The heaps of glittering stones are an impressive sight.

These large-scale and elaborate mining and processing methods are only justified if they can be continuous, that is, if the excavated ore persists in yielding an adequate amount of gemstones over many years. With most river gravels this is not the case. Though the river may have concentrated the heavier gemstones quite appreciably and the yield per ton may therefore be relatively high, the beds in which the gems occur are shallow and soon exhausted. The lower value of most gemstones other than diamonds also precludes a capital-intensive exploitation and difficulties may arise from the inaccessibility of the mines. Moreover, in many gem areas labour is so cheap that it is more economical to employ a number of men using shovels than to bring in a bulldozer, perhaps over impossible terrain.

In several parts of Africa diamond-bearing gravel is scooped from the beds of existing or extinct rivers, then concentrated by means of screens, sieves or pans, using water where possible, and the diamonds picked out by hand from the bottom of the concentrate. Excavated ground is often left in a desolate condition. Though governments try to control such mining, it is often carried on illicitly. The miners disappear fast when patrols are signalled but they pay no heed to aeroplanes since these cannot land and can only carry a few men.

In Ceylon and some parts of Burma the gem-bearing gravel (called illam in Ceylon and byam in Burma) is often below the surface so that it is necessary to sink a shaft which may, though rarely, reach a depth of as much as thirty feet. The sides of the shaft are shored up with timber since the ground is often waterlogged. The gravel and ground water are raised in buckets either on a windlass or dangling from the end of a long pivoted pole that is counterweighted at its other end. Small petrol-driven pumps are also used to bail out the water. In some places the illam is merely scraped from the dips in a river bottom with long rakes and then swirled round in plaited fibre baskets. By this process the clay, sand and stones too small to matter are washed away and the denser gemstones concentrated at the bottom. They are then sorted out by hand. In some parts of Thailand and Cambodia where there is no water, all the soil dug out is sifted and examined for gems, but then the soil is finer and more crumbly and the gemstones stand out more clearly.

Water played an important part in the (now largely inoperative) ruby mines of Burma where the gems were deposited in a relatively soft soil which could be disintegrated with monitors (high pressure

*Above left* Illicit diamond miners using primitive panning.

*Above middle* Illicit diamond miners leaving—in a hurry!

*Above right* Police rounding up illicit diamond miners in Sierra Leone.

*Below left* A shallow gem pit in Ceylon. The gem-bearing gravel is raised with the aid of counterweighted bamboo poles or with winches.

*Below right* Recovering ruby-bearing gravel from the bottom of a sluice near Mogok, Burma.

*Above* Various ornamental
stones: moss agates, onyx,
jaspers, ruin marble, Egyptian
marble and fossilized plants.

*Above right* Chalcedony group:
a bloodstone cameo, mocha
stone, banded agates, cornelian
and chrysoprase.

*Below right* Turquoise from
Sweden, USA and Canada. The
cut or carved specimens are
mostly made of Iranian turquoise.

water jets). The soil with its gemstones was then pumped as a slurry to a series of sluices which separated the stones retrieved in accordance with their density and carried away all the soil and fine matter. But the primitive methods already described were – and are – also in use.

In the Colombian emerald mines the gemstones occur in veins in a limestone that is quarried away in terraces which mount like steps up the sides of hills. Density separation is impracticable because of the low specific gravity of emeralds, so the rock is scrutinized carefully when a vein is struck and the emeralds are picked out by hand. Streams are diverted to the working points and used to wash the waste rock down the hillside. Extracting the many other gemstones found in South America is largely pick-and-shovel work, feasible because only relatively large crystals of quartz and agate, for example, are worth gathering.

Picks and shovels are also used to secure the opals of Australia. Mining and prospecting for opal in the blistering heat of the Australian outback is a pursuit which appeals only to the addict. At the famous Coober Pedy field (Coober Pedy means 'white man underground' in the aboriginal language), miners live underground in dugouts; all their water and other supplies have to be brought in by lorries and planes.

In Burma some jadeite boulders are found in the beds of streams that have cut their way through the deposits, while others are dug out from adjacent soil. It is said that the men collecting the boulders from the stream beds can tell pieces of jadeite from other rocks by feeling for them with their feet. In other parts of the world nephrite and lapis lazuli were formerly released from the rock by pouring water on to the fire-heated surface so that it cracked, but this process wastes and disfigures much material and explosives are now used more commonly. Several sites are in mountain ranges that are very difficult to reach.

Gemstones are sometimes found as a by-product of other mining activities. A little beryl of gem quality is found with the opaque beryl mined as an ore of the industrially important metal beryllium, but the quantities are so small that it does not pay to separate out the gems. As another instance, clear hessonite garnets of a most attractive pale reddish-brown colour occur as euhedral crystals in asbestos mined in Quebec. They are a nuisance to mining engineers, however, for the hard and bulky crystals can damage the machines that separate and purify the soft asbestos fibres. The garnets are therefore eliminated as a waste product.

Almost all rough gem material is sold to cutters though in recent years there has been a remarkable increase in sales of rough crystals

Opal digging at Lightning Ridge, Australia.

in their natural state for display. The finest of such items are bought by an ever-increasing number of museums and collectors but this still leaves a goodly number of colourful and well-shaped specimens that form delightful ornaments for private buyers.

Gemstone cutters usually specialize to some extent. Diamonds are cut by quite different methods from those used on other gems and entirely separate establishments deal with them. Certain individual cutters may acquire a reputation for cutting particular kinds of stone exceptionally well but firms cutting transparent stones will not normally fashion stone articles like ashtrays, pen stands and boxes. Each cutting firm will be in touch with mining and importing firms which can supply their requirements; fine rubies, emeralds or opals, however, cannot be produced to order and cutters must take what becomes available. It may take a long time and much searching to complete a matching parure or even a necklace of good stones. Some large firms maintain buying agencies in gem-producing countries. In addition there are auctions, specially of ornamental stones, where material can be inspected prior to sale. At the important gem-cutting centre of Idar-Oberstein in Germany auctions of agates and chalcedonies are held regularly. Specimens of agate are stained in a standard manner to show the potentialities of each batch.

Sorting uncut diamonds by size and quality.

Topaz (left) and tourmaline
(right), illustrating some of the
shades in which these colourful
gemstones occur.

Zircon: crystals and cut stones.

Sales of gem diamonds are organized quite differently. Some four-fifths of all diamonds produced pass through the Diamond Trading Company who accept orders only from some 250 selected customers, mainly diamond cutters, from all over the world. The Company then prepares parcels of rough stones matching these orders as nearly as possible and invites the customers to view them at special 'sights' held in London ten times a year. The buyer cannot select from the stones offered to him. He has to buy the whole lot (on average over £100 000's worth), the only point at issue being the assessment of quality and hence of value. The buyers sell what they do not require for their own use. The stones may thus pass through the hands of several dealers organized in the 'Diamond Club'. Some African and South American diamond-producing countries maintain their own sales organizations. The Russians also made different marketing arrangements after their trade boycott of South Africa. Industrial diamonds are sold through another section of the Diamond Corporation.

The main differences between the cutting of diamond and the cutting of other stones arise from the very much greater hardness of diamond. This makes its sawing, grinding and cutting a much lengthier and more complex process and necessitates the employment of specialists at each stage, whereas the cutting of other gemstones can be carried out by the same person from start to finish, though some specialization is common.

The first stage in the production of a gem diamond is a careful inspection for inclusions and strain, often under a polarizing microscope. The crystal lattice of some diamonds is under strain through imperfect crystallization or inclusions. Such strain may cause the stone to shatter when it is sawn or cut. The inspection will determine the size, shape and orientation within the crystal of the gems to be cut from it. It is a most important operation at which the strategy of obtaining the optimum yield for the minimum expense is decided. It is performed by a senior member of the staff. He may indicate with an Indian ink line where the stone is to be cleaved if it is desired to separate off a faulty portion or to divide the stone into more convenient units; the sawing plane will also be indicated.

To cleave a diamond, a narrow V-shaped groove is scratched into the

*Below left* Polishing gems at Ratnapura, Ceylon. The polishing disc is rotated to and fro by means of the stringed stick.

*Below right* Cleaving a diamond. The receptacle on the right receives the diamond dust from the previous operation of scratching a nick (kerf) into which the cleaving blade can be inserted.

crystal with a sharp diamond point, following one of the four cleavage directions very precisely. A steel blade is inserted when the groove is sufficiently deep and is given a smart blow with a steel rod or mallet. This is very much a specialist's job requiring steady hands and nerves, for faulty cleaving can shatter a stone.

Normally, it is not necessary to cleave well-formed octahedral crystals; they are sawn into two parts, either across the middle to provide two equal stones or higher up the octahedron, to yield one larger and one smaller stone. Imperfections may also be sawn out. In all these and the following operations advantage is taken of the greatly varying hardness of diamond. In some directions it cannot be abraded at all, in others it can be cut quite readily. The chief skill each diamond worker must possess is the ability to determine the 'soft' directions accurately. These directions are invariably related to the crystal structure of the diamond. In sawing and in polishing one of the soft directions is exposed to the diamond powder on the saw or on the 'scaife', a horizontal disc of cast iron about one foot in diameter charged with diamond powder

Sawing through a rough gem diamond.

*Above* Mother of pearl cat's-eyes and pearls of various colours.

*Above right* Carvings of tortoiseshell, ivory, coral and jet.

*Below right* Some rare gemstones; top row: sillimanite, danburite and zoisite, bottom row: taaffeite (the original specimen), andalusite and rhodochrosite.

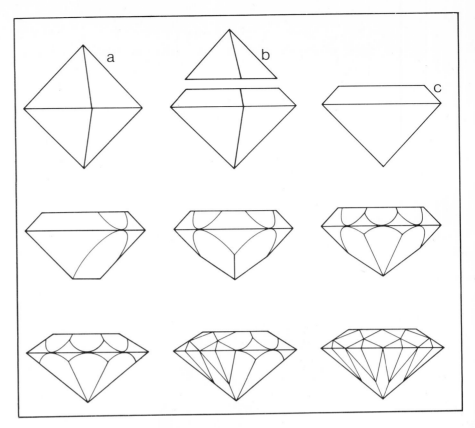

Cutting a brilliant. Top row:
(a) octahedron (b) after sawing
(c) round shape after bruting.
Middle row: the first facets are
applied, in the order shown, by
the cross-cutter. Bottom row: the
remaining facets are added by the
brillianteerer.

suspended in olive oil. These powder particles lie at random – roughly half in a soft direction and half in a 'hard' direction. It is these latter particles that do most of the abrading and cutting.

The saw employed in cutting diamonds is an exceedingly thin disc of phosphor bronze, three to four inches in diameter (it wears down in use), revolving vertically at 5 000 to 6 000 revolutions per minute. Diamond powder mixed with olive oil to form a paste is applied to its rim. All the cutting is done by this powder; the saw merely holds it in its pores. The stone to be sawn is held in a clamp that can be weighted to give more rapid cutting. Several saws are placed in a row and attended by one man who watches continuously to prevent them 'wandering' off the right course or being caught in an extra hard patch in the crystal, a 'naat'. Sawing a one-carat diamond may take anything up to eight hours.

Sawing for round brilliants leaves two small pyramids which now need to have their corners and edges removed. This is done by 'bruting'. One diamond is fixed to a rotating spindle and another to the end of a stick held on a fulcrum and under the bruter's arm. The two stones are forced against each other and turned until they are reduced to a shape appropriate to the final form of the gem.

The next process is grinding. This is done on a scaife. The diamond to be ground is held in a steel grip tightened by screws called a 'dop'. This is attached to a soft copper stalk by means of which it is held in a clamp or 'tang'. The tang stands on the platform that surrounds the scaife and it can be weighted if more pressure is required. The copper stalk can be bent so that the diamond is placed on the scaife in exactly the right position. This is essential if the facets are to be accurately symmetrical and if the grinding process is to proceed as fast as possible. If the diamond is positioned even a few degrees off the softest direction, grinding may be slowed up considerably. Some experiment is usually

# Gold again a by guess and by golly investment bet, thanks to politics

**Jane Bryant Quinn**

NEW YORK—Today, gold investing is an up-or-down bet on the politics of the Middle East.

Before Iraq swallowed up Kuwait, the gold bulls had been making a case for buying the metal at around $350 an ounce. Rising U.S. inflation and a devaluing dollar were two of the many reasons they gave.

John Sack, a precious-metals trader at Shearson Lehman Hutton Inc., says a lot of heavy hitters stepped in when the Dow Jones industrial average touched 3000, because they thought that was too high. Often, gold and gold stocks go up when other stocks are going down.

Now, however, with gold seesawing above $400 and on wartime alert, its future is anybody's guess. Judging by the rise in sales, a lot of guessing is going on.

Not all of the vendors are at their old stands. Citibank, for example, is dropping its retail gold-selling operation after several years of yawning disinterest on the part of the public.

By contrast, two new no-load (no-sales-charge) mutual funds started up just in time to catch the wave.

Gold mutual funds buy the stocks of companies that mine and process gold. They're an especially speculative play. When gold prices rise, the stocks of gold-mining companies rise even faster. And they drop even faster on the downside.

One recent top performer: The year-old, $116 million Benham Gold Equities Index Fund in Mountain View, Calif.—up 11 percent since Aug. 1, the day before Iraqi tanks rumbled into Kuwait. Benham has created a "gold-shares index," made up of 35 major U.S. and Canadian companies. The fund invests proportionately in all of them, so you'll match the moves in the market, up and down.

Ironically, Benham's market-matching fund has been outperforming most of the gold funds that try to beat the market. The main reason for this, says portfolio manager Steven Colton, is that index funds are fully invested in stocks when the market moves up, while other funds may be holding cash reserves.

In theory, index funds should fall harder than the other funds do when gold shares decline. But in practice, the mutual funds indexed to other types of securities have proven pretty resilient on the downside, too.

But there are indexes and indexes. The Rushmore group's year-old, $8 million Precious Metals Index Plus Portfolio in Bethesda, Md., which owns shares in 25 North American companies, has been running more toward the middle of the pack.

Gains since the day before the invasion: 9.1 percent.

Mutual funds are used principally by gunslingers, who buy now and sell later, when they think that gold prices will fall. But if you're bullish on gold long-term, you could accumulate mutual funds slowly, buying some shares every month, so as to dollar-average your position. Gold companies may pay dividends, which the metal itself does not.

Long-term holders, however, are more likely to turn to the gold itself. Best buys for investors are one-ounce "bullion" coins, meaning coins sold for their gold alone, with no special numismatic value.

Shop around, because the market is highly competitive. Last week, five one-ounce gold American Eagles, the U.S.-minted coin, could be had (by phone) at 4.75 percent over the spot price of gold both from Benham Certified Metals, also in Mountain View, and the Rhode Island Hospital Trust National Bank in Providence.

If you wanted to sell the same order back, however, Benham offered 1.5 percent over the gold price (after sales commissions), and Hospital Trust offered 2.25 percent over. So on a round trip—both buying and selling—the bank was cheaper. Still, these prices are good. Some vendors charge retail customers more. When shopping, also compare shipping charges and any other fees.

# ls on trust

at a local building-materials plant. He regaled me for an hour or so with tales of pettiness and mistrust on the part of management (returned in kind by the employees). I respect him immensely and know his employer too: His every word rang true.

Why must we be so mistrustful? Underestimate people so badly? I'm not in the least bit irritated at American's counter person or the yellow-clad Hertzies. But I'm mad as hell at their managements. When I encounter pettiness at the front line, I get white hot at the people on top—all, of course, preaching about their "bone-deep belief in people." Wanna bet?

American claims that its front-line people have lots of leeway. If so, why didn't the front-line person act like it? There's a chance that she was having a lousy day. But I suspect it's the result of an iron-fisted, untrusting approach to employees.

I'm no Pollyanna. People do have bad days. (I sure do.) And some people don't live up to trust when it is given, even at IBM let alone at my friend's factory. But by and large, everything I write about— such as installing exotic organization structures and pursuing constant quality improvement—rises or falls on the basis of trust: a belief in the potential and inherent decency of front-line people (and customers, too).

I'll bet my last dollar you've got dozens or hundreds or thousands in your outfit capable of remembering 500 names and habits of customers, and a handful who doubtless could give that bionic Mr. 2,000 a run for his money. But you'll never know

## Bailey. Controls Company

29801 Euclid Avenue • Wickliffe, Ohio 44092
Phone: (216) 585-8500 • Telex: 980621 • Fax: (216) 943-4609

August, 1990

### Keeping Good Company...Worldwide!

It's been said that a company is known by the custo has helped to keep thousands of world leaders in com profits through seamless, real-time solutions to distrib I am pleased to announce a significant addition to this

Bailey Controls and E.I. DuPont De Nemours and C a strategic business agreement whereby Bailey will se preferred suppliers of distributed controls to DuPont f for the coming decade. This relationship applies to ove locations in over 50 countries around the world and en Bailey INFI 90° distributed, digital systems plus a wide field instrumentation.

The DuPont-Bailey Initiative (DBI) marks a significa well-established relationship between our two compani ago, we were one of more than 18 DCS suppliers to Du number was pared to five vendors. The current strateg from a continued focus by DuPont on greater quality, s cost effectiveness through consolidation of its supplier relationships.

From a business world filled with fierce competition, have forged a team with unique synergy. We will excha and business information as required to support our m including the common objective to relentlessly improve customers' operations. We will bring control consistenc and ever-increasing quality to a myriad of processes. T address issues which affect not just our respective com

Bruting two diamonds by grinding them against each other.

required and this is done near the centre of the scaife, where it turns most slowly, so that errors can be adjusted before grinding has gone too far. Once the correct angle has been established, grinding can proceed faster, in a position halfway to the edge of the scaife. Grinding leaves some grooves on the facet and these are then polished off by swinging the stone to and fro across the fast outer part of the scaife. The main facets which determine the position of the others are put on by a specialist, the 'cross cutter', the smaller facets by the 'brillianteerer'. Both proceed by eye only, employing an uncanny degree of skill, for

*Below left* Securing a diamond in a 'dop' which will hold it during cutting.
*Below right* Diamond being faceted on a 'scaife'.

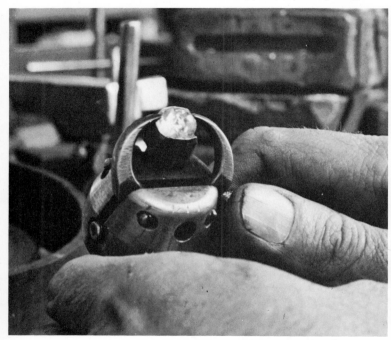

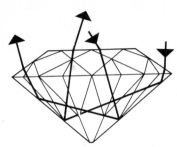

In a brilliant of perfect proportions as much light as possible is reflected out through the crown.

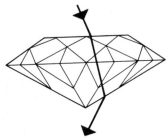

Too shallow a brilliant looks empty—a 'fish-eye'—since light passes straight through it.

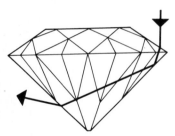

A brilliant cut too deeply looks dark since most of the incident light is lost through the pavilion.

*Right* Names of the facets in a standard brilliant cut.

their tools are basically simple. An account written by Benvenuto Cellini in the sixteenth century shows that in principle the methods now used are the same as those employed 400 years ago; the discovery of electrical power and the resulting mechanization and the invention of sawing have merely eased and speeded up the work. Experience, guided by science, has produced much more pleasing stones.

The proportions and angles required for maximum brilliance have been illustrated in the previous chapter. The essential features to ensure maximum brilliance are that the pavilion facets should be inclined to the girdle plane as nearly as possible at 41°, the crown facets at 34°, and that the diameter of the table facet should be just over half that of the girdle. It is a remarkable fact that cutters can achieve these angles, within minutes of a degree, by inspection alone. Deviations from these desiderata spoil the 'make', as do extra facets produced by polishing off a flaw near the surface, a girdle that shows damage, 'bearding' (tiny cracks extending into the stone), or an obvious 'natural' (an unbruted spot, usually on the girdle).

The normal brilliant cut consists of fifty-eight facets. On the upper part or crown of the stone there is the table, eight star facets, eight kites, and sixteen upper girdle or cross facets; on the lower part or pavilion there are the culet, eight pavilion facets and sixteen lower girdle facets. The culet should be quite small and is sometimes omitted altogether, but the sharp point left may then splinter off. The girdle is usually left rough, as bruted; too thick a girdle reduces brilliance, too thin a girdle may chip when the stone is set. A recent fashion is to polish facets on the girdle. Contrary to the claims made, this does not enhance brilliance appreciably. As can be seen from the drawings on page 131, it is possible to adapt the facets of the brilliant cut to stones that are not round but oval, cushion-, boat- or drop-shaped. These are variants designed to make the best use of the many oddly-shaped rough diamonds and also to produce stones appropriate to a particular setting. A boat-shaped marquise runs along the finger; a pendeloque is ideal for an ear drop or pendant from a necklace.

The main alternative to the brilliant cut is the step or trap cut. This is obviously much simpler and therefore cheaper to produce and it may also waste less material. Its simplicity is in line with modern taste, but with diamond it has one great drawback: it greatly reduces its fire and sparkle because small facets are absent. There are several variants on the basic idea; in some cuts used with coloured gemstones the facet edges do not run parallel and there are also combined forms in which the top of a stone may be based on the brilliant cut and the pavilion on the step cut, producing the so-called 'mixed cut'.

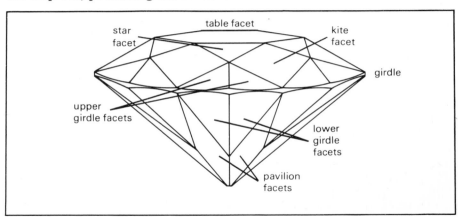

The domed cabochon cut is perhaps the most ancient method of cutting stones. It is used for coloured stones only, both opaque and transparent, and it is essential for the display of asterism and chatoyance. Star stones and cat's-eyes are often cut with a fairly steep and high dome; the base is usually left unpolished but is also domed, though less steeply. Turquoises, opals, garnets, chalcedonies and agates are often cut as cabochons with a flat base. Dark garnets may have their base hollowed out to lighten their colour. Opals are often formed into very shallow cabochons ('tallow topped') since the material from which they are cut frequently exists in thin layers only. These may be cemented on to poor quality opal, onyx or even black glass to form opal doublets. Chrysoprase is also sometimes cut as a flat cabochon with some facets round the girdle. The cabochon is the easiest and cheapest style of cutting.

The rose cut, broadly a flat-based steep cabochon covered in little triangular facets, is an old style much used for small transparent stones. It is the normal cut for Bohemian garnets and was also extensively employed for pale zircons from Ceylon ('Matara diamonds'). It was used for small diamonds, particularly in the days before diamond sawing was invented. Diamond octahedra were cleaved and the two halves were then formed into roses. It could also be used with advantage on flat diamond crystals. Nowadays small diamonds are more usually cut to form baguettes, trapezes, or square cuts; if round, only eight or sixteen facets may be applied.

Calculations and experiments are still proceeding to evolve new styles of cutting, particularly for diamonds and their newer substitutes. It is claimed that fire can be greatly enhanced by covering the stone with small facets set at very small angles (4–7°) to each other. The resulting shapes have not yet been generally accepted either by the trade or by the public but there has been some support for another fairly recent innovation, the profile cut. This makes good use of flat stones by forming their base into a series of parallel ridges sloped at an angle to give maximum brilliance. Bright stones of considerable 'spread' in relation to their weight can be produced by this means.

The brilliant cut has been applied to most transparent stones though it is, strictly speaking, necessary only for stones with a high dispersion. These include, apart from diamond and its imitations, the paler varieties

Variations on the brilliant cut.

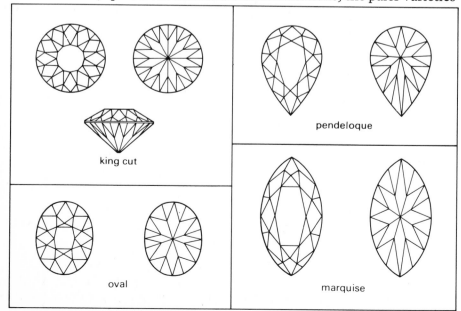

king cut

pendeloque

oval

marquise

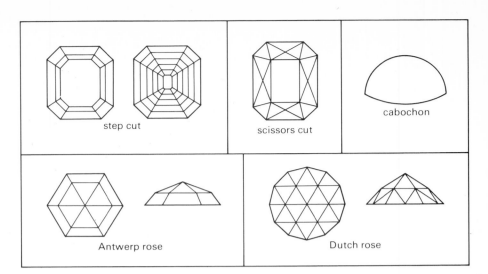

Some other styles of cutting gemstones.

of zircon and a few rarer gems such as sphene and demantoid garnet. The brilliant cut displays their fire splendidly. A sparkling brightness can be imparted to any clear stone that has a reasonably high refractive index and this can be done as easily by the step cut as by the brilliant cut. It is only necessary to cut the reflecting pavilion facets at a steeper angle than is correct for diamond, and some cutters maintain that the step cut displays the colour of a stone better. But since the brilliant cut has become established by tradition, people have come to expect it in gemstones. With its multitude of facets it certainly tends to make stones sparkle, but it is wasted on stones that are at all cloudy or of a deep colour. For this reason emeralds are usually shaped in their traditional step cut for they are very rarely fully transparent and have a relatively low refractive index and dispersion. The shape of their crystals also lends itself better to the step cut. This is also true of several other gem minerals that crystallize with a prismatic habit, for example, the other beryls, tourmaline and topaz.

Quite different skills and working methods are required for cutting gemstones that are not diamonds. Differential hardness and the strict observance of cutting directions is of little importance. Instead, the cutter of coloured stones, the lapidary, is mainly concerned to display colour to the best advantage. He has to place the crown of a stone in such a way that the palest aspect is presented in a dark stone and the darkest aspect in a pale one. The number and placement of the pavilion facets can make an enormous difference both to the brilliance of a gem and to the intensity and purity of its colour. The symmetry and equality of facets are still of the greatest consequence and this is a respect in which many stones cut in the East are found wanting. They are often cut so as to produce as heavy a stone as possible, with insufficient attention to symmetry. Far less importance attaches to the avoidance of small flaws and inclusions – indeed, in some stones these may be desirable. Stars and cat's-eyes must be placed centrally; the sheen of, say, feldspar gems must be shown to best advantage and the play of colour in opal displayed at its most colourful aspect. The lapidary has therefore to command expertise over a much wider field than the diamond cutter but on the other hand he normally has far less intractable materials with which to deal. The cutting and polishing of a non-diamond gem may only take an hour or two from start to finish while the time taken in cutting a diamond may run into days or even weeks. Most of the material handled by the lapidary is also rather less costly than diamonds are.

A lapidary's first step in fashioning a gem is to outline its shape on the rough material from which it is to be cut. Unwanted portions may then be trimmed off by skilful blows with a small hammer or by sawing. A saw is also used to divide the rough into usable portions. The saws are thin discs of steel with small industrial diamonds set into their rims and the stones to be sawn are usually held in the hand against the saw, a procedure that looks more dangerous than it actually is. Sawing takes seconds, or at most minutes, as compared with hours or days for diamonds, but the much slower 'mud saws' employing a slurry of carborundum (silicon carbide) are also still in use. In the East hand-operated hacksaws and carborundum are used in the absence of electric power. Large jade boulders are sawn by means of wires stretched across a bow suspended from the ceiling: two men draw the bow to and fro while a third drips in the carborundum.

The broad wetted rims of abrasive wheels rotating vertically are next used to shape the stones which are again held in the fingers and ground ('sanded') to a close approximation of their final shape. Subsequent processes need a more accurate control over the stone. It is therefore cemented to the end of a 'dop stick' (a wooden stick the size of a pencil shaped to a point at the other end). The facets are now ground on precisely by 'laps' (metal wheels rotating horizontally). From a wide range of laps and abrasive powders the grinder selects those most appropriate to the stone on which he is working; diamond powder may be used for the hardest minerals. As a help in grinding on the facets at the correct angles the pointed end of the dop stick is inserted into holes drilled in a 'jamb peg' fitted by the side of the lap. It takes considerable skill to produce perfectly flat facets by eye and touch alone, yet professionals scorn to use faceting machines by the aid of which amateur lapidaries can obtain quite creditable results.

Grinding produces a stone completely and correctly shaped in every particular but with a matt surface. It has now to be polished, a job done by specialists in the larger establishments. Polishing is carried out on a different set of laps, still with a dop stick and jamb peg but using polishing powders which are not abrasive. Soft materials with a high melting point are employed such as jewellers' rouge (iron oxide), tripoli (a diatomaceous earth), tin oxide and cerium oxide. These powders and the frictional heat they produce make the surface of the stone flow, spreading it out in an extremely thin transparent layer. Polishing does not reduce the weight of a gem but imparts to it the familiar smooth and shiny appearance. Diamond does not have this layer; its polish is acquired by the abrasion of any roughness left and this process is not so critical as with other gemstones. Curiously, it is much more difficult to impart a good polish to a soft mineral than a hard one. Overheating a stone in polishing is the great danger and more stones cleave and fracture during this process than during previous ones. Electric power drives the laps but for really fine work some polishers still prefer to crank the lap with one hand and hold the dop stick in the other.

Faceting is a relatively recent practice – it only became common during the seventeenth century – but stones have been polished since neolithic times. Presumably it was noticed how much prettier some pebbles looked when wet and workers in stone learned that a similar improvement could be produced by first grinding off the rough outside of a stone and then smoothing the flat surface produced. The tools and materials used were simple and polishing required long hours of labour. That quite ambitious stone carving was nevertheless undertaken, even without the use of metals, is proved by surviving artefacts and by the observed procedures of the Maoris of New Zealand or the inhabitants of Easter Island as reported by Thor Heyerdahl. As recently as 1842 two travellers came across a Maori village that lived by carving 'pounamu', green nephrite. They used various grades of sandstone for grinding away unwanted portions and a very fine-grained sandstone with shark oil for polishing.

Primitive people drilled stones first by twirling a stick charged with abrasive between their hands; then by pressing such a stick down on the workpiece while imparting a rotary motion to it with a string wound round it and pulled to and fro by means of a bowed piece of wood. Later, tools were made of bronze and ever more elaborate carvings and engravings were accomplished. First designs were cut into flat surfaces, often for use as seals. These developed into inscriptions, portraits and representations of factual or mythical scenes which could only be fully appreciated when the carved stone was pressed into soft clay or wax. Such a carving is known as intaglio from the Italian meaning 'cut into'. Later the design or picture was left in relief against a flat background that had been cut away, thus producing a cameo. For cameo carving the most popular gems were those with a layered structure such as agate, onyx and sardonyx. The coloured layers were used for carving hair, clothing or ornamental features, leaving the white layers for the face and skin, so accentuating the three-dimensional character of the carving. Supreme artistry in the production of these miniatures in stone was achieved in the sixteenth and seventeenth centuries, largely by Italian craftsmen. One of these, Benedetto Pistrucci, worked at the Royal Mint in London and his cameo of St George and the dragon was used to form the obverse of British golden sovereigns. The art is not practised much at present; there appears to be little demand for fine cameos and very few craftsmen are left. Until the early part of the present century there was a market for seal intaglios incorporating monograms, coats of arms and regimental badges, and masonic and zodiacal emblems.

The engraver works nowadays with an array of diamond-tipped tools that can be attached to the spindle of a smoothly running electric motor. The stone to be carved is pressed against the revolving tip of the tool. For fine work the engraver may steady his body and hands with a kind of harness. Otherwise he may merely brace himself against an upright support. Stones are now drilled with ultrasonic appliances or, in the case of diamonds, with laser beams.

The bulk of the output of gemstone cutters and engravers is sold to manufacturing jewellers, either directly or through dealers. Sales range from single stones of special quality or required for replacement to parcels of several hundred carats.

Most gemstones are sold by weight and prices are quoted as so much per carat (abbreviated ct). This now refers universally to the metric carat of one-fifth (0.2) of a gram. There are approximately 142 carats in one ounce avoirdupois or 7.77 carats in a pennyweight. The weight of a gemstone is always given to the nearest hundredth of a carat, that is, to two decimal places. A stone of eight and one third carats would be referred to as an 'eight point three three' (8.33) stone and one of 0.10 carats as a 'ten point' stone or as ten stones to the carat. Confusingly, the word 'carat' is also used to measure the purity of gold – an entirely different concept explained in the glossary. Pastes, doublets, synthetic and most ornamental stones are sold by their measurements in millimetres. The approximate diameters of various gemstones of the same cut

St George and the dragon. Obverse of coin based on a cameo carved by Benedetto Pistrucci.

|  | 0·5 carat | 1 carat | 2 carats | 3 carats | 5 carats |
|---|---|---|---|---|---|
| zircon S.G. 4·69 | ○ | ○ | ○ | ○ | ○ |
| beryl S.G. 2·71 | ○ | ○ | ○ | ○ | ○ |
| diamond S.G. 3·52 | ○ | ○ | ○ | ○ | ○ |

Approximate sizes of different brilliant cut gemstones.

and weight are indicated on this page. These sizes vary inversely with the density of the stones. For stones in the popular range of weights, say from a half to five carats, the value tends to increase rather more than in proportion to the weight. For the best qualities of the truly precious stones (emerald, ruby, diamond, natural pearl, opal, sapphire) it may increase as the square of the weight, but less steep multipliers apply to gems too large to be worn conveniently. Perfection of cut, a fine colour, or absolute colourlessness in diamond, flaws and inclusions, also affect the price considerably, as does the quantity bought. A parcel of gemstones sold as a whole will go for an appreciably lower price per carat than stones selected individually from a parcel. One must also expect to pay rather more for sets of fine gemstones exactly matched for size and colour than for single stones. Prices are affected by world trends in demand and supply as well as by the stock held by the jeweller concerned. For all these reasons there is no standard or fixed price that can be assigned to a gemstone and bargaining is common.

A curious method of bargaining is in use in Ceylon and other eastern countries. Bidding is by touch and not a word is spoken. The buyer and the seller clasp one hand under a cloth, concealing the bidding from an interested ring of bystanders. Bids are conveyed by squeezing the joints of fingers, each joint representing a different figure. When agreement is reached the onlookers expect a small gift for their sympathetic participation though they are not told the price agreed. The export of stones from most gem-producing countries is controlled and usually taxes are levied on their value.

The making of gem-set jewellery begins with a design, first on paper and then often on a wax plate. The designer must have practical experience in goldsmithing and a good knowledge of the peculiarities of gemstones. Often he or she works up the design to the finished product but large firms may employ or commission specialist designers. Large retail jewellers may also have their own workshops. These and the individual workers produce the bulk of high-class jewellery. They may send out some of their work to specialists such as diamond setters. The setting of diamonds is an exacting task calling for special training and skill, for the settings have to be strong and yet not obtrusive. Quite a range of other specialists operate in the jewellery industry: casters, platers, setters, engravers in stone and metal, jobbing repairers, workers in ivory, mother-of-pearl and tortoiseshell, pearl threaders,

Jewellery designer at work.

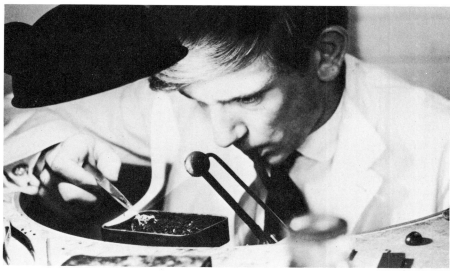

Goldsmith soldering a piece of jewellery.

and many others. Many jewellers can carry out repairs on their own premises and only have to send unusual work away for a specialist's attention. The replacement of gemstones lost from a setting is usually a task for a specialist, for few shops can carry the wide range of stones that may be needed.

Mechanization has affected only a part of these ancient crafts. Mechanical stamping and die casting has been in use for over 150 years, replacing some of the work that was formerly 'chased' by hand. Ultrasonic cleaning can remove dirt from crevices inaccessible to a brush (but it must be used with caution on stone-set jewellery). Otherwise the working jeweller still relies largely on his soldering blowpipe (which may now be blown by compressed air instead of his lungs), on his files,

A modern gemmological laboratory.

gravers, punches, saws and drills, as did his ancestors for hundreds of years.

Cheap jewellery is mass produced by wholesale firms and their designers need to be conversant with the special casting methods used. Goods are turned out by the gross, but few items are set with stones and these are usually paste, plastics or synthetics. On a smaller scale, cheap jewellery is made up from a large range of ready-made 'findings', that is, standard-sized settings such as ring shanks, ear clips, brooch fittings and cuff links that need only a minimum of adaptation or soldering to turn them into wearable jewellery.

An ancillary service of some importance in the present context is gem testing. The average jeweller has little contact with the newer and rarer gemstones and in the past he acquired a more or less adequate knowledge of the few gem species that came his way. This situation was drastically changed by the advent of synthetic gem rubies, sapphires, emeralds and the cultured pearl. These could no longer be distinguished with certainty by sight or with the simple instruments then available and from 1925 onward, laboratories were established in several western countries to which jewellers could refer doubtful items brought in for sale, valuation or repair. Gem-testing laboratories now exist in many countries; they can usually be consulted by the public through a competent jeweller. Some of them test many tens of thousands of gems and pearls in a year, applying the tests outlined in chapter three. A few museums also provide a testing and identification service.

This chapter has set out to describe the main processes by which gemstones are mined, fashioned and marketed. The picture that emerges is one of contrast between the efficient and highly mechanized part of the diamond mining industry and the very primitive methods used in the small-scale mining of most other gemstones. The cutting of all gemstones is still a trade in which skill and experience is of paramount importance and where thorough familiarity with the materials worked matters supremely. No two gemstones are ever exactly alike; small wonder then that the gem trades also have their fair share of individualists.

# The Evolution of Gems and Jewels

The use of gemstones goes back to remote antiquity. Archaeology has proved that wherever suitable minerals were available they were used for ornament. Most primitive peoples acquired the skills necessary to polish and perforate ornamental stones long before they learned to use metals. This 'neolithic' stage was reached by different communities at different times. The earliest ornaments of stone found in a few European and Asian localities appear to date back up to 10 000 years, but the more general use of gemstones runs parallel with the development of local civilizations and their technologies.

It is also clear that societies in frequent contact with each other obtained new gem materials and learned how to shape and use them while those cut off by the sea or natural obstacles progressed more slowly. Thus the use of metal-set gemstones in jewellery spread throughout the inter-communicating areas of southern Asia and the Mediterranean lands as far back as the fourth millennium BC, while the Maoris of New Zealand, though expert carvers of jade, were not yet using metals by the time of Captain Cook's arrival in 1769. The natives of the interior of New Guinea even now live in a Stone Age culture. Like other primitive tribes they use such items as feathers, shells, seeds and bones for adornment and these materials can therefore claim to antecede gemstones as ornaments.

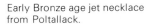

Early Bronze age jet necklace from Poltallack.

Maori carvings in nephrite, jade and other materials.

There are at least three reasons why minerals with the right attributes came to be accepted as gemstones. The most obvious is by their appeal to our sense of beauty, for example, by their colour. The oldest civilizations singled out minerals that were relatively soft and therefore easy to shape and polish, outstandingly amber, turquoise and lapis lazuli. The harder gem minerals were not used ornamentally until much later; at first such stones were mainly sought and treasured as talismans. On account of their hardness, colour and lustre, popular regard endowed them with mystic powers, particularly the corundums and diamond above all. They were worn by men in battle or to bring success on important occasions and were only later appropriated for adornment by women. Finally, there were minerals such as jade and obsidian that had been found useful when shaped for employment as tools and which had rarity and beauty as well. When their use as tools was superseded by metals, their prestige, often amounting to veneration, remained.

Whatever the reason, the desire for gemstones was sufficiently strong to promote their trade and transport over many hundreds of miles even in neolithic communities, and over whole continents in later periods. Nephrite from Silesia has been found in neolithic lakeside dwellings in Switzerland; it travelled to China and India from Turkestan. Amber reached Homer's Troy and other Mediterranean settlements from the Baltic over 1 000 BC, both overland and by sea. Alexander the Great's incursion into India brought the gems of that fabulous land to Europe. As time went on trade became worldwide and many new species of gems were discovered and adapted for use.

At first coloured stones merely had their outer roughness removed, but in time, polishing, perforating, the shaping of beads and cylinders and the carving of designs followed. The combination of gold with precious stones dates back some 5 000 years in Sumer, Egypt and the Indus valley, and probably also in South-east Asia.

Gold was the earliest metal to be used wherever it occurred in a pure, native state, that is, when it could be extracted relatively easily from rocks by crushing or collected from river and stream beds by panning. Another ancient method of collection was the suspension of a sheep's fleece in the current of a gold-bearing stream. The current would carry away the sand while the gold was trapped in the woolly fleece, producing the Golden Fleece of Homer's Odyssey and other tales. Gold is by far the most malleable metal and is easy to work. It can be beaten into gold leaf 1/200 000 of an inch thick or one ounce troy can be drawn into a fine wire some sixty miles long. Pure gold is, however, too soft for normal use in jewellery and it is therefore alloyed with other harder metals, a process which the ancients soon mastered.

Silver is harder and not nearly so plastic as gold, though it exceeds most other metals in this respect. It sometimes occurs in a native state, usually as branching or wire-like incrustations on certain rocks. Like gold it does not oxidize, but it tarnishes, especially in air containing traces of sulphur. The ancient civilizations that had access to native silver learned to use it for ornament, either alone or alloyed with gold to form 'electrum'; ornaments made from this alloy have been found at Ur. Trade in both these precious metals goes back well before 2 000 BC. By contrast platinum was only discovered by the Spaniards in South America in 1735. They found it in small alluvial deposits in Colombia and called it *platina del Pinto*, 'silver-like metal from the Pinto river'. Its extremely high melting point (1 773°C) and the consequent difficulties of working it, as well as its rarity, precluded it from wide use in jewellery till the end of the nineteenth century.

Craftsmen and artists in ancient times knew how to produce beautiful ornaments by setting off lapis lazuli, turquoise, faience (glazed earthenware) and other materials against gold and silver. Most of our knowledge of ancient jewels and the skills of the artisans who produced them is derived from excavations of tombs and burials. Items handed down do not usually survive for long in their original shape; they are lost, broken or refashioned over and over again. Unfortunately, tomb robbers have been active over the millennia and only a very small proportion of the gems buried with their owners have survived.

These suffice to prove the excellence of design and the high degree of skill attained in Egypt, Babylon and later in the Mediterranean lands. The Tutankhamen treasures how that by the twelfth century BC elaborate gold work was being inlaid with coloured gemstones and faience. Practically all goldsmithing processes had been developed: casting, soldering, enamelling, piercing, chasing, engraving, and the setting of stones in collets or as inlay. All these techniques were combined to produce jewels of breathtaking beauty.

The lapidary's art had also progressed with the improvement of bronze tools and the discovery of harder abrasives. In addition to silica, powdered garnet and corundum were used and some authorities even think that the finer gem engravings of the first millenium BC could not have been carried out without the use of diamonds either mounted as pointed cutting instruments or as abrasive powder tipping bronze tools. To the softer stones previously used were added the chalcedonies – cornelian, chrysoprase, onyx, agate, bloodstone and jasper – as well as amethyst, rock crystal, garnet and haematite. Many of these gems were also used in Babylonia to fashion seal rings which remained in vogue for centuries. Herodotus reports that almost every Babylonian wore a seal ring. The seals were either in the form of a pierced cylinder which turned on a pivot and produced an oblong impression or in the form of the familiar flat seal.

Egypt was in contact with Asia Minor and the islands and shores of the Mediterranean Sea where elaborate and expressive jewellery was made as far back as the second millenium BC. Helen of Troy appears to have been a Mycenaean heiress abducted to Asia Minor at about the time of Tutankhamen or a little later and fine gold work with filigree was found when the site of Troy was excavated. Later the Phoenicians traded for tin and copper as far as Cornwall and for all sorts of goods, including gemstones, eastward to India and Ceylon. They brought back rubies, sapphires and emeralds but these were so hard that their craftsmen, limited by a lack of technology, could achieve no more than a rough shaping and polishing as baroque cabochons.

The flowering of Greek civilization brought with it a wonderful development of the jeweller's arts all round the Mediterranean, the consummation of 2000 years of experience and development. It is still true that some of the jewellery made at that time, for example by the Etruscans in Italy, has never been excelled. Their fine filigree work has not been equalled, let alone surpassed. The process by which they soldered the tiniest granules of gold to form intricate patterns completely covering a gold base has been lost and never re-identified with certainty. This was a period when men really mastered the fashioning of gold and revelled in its use at the expense of gemstones, many of which were still proving intractable and were to remain so for many centuries.

More use was made of gemstones in the eastern countries nearer their sources. Lapidary crafts flourished wherever stable political conditions

*Above* An intaglio seal of Diomede and Odysseus and its impression.

*Left* Ganymede and the eagle. A Greek garnet intaglio from the first century BC.

prevailed. The use of coloured stones can be traced back in various parts of India for well over 6 000 years but the turbulent history of the subcontinent and the custom of disposing of dead bodies by fire or later by exposure to birds of prey meant that no burial finds comparable to the tombs of Egypt could be expected. Old jewellery has been refashioned over and over again to suit the needs of the time. As elsewhere, gemstones were used to add colour to jewellery by means of inlay work or as cabochons; no faceting was attempted until much later. Stress was laid on producing bright and intricate ornaments full of glorious colour.

In China, different trends prevailed, conditioned by the veneration for jade. The art of carving nephrite of all colours was well developed 2 000 years or more BC and simple but wonderfully expressive objects of quasi-religious and talismanic significance survive, partly from burials but also because they were treasured and preserved carefully. Jade was at first carved with bamboo sticks impregnated with garnet powder. It must have been an excruciatingly slow process, but then jade was credited, among other things, with conferring incorruptability and even immortality. The mythical Queen Hsi Wang Mu, who knew the secret of preparing the elixir of life from it, lived several thousand years! Mummy cases of the Tang period (618–906 AD), completely enclosing the bodies of a king and queen and composed of jade fragments polished and closely fitted together, have recently been exhibited. Long burial in contact with soil gives jade subtle shades of brown and a peculiar patina greatly prized and treasured in China and elsewhere. But there have been reports of 'burial jade' coloured artificially by chemical means.

Ploughing scene with two of the eight immortals, carved in Chinese jade during the eighteenth or nineteenth century.

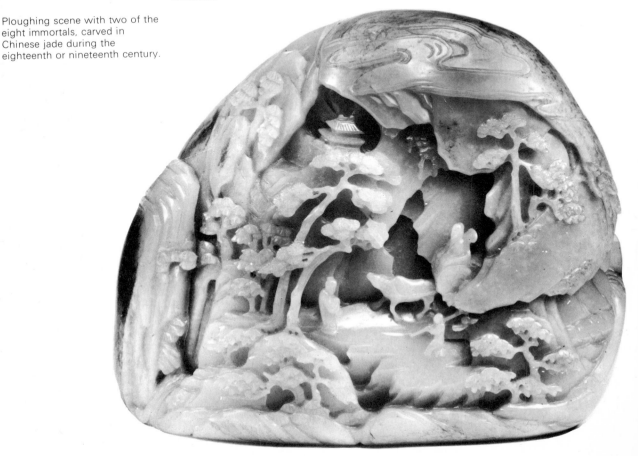

142

When Rome took over as the main Mediterranean power, the lightness of touch so evident in Greek work was lost. Although fine work was still produced, Roman designs were on the whole heavier and less imaginative.

An art in which the Greeks excelled and the Romans were also adept was the carving of cameos and intaglios. Lifelike portraits and figures were carved in the minutest detail in Greece from the fifth century BC onwards. The most famous engraver, Pyrgoteles, was honoured by Alexander the Great who allowed him alone to carve his portrait as a cameo, now, alas lost. He is reputed to have carved it in emerald – an astonishing achievement if true. Greek and Roman cameos have been held in the highest esteem ever since. In the Middle Ages they were used to adorn sacred relics, treasures and book bindings, often quite incongruously, the pagan deities being identified with Christian saints. Even the superb engravers of the sixteenth and seventeenth centuries did not scruple to copy antique cameos, complete with their Greek signatures.

At the height of the Roman Empire the use of jewels for personal adornment was fairly widespread and the possession of jewellery – whether bronze, silver or gold – set with gems, was not necessarily an attribute of the rich or powerful. With the fall of Rome, however, there was a sharp reduction in the scope for jewellers' and lapidaries' products, and the centre of Mediterranean civilization moved to Byzantium (Istanbul). Some jewellery continued to be made there until the city was sacked by the Crusaders in 1204.

The races that surged across Europe during the early Middle Ages knew nothing of the finesse with which the Greeks had assembled gold and gems hundreds of years earlier and nearly a thousand years passed before the Renaissance inspired another supreme flowering of the jeweller's art. Meanwhile designs were crude and heavy, craftsmanship declined sadly and the stone engraver's knowledge was lost.

This lacuna in the history of the jeweller's skills was redeemed, however, by the introduction into Europe from the East of the art of enamelling, a skill which was further perfected during these dark ages, endowing jewels with bright colour. The little cells of gold strips (cloisons) which contained the enamel could also be made to hold small gemstones; garnets and other coloured gems were often set in this way.

In time, jewellery became the prerogative of rank in the three main domains wielding power: the church, the royal court and the nobility. The insignia and ornaments now associated with these institutions, such as the crown, gradually evolved during this period. The Roman emperors had worn laurel wreaths and later, diadems – circlets set with a band of gemstones between rows of pearls at the top and bottom. In Byzantium the diadem was expanded with hoops which were finally joined to cover the entire head, sometimes with pendant pieces over the ears. This head cover developed into an ornamental cap under the hoops or a solid dome of a shape that survives in the crowns of the patriarchs of the Eastern Church and in the papal crown of Rome.

The crusades brought further contact with the East and both gemstones and the techniques of shaping them began to be imported as soon as the more settled conditions from the thirteenth century onward allowed trade once more to flourish. We find the first records of agate polishing mills driven by horse and water power in Germany. Goldsmiths' guilds were established in London, Paris, Nuremberg and other centres in Europe. Goldsmiths and jewellers (that is, those who set gemstones in precious metals) usually belonged to the same guilds and employed the same skills, but lapidaries (gemstone polishers and engravers) had their own separate organizations which also date back to the fourteenth century.

Throughout the Middle Ages gemcraft had progressed in the East and contact through the crusades may have inspired its re-establishment in the West. It is likely that the first experiments in faceting originated in India, though it seems that the aim was merely to produce pleasing surfaces; the power of the back facets to give brilliance to a stone does not appear to have been appreciated. It is, however, quite likely that Indian craftsmen managed to polish facets even on diamonds a thousand years ago.

Other gem-using civilizations that developed during the Middle Ages were those that succeeded each other in Central America. First the Mayas, then the Tolmecs and Aztecs established cities and temples in which many art forms flourished, including those of the lapidary. They all valued gold, silver and gemstones, of which they had emerald, jadeite, nephrite, garnet, amethyst, rock crystal, obsidian, amazonite, turquoise and cornelian. The Aztecs treasured green jadeite and emerald above all others. A hand-sized piece of jadeite equalled in value as much gold as two men could carry. They carved and drilled beads of many shapes; they portrayed their many gods in jade, including the tutelary deities of the stone carvers. Large crystals of quartz were used as badges of office and with the primitive tools in use – though gold was used for ornament, metal tools were unknown – it might take

Gemstones and enamel openwork broach, eleventh century Ottonian art.

*Left* A jade plaque (seventh to tenth century) shows a Mayan dignitary sitting on a throne. The workmanship represents the peak of the Mayan jade carvers' skill.

*Below* Diopside-jadeite Olmec celts from El Mangal, Mexico, made in about 1500.

two lifetimes to drill through one such crystal. Many of their elaborate and expressive carvings were smashed as idolatrous by the Conquistadors; golden artifacts were melted down for easier transport. Relatively little survives though more is being recovered from ancient temples and cities abandoned to the jungle.

In Europe a revival of more general interest in gemstones is much in evidence from contemporary manuscripts of the thirteenth and fourteenth centuries, but these concentrate on the medicinal and talismanic properties of gems, drawing mainly on tradition and on classical and Arab sources. Several edicts surviving from the same period and issued in different countries restrict the wearing of jewels to people of rank, thereby implying that by this time commoners were once more bold and rich enough to wear gems. We can also trace the first essays in the accurate and symmetrical faceting of gemstones to the fourteenth century. Before then lapidaries had had to be content with polishing the surface only, but now even diamonds were faceted in ever more elaborate patterns and there are the first literary references to diamonds being worn by women. The design of jewellery became lighter, craftsmanship improved and there are interesting similarities to the graceful architectural styles of the period.

The next two centuries witnessed the effulgence of the Renaissance, with a dramatic development and proliferation of jewellery. Freed from the limiting influence of church and court and appealing to a much wider market, jewellery reflected the new interest in classical forms and themes. Saints were replaced by nymphs and satyrs; jewels of the most intricate design adorned every conceivable part of the body and dress. Some of the greatest artists of the time started their training as goldsmiths, including Botticelli, della Robbia, Pollaiuolo, Brunelleschi, Verocchio, del Sarto and Dürer. Benvenuto Cellini made notable jewels and Holbein designed them.

At first the goldsmiths' work merely echoed simple Roman designs but soon there were broad necklaces, rings on every finger, earrings for both sexes, richly ornamented buttons, clasps to hold the fashionable split sleeves together, and most elaborate hat ornaments, brooches and pendants. Henry VIII and Elizabeth I both loved jewels as contemporary portraits show. Henry acquired a great wealth of gems when he dissolved the monasteries. From Canterbury alone came two large chests each of which eight men could barely carry. Elizabeth employed a court jeweller; she was particularly fond of pearls and did not disdain wearing the imitation pearls which began to be produced during her reign. Among the courtiers who presented her with jewels was her treasurer, Sir Christopher Hatton, whose garden, still so called, is now the centre of London's jewellery trade. The same garden had already been famous in the fifteenth century – for its strawberries!

Jewels of this period were made to be looked at in the round so care was taken to finish even the hidden backs of rings and brooches, often with elaborate enamelling, an art in which great mastery was attained. The exploits of navigators and explorers introduced oriental gems and designs; ships and fabulous animals were minutely reproduced in enamelled jewels of which the centre piece was sometimes formed by a huge baroque pearl skilfully placed to make use of its irregular shape.

The classic revival brought with it renewed interest in cameo carvings. During the sixteenth and seventeenth centuries this art reached a level that has never been equalled since. Among many famous names in this field that of the family Miseroni of Naples, members of which settled and worked in several countries, is one of the most renowned.

The cameos were set in elaborately enamelled brooches and pendants.

The technique of faceting gemstones was evolving throughout this period and cabochons became rarer. There was an increasing realization of how greatly skilful cutting and polishing could enhance the lustre and brilliance of a gemstone and improve the scope for setting and displaying it, but it was not until the seventeenth century that gemstones displaced enamel as the most important feature of jewels. From then on they predominated, smaller stones often being pavé set (placed so closely together that the setting was hidden entirely). Very accurate cutting was required for this type of setting.

The seventeenth century also witnessed the achievement of the full brilliant cut of diamonds. This discovery is usually attributed to the Venetian Vincenzio Peruzzi, about 1670, but even at the end of the fifteenth century Louis de Berquem of Bruges had realized what fire lay hidden in diamonds. His attempts to reveal it started a series of experiments that continued for centuries and is not concluded even yet. Cardinal Mazarin is sometimes credited with having promoted the rose cut about 1630, but this was also known long before his time.

Unfortunately, few examples of seventeenth-century jewellery survive in Britain. Charles I and Cromwell both extracted forced loans from jewellers, livery companies and wealthy citizens to finance the Civil War and many jewels were destroyed to raise ready cash from the gold and stones. The Commonwealth and Puritanism had a depressing effect on design. Jewels became less exuberant and macabre themes such as skulls, coffins and other reminders of death were worn as a compromise between the desire for adornment and the rejection of earthly pleasures. In France, however, matters were very different. Louis XIV – the Sun King – loved jewels and wore them profusely, imitated by his court. Their design was rich and elegant, with use of many colourful stones in elaborate settings.

In India the Mogul Empire reached its climax and this was reflected

From left to right: agate, rock crystal and onyx Renaissance amphorae.

in the sumptuous jewellery produced for the royal court and the tributary potentates. Gem-encrusted thrones of ivory inlaid with gold (chryselephantine) and rich ornaments of every conceivable kind were produced in abundance. Even the royal horses were caparisoned in emeralds. Enormous pearl necklaces and belts were worn and beakers, flasks, bowls, and sword hilts were richly inlaid with coloured gems and gold. Jaipur was a notable centre for this inlay work, as it was for the carving of nephrite. Exquisite translucent bowls and plates dating from the seventeenth century can be admired in the Victoria and Albert Museum, London, and other collections, including those in the East. Some of the Mogul emperors were experts in the knowledge of gems. They were the original owners of the Koh-i-nur and many more of the world's largest and most famous gems, by now faceted and sometimes engraved with their names. This love of gems has remained with eastern princes; Indian rajahs and especially the Shah of Persia (Iran) have fabulous treasuries of jewellery.

Back in Europe, the eighteenth century saw the rise to affluence of the merchant class. Jewellery was no longer confined mainly to the court and land-owning gentry; ever-widening markets opened among the nouveaux riches, or rather their wives, for from now on the wearing of jewels became largely the preserve of women, though jewellery was still worn by men, particularly in the form of ornate and jewelled sets of buttons and buckles. Changes in fashion became increasingly frequent, but it is beyond the scope of this book to follow them in detail. One can but wonder why a gentleman of the sixteenth century should have felt practically nude without his earrings while in 1860, just before earscrews were invented, a young lady would have been distinctly overdressed if she wore earrings.

Under the influence of the splendours of the royal court in France, Paris became the arbiter of fashion and good taste in jewellery and many other arts, a position it has held for well over 200 years. The rococo period produced intricate asymmetrical flourishes, the so-called *rocaille* style in jewellery; its chief exponent was a Paris jeweller, Paul de Lamarie. For the first time different jewels were designed to be worn on different occasions. Brightly coloured gemstones were worn by day. According to the wealth of the owner they could range from chalcedonies, through garnets, to the more expensive coloured stones. Fully transparent coloured stones, often foiled, and above all diamonds, were reserved for evening wear when the light of hundreds of candles would make them sparkle and glitter in multiple reflections. Instead of the colourful riot of previous centuries, stones of one colour only were now increasingly used for individual pieces of jewellery and even for entire suites or parures of necklace, bracelets, earrings, brooches, rings and perhaps a hair ornament, each piece being carefully matched with the rest in both design and colour.

Other French fashions included the *girandole,* earrings consisting of round gems or clusters on the earlobe from which hung pear-shaped pendants; the *aigrette,* a spray clip worn in the hair in the form of a plume, leaves or flowers, adorned with birds or butterflies and often mounted on springs or thin wires to make the ornament oscillate with each movement; and the *sévigné,* a large bow-shaped brooch of open scrollwork. The finest examples were set with diamonds mounted almost invariably in silver. Small pomanders that could be worn as freely swinging pendants on necklaces or chatelaines were also popular. Jean Bourguet and George Michael Moser (a Swiss) produced Paris enamel – on ring shanks, for example – that is of outstanding quality.

Repelled by political and religous oppression in their own countries and attracted by the rising affluence of England and America, many fine craftsmen fled from Italy, France, Germany and the Netherlands to lands which offered more freedom. Among them were jewellers who brought their native styles with them and influenced design so profoundly that it is quite difficult to judge where some eighteenth-century jewellery was made. On the whole the more extravagant rococo styles had only a limited appeal in the English-speaking countries.

The opening up of new sea routes and the more thorough exploration of lands discovered earlier led to fresh gem sources of which South America was the most important. Previously, all diamonds and most coloured stones had come from India and the East. Now diamonds, emeralds, topazes, aquamarines, chrysoberyls, amethysts and all other kinds of quartz came from the New World. The settings made to hold this new wealth of gems were of much lighter, more open design than those of the seventeenth century which tended to emphasize opulence.

Those who could not afford diamonds were able for the first time to buy excellent glass substitutes. Ravenscroft in England and Strasser in Germany perfected a strongly dispersive lead glass that could not easily be distinguished from diamonds by candlelight. Diamond suites were sometimes copied in paste, often with equally painstaking work-manship. Such pieces can still be admired in several collections, but it is noticeable that in almost every case the old paste is somewhat tarnished. The manufacture of glass jewellery was forbidden in Germany but encouraged in France and England.

Another poor man's friend was a certain Christopher Pinchbeck who in 1732 invented an alloy of copper and zinc which looked like a gold alloy, did not tarnish readily and was cheap to produce. Much of it was cast and some contemporary well-finished jewellery made of this material still survives, though many more less well-made pieces date from the nineteenth century.

Cameos and intaglios, which were still very much in vogue, were reproduced from classical designs by Josiah Wedgwood in 'jasper' ware, a form of fine-grained stoneware in which the white design stands in relief against a coloured background, and by Tassie who produced transparent glass casts of intaglios which preserve the finest detail. Both are now valued collectors' items.

The end of the eighteenth century also saw the wider use of jadeite of a bright green and other colours emanating particularly from China. Up to this time jade carvings had been made almost exclusively of nephrite, but in 1784 a treaty was signed between Burma, by then the only substantial source of jadeite in Asia, and China. China had gone to war to secure this course of jadeite and Burma undertook to export to her all the jadeite produced. Jadeite then became, and has remained to the present day, the most highly valued species of jade. Among the great lovers of gems the nineteenth-century Empress Chu Hsi ranks high. She amassed a vast treasure of gems and is said to have been able to pick out jades of different kinds and colours merely by handling them in bowls of warm scented water.

In the eighteenth and nineteenth centuries the Chinese and Japanese enlarged their production of gemstone carvings greatly. Pendants, buttons denoting mandarin rank, snuff bottles, belt buckles and a wide range of other ornamental objects were made from jade, the silica gems, tourmaline, grossular garnet and many other ornamental stones.

The wars at the end of the eighteenth century and the French Revolution depressed the jewellery trades in Europe. As in all wars, money was scarce, so materials of low intrinsic value came into vogue. It became fashionable to wear black jewellery, often as a sign of mourning, and Whitby jet was much in demand. The early nineteenth century also saw the rise of the Berlin iron foundry which made fine lace-like jewels of black cast iron. In France, the Directorate frowned upon the wearing of jewellery and suppressed the Paris goldsmiths, but this did not last long as Napoleon had no such inhibitions. He established an imperial court and encouraged a lavish display commensurate with its grandeur. By the turn of the century it was no longer an insult to democracy to wear diamonds; by 1810 they were again supreme. The old French royal treasury had, however, been looted in the revolution and most of its contents had disappeared. New jewellery, conforming to the Directoire style was therefore produced. Its craftsmanship was not quite so good as older work but the jewels were of a classical simplicity in outline, however rich the material might be, and reflected current themes – imperial eagles, laurel wreaths, cameos in which the letter N figured prominently. However, poverty marked the first decades of the nineteenth century and there was a vogue for cheap and colourful gemstones such as coral and malachite. When the Duc de Barry married, the City of Paris gave him a wedding present of jewellery – set with paste.

The discoveries of Roman antiquities, when Pompeii was excavated thoroughly under the French occupation of Naples between 1806 and 1814, had a profound influence on jewellery design. Classical themes became the fashion and the arts of mosaic and stone inlay were greatly stimulated in Italy, France and in England. Medallions for brooches, necklets and bracelets were produced in exquisite detail. Mosaic work in Naples and inlay in Florence has survived to the present day.

As the nineteenth century progressed new techniques developed that helped to cheapen jewellery, in both senses of the word. This was

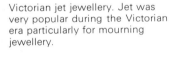

Victorian jet jewellery. Jet was very popular during the Victorian era particularly for mourning jewellery.

true particularly of increasing mechanization. Instead of making each piece of jewellery individually, it now became possible to stamp out components or entire pieces with great precision, so initiating the age of mass production in this as in many other fields. Quite elaborate designs could be reproduced in large numbers and sold cheaply, using paste, the cheaper silica gems, garnets or imitation pearls. Electroplating was perfected during the first half of the nineteenth century providing a cheaper and more reliable means of covering base metals with gold and silver. Design and craftsmanship suffered as a result of mass production; it was not worth spending the time necessary to produce good quality workmanship on such cheap jewellery.

After the Napoleonic wars more opulent jewellery and gemstones once more came into wider use and the jewellery trades recovered. Costly gemstones were again mounted in elaborate well-finished settings. Necklaces and tiaras were made to take apart, so that the constituent pieces could be worn separately as clasps, brooches, pendants or bracelets. Fashions changed with great rapidity; at one stage jewels were highly ornate – to our taste unduly so – at another they were subdued and simple. Sometimes entire parures were worn, at others it was fashionable to wear hardly any jewellery at all.

The great exhibitions in London (1851) and Paris (1867) gave prominence to the outstanding jewellery designers of the time, two of whom must be mentioned by name because they produced jewels of such impeccable artistry and superb workmanship, using fine gems and enamel. The earlier of them was Castellani of Rome. His firm flourished for several decades and his success inspired others, notable among whom was a Neapolitan, Giuliano, who settled in London. Both based themselves largely on classical motifs, reproducing Greek and Etruscan work with great exactitude. Their products are now collectors' pieces of great value. Taste then shifted to Turkish, Chinese and Egyptian designs (inspired by the opening of the Suez canal).

In the seventies and eighties diamonds were considered to be in better taste than coloured stones, a belief influenced, no doubt, by the development of the South African diamond fields. These discoveries greatly stimulated the interest in the cutting of diamonds and the design of diamond jewellery, an interest which has lasted to the present day. The revulsion from coloured stones also led to the popularity of jet, ivory and amber. Popular jewellery, mass produced in Birmingham, reproduced an immense range of floral and animal designs. Flowers of all kinds, snakes, lizards and insects of every description proliferated, as did sporting motifs such as horses, dogs, stirrups, whips and horseshoes. Jewellery was now made almost solely for women; men had to be content with a watch chain and the odd ring or perhaps a tiepin or cuff links.

The discovery of major platinum deposits in the Ural mountains and their exploitation from 1822 onwards should also be mentioned here. Earlier in the nineteenth century platinum had been used as a substitute for silver in the Russian currency, but with its matt lustre, its utter resistance to corrosion and its rarity value it ultimately became the ideal metal in which to set diamonds. Even the newly discovered aluminium was, for a short time before 1850, treated as a precious metal and some jewellery was made of it.

Paris remained the centre of fashion throughout the nineteenth century, attracting custom from all over the world. In England, Queen Victoria had little interest in jewels, but Napoleon III's Queen Eugenie took a great delight in them and particularly loved diamonds and pearls.

French diamond jewellery designs were often exuberant with settings so contrived as to be almost invisible, giving the glittering stones full predominance. Settings were of gold but faced with silver or, later, platinum. The standard of craftsmanship was high where important items were concerned. For simpler jewellery, star and crescent designs, bar brooches and heart motifs were in vogue. Necklaces in the form of 'rivières' came into fashion. They were composed of large single topazes, emeralds, amethysts or even diamonds. After the South African discoveries, diamond solitaire rings became popular. In New York the house of Tiffany rose to prominence, attracting craftsmen and experts of all kinds, including the great mineralogist and gemmologist G. F. Kunz. Their designs were among the finest and most elaborate. Increasingly, jewel art forms became identified with the great jewellery houses rather than with national character, though local traditional designs were fostered and occasionally favoured by fashion; for example, Chinese, Indian, Egyptian and Mexican influences all had temporary vogues.

So great was the proliferation of designs that a natural reaction set in, from 1880 onward, inspired by the Aesthetic Movement and the Art Nouveau. The aim was to get away from traditional styles and materials; the exponents of the new styles delighted in natural forms, in wavy, asymmetrical shapes and in using bronze, glass, ivory, and mother-of-pearl in preference to gemstones. The movement flourished in England, France, Germany and the Low Countries. Both Art Nouveau and traditional forms developed, influencing each other, up to the outbreak of the First World War.

The early twentieth century was a period of ostentation and, on the whole, undistinguished design except for one outstanding manufacturer: Peter Carl Fabergé, a Russian of Huguenot extraction. He was patronized by the Russian court and acclaimed all over the world for his highly original designs and excellent workmanship. At the height of his fame he had five factories, including one in London, and employed some 700 workmen—a vast enterprise by the standards of that time. He used gemstones extensively, including the more colourful ornamental stones which were exquisitely carved into flowers. One of the Easter eggs made for the Tsar was auctioned about twenty years ago. It was made of hollowed rock crystal on a base of the same material, the whole etched with ice and snow crystals. The cold glitter was enhanced with diamonds. When opened, the egg disclosed a golden basket of spring flowers carved in minute detail from coloured stones. Fabergé's factories were converted to manufacture munitions during the First World War and most of his products were lost. Much of the output of his contemporaries suffered the same fate, for there was a period in the 1930s when gold greatly rose in value and when jewellery, particularly of the pre-war years, was melted down on a vast scale. The recovered gemstones, except diamonds, were often sold at giveaway prices.

All wars disorganize the jewellery trades and impoverish their usual customers; the two World Wars were no exceptions. After the First War, new trends in fashion aided the mass production of inexpensive 'costume jewellery', designed more as accessories to dresses than as ornaments in their own right. There were also long bead necklaces in ivory, coral or amber, heavy bangles and bracelets on the wrists, pendant earrings and large rings made of silver and base metals. A few original designers arose out of the 'Arts and Crafts' movement of the 1920s. They used silver set with such stones as chrysoprase, cornelian, agate and garnets in a variety of forms reflecting national traditions. Some jewel designs were also influenced by the Cubist movement, Picasso contributing notable examples of work some of which were executed in platinum set with diamonds, rubies and emeralds. Pearls were more popular than ever under the dominant influence of the Japanese cultured pearl industry and the imitation pearls made in France and Czechoslovakia. Tiny watches, concealed in bracelets and rings were manufactured in Switzerland, Paris and New York, as were composite pieces, such as brooches that could be taken apart to form two or three clips.

Further technical advances were made after the Second World War. The technology of palladium advanced, largely as a consequence of research in the USA, to a point where it began to supersede its allied metal, platinum. Both are extremely resistant to corrosion and show a bright white lustre, but palladium is lighter in weight and much cheaper. Workable alloys were produced that enabled it to be readily manufactured into jewellery. New surfaces could also be given to base metals by anodizing, for example, which produces matt coloured films on metals, or by rhodium plating, which gives a bright un-tarnishable finish. Fine films were 'sputtered' on glass to give novel effects to beads. Designers delighted in experimenting with these and other new materials, particularly plastics.

In the high-class ranges of jewellery, artists like Braque, Calder, and Giacometti joined Picasso. Salvador Dali designed mobile jewellery – flowers of precious stones and metals that opened and closed, a ruby heart that beat. Leading international jewellery houses such as Boucheron, Bulgari, Cartier, Garrard, Tiffany, Van Cleef and Arpels produced designs that broke right away from conventional outlines as well as more traditional forms, all executed with fine craftsmanship.

Some experiments of this period may not have succeeded, producing a heavy and pretentious effect, but much has been produced that is striking and impressive. Ever wider circles are being attracted to practical participation in gemcraft and jewellery making. These arts may well be lifted to new levels and acquire new patrons who are both informed and discerning.

# The History and Lore of Gemstones

An aura of admiration, wonder and curiosity such as no other objects have created, surrounds the great and famous gemstones of the world. Tragedy and adventure, often directly inspired by these treasures, mark the lives of their owners, who were often of royal birth. Stories, both authentic and apocryphal, have grown round the more ancient among them. Those accessible to the public always attract long queues of admirers. Most of them have been fully documented, but no account of gems would be complete without reference to the origins of the most famous stones.

The largest diamond discovered so far was called the Cullinan, after a president of the South African Premier Diamond Mining Company. It was found by Mr Frederick Wells, the manager of the Premier mine, who noticed a glint in the wall of the mine one evening in 1905 and extracted a massive diamond of 3 106 carats, almost flawless and of superb quality. News of the discovery spread quickly and the great stone had to be guarded carefully and insured. When it was sent to headquarters in London, an armed guard was ostentatiously mounted night and day over the ship's safe supposed to contain it, but the Cullinan was actually despatched by the normal postal route with other stones. In London the insurance premium for removing it from safe custody for two hours to show it to King Edward VII ran to £150, but it is reported that the King was not impressed by the appearance of the rough stone. It was bought by the Transvaal Government for £150 000 and at the suggestion of Premier Botha, who had been a famous general fighting the British in the Boer war, was presented to King Edward in 1907. Cutting the stone was entrusted to the Dutch firm of I. J. Asscher and Co. who suggested that it be cleaved into five parts. This operation was so tense that the expert performing it had to have medical attention immediately after it was successfully accomplished. Nine large and ninety-six smaller brilliants were cut from the Cullinan, but together they represent only about one third of the weight of the original

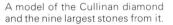
A model of the Cullinan diamond and the nine largest stones from it.

154

stone, two thirds having been lost in the cutting. The largest brilliant is drop-shaped. It weighs 530.2 carats and is the largest cut diamond in the world. It is known as the Star of Africa and it adorns the British royal sceptre kept at the Tower of London.

The Cullinan had a large cleavage surface and must therefore have been part of an even larger crystal. This has never been found in spite of diligent search, but there was a report in 1919 that a diamond of approximately 1 500 carats had been crushed by machines in the Premier mine. This may have been part of the missing half. Another case is known where the cleaved parts of a single diamond were found in widely separated sites.

The second largest among the gem diamonds of known original weight was the Excelsior, discovered in South Africa in 1893. It weighed 995.2 carats and was cut into twenty-two brilliants, the largest weighing nearly 70 carats. The third largest diamond, the Star of Sierra Leone, came from that country as recently as February 1972. It weighs 968.8 carats (nearly ½ lb) and has not yet been cut.

The history of these stones is short and is known in minute detail. Very different are the sketchy and often conflicting accounts of some of the truly historic stones. Their origins can only be surmised; the tales told about their passage from one owner to the next are often at variance, there are long gaps during which their whereabouts were uncertain and some have disappeared for good. Records of a sort exist concerning some fifty famous stones, mainly large diamonds. Several have been the causes of wars, murders and great misfortunes of all kinds. They certainly have not justified the ancient belief that gemstones necessarily bring good fortune, health and happiness. Most of these stones now adorn regalia or rest in private treasuries, including those of some Indian princes.

The longest known history is probably that of the Koh-i-nur (sometimes Koh-i-noor or Kohinoor) which means 'mountain of light'.

Star of Sierra Leone.

Grand Mogul diamond.

Tradition traces it back for more than 4000 years, but it is known for certain to have come by conquest into the possession of a Mogul king in 1304 and to have remained in that royal house until Nadir Shah of Persia invaded India in 1739. The story goes that Nadir exchanged turbans with his beaten foe as a sign of favour and forgiveness, fully aware that the Mogul kept the great diamond hidden in his turban. Nadir was murdered a few years later, his empire disintegrated and the Koh-i-nur passed for sixty years to the royal house of Afghanistan. Forced to flee by a revolt, the Afghan ruler of the time obtained sanctuary with Ranjit Singh in India, who, however, relieved him of all his jewels, including the Koh-i-nur which he wore in an armlet for many years. At his death in 1839 it passed into the treasury of Lahore. The stone was then seized by the East India company, with other gems, after a war with the Sikhs and presented to Queen Victoria in 1850.

Tiffany diamond.

156

It has been set in the crowns of the Queens of England ever since, for according to tradition it brings good fortune to women but bad fortune to men. It can be taken out of the crown and worn separately as a brooch.

The stone is thought to have weighed some 800 carats originally. The Mogul Emperor Shah Jahan (the builder of the Taj Mahal) had it recut by a Venetian diamond cutter but this craftsman did his work so badly that the Shah fined him all he possessed. When it came to Queen Victoria it weighed 191 carats. She had it recut yet again, a course that has been much criticized; both Prince Albert and the Duke of Wellington are said to have assisted at the cutting. The stone now weighs 108.9 carats and is in the form of a standard brilliant, not quite round and not of the correct proportions.

Another large diamond of superb quality that finished up in a royal sceptre after a turbulent career is the 199.6 carat Orlov. Mined at Collur in India some 350 years ago, it was acquired by Shah Jahan and cut to a domed shape which it still retains, greatly enhancing its historical interest. It passed to Nadir Shah with the Koh-i-nur and the Timur Ruby and is said to have been mounted as an eye in a statue of Buddha after Nadir's assassination. A French soldier posing as a wor-

Koh i nur diamond.

shipper then stole the jewel and sold it to an English sea captain who brought it to Holland. From there it was sold to Prince Orlov who presented it to the Empress Catherine of Russia. She had the stone mounted in her sceptre and it is still housed in the Diamond Treasury at Moscow, together with another fine and historic diamond, the 88.7 carat Shah. This stone also once belonged to Shah Jahan and is engraved with his name and that of two other Indian rulers.

The National Collection at the Louvre in Paris holds the Pitt or Regent diamond, mined in India in 1701 and bought by Sir Thomas Pitt, Governor of Madras. He had it cut to a fine brilliant weighing 140.5 carats, a task that took two years to accomplish and involved the loss of two thirds of the original weight. Pitt sold the stone to the Regent of France, the Duc d'Orléans, but it was looted together with the rest of the French royal treasure during the French Revolution. Unlike the other treasures it was returned intact; it had been found unharmed in a ditch.

Sancy diamond.

The equally famous Sancy diamond and the original of the Hope blue diamond were looted at the same time. The 55 carat Sancy, whose origin is uncertain, reappeared on the market much later and, after passing through many hands, is now owned by Lady Astor. The blue diamond disappeared completely but three blue stones were marketed later and these would together account for the missing stone. The largest of these, a stone of a fine sapphire-blue and weighing 44 carats was bought by H. P. Hope, a London banker, in 1830. It is now at the Smithsonian Institution at Washington. There appears to be little foundation for the many tales of ill-luck associated with this stone.

Several other coloured diamonds are famed for their size and beauty. One of the largest is the Florentine or Austrian Yellow, a nine-pointed briolette weighing 137.27 carats. Its origin is unknown but it certainly belonged to the Medici family of Florence, the great patrons of Renaissance art. The Austrian Empress Maria Theresa obtained it as part of a marriage settlement in 1743 and it remained in the personal possession of the Habsburg imperial house even after their overthrow in 1918. It disappeared during the Second World War but was recovered by the American Third Army and restored to Vienna by General Mark Clark.

The famous Green Vault at Dresden, which contained the royal treasures of Saxony, still contains the flawless Dresden Green diamond of 41 carats and four or five yellow brilliants, the largest of 38 carats, as well as a fine colourless stone of over 48 carats.

No gemstone can have passed through more great adventures than the Black Prince's Ruby which occupies a prominent place in the British Imperial State Crown. It is in fact a rich red spinel, polished but irregular in shape and some two inches long. It probably originated in the East but makes its first authentic appearance in 1367, when the King of Castile slew the King of Grenada to obtain it. Within a year, however, he gave it to the Black Prince (Edward, the valiant son of Edward III) as a reward for vital help in a battle. The stone was then seized from Richard II by Henry IV; Henry V wore it in his coronet at the battle of Agincourt where it is said to have deflected a heavy blow aimed at the king. It may also have been worn in Richard III's crown at Bosworth field and so have featured in the coronation of Henry VII immediately after this battle. The Ruby is next recorded when it was sold together with the Crown Jewels during the Commonwealth, fetching a mere £4! It may have been acquired by a royalist for it reappeared in Charles II's crown. When an adventurer, Colonel Blood, attempted to steal the crown the stone fell from its setting, but the plot was foiled and the stone recovered; King Charles is said to have roared with laughter and made Colonel Blood one of his bodyguard with a sizeable salary.

An even larger red spinel is among the British Crown Jewels, the Timur Ruby of 361 carats which was presented to Queen Victoria by the East India Company in 1851. It still bears inscriptions which prove that it once belonged to the great Tartar emperor Timur, perhaps better known as Tamerlane, who ruled over a large part of Asia. The names of several Mogul emperors are also engraved on it, showing that it passed through the same hands as the Koh-i-nur.

Perhaps the 'oldest' stone in the British regalia is St Edward's Sapphire, a fine blue rose-cut stone of unrecorded weight, said to have been worn in a ring by Edward the Confessor in 1042. It was credited with great healing powers. The Stuart Sapphire, also in the Imperial State Crown passed from James II to the Old Pretender but was returned to George III by the Pretender's son, Cardinal York.

The most famous – though not the largest – of emeralds is a hexagonal crystal of excellent colour but no great purity belonging to the Duke of Devonshire. It comes from Colombia and weighs nearly ten ounces. It was presented to the Duke by Dom Pedro, the last Emperor of Brazil, after his abdication in 1831.

There are several legendary references to large emeralds, notably to stones carved as bowls or phials reputed to have held the blood of Christ, the Holy Grail. One version relates that the Holy Grail was brought to Glastonbury in England by Joseph of Arimathea but no such relic is now held there. Another story connects the Holy Grail with a green bowl at Sacro Catino in Genoa, Italy, but this is made of glass. The bowl is said to have been pawned when the Genoese needed some money in the Middle Ages. When they came to redeem the pledge some years later, the original broker had disappeared but several other men claimed the money, each presenting a similar bowl that had been repawned with them. There is also a report of a fabulous 'emerald goddess', as large as an ostrich egg, once worshipped by Indians in Peru. Their priests persuaded them that a gift of emeralds, the goddess's 'children', would secure special favour. The Spaniards found quite a hoard of emeralds but rather than let this fall into the enemy's hands, the Indians prompted them to apply a 'hardness test' with a hammer. Many fine stones must have been destroyed. The goddess was spirited away and has never been found.

Some of these stories show how tenuous is the distinction between history and the lore founded on tradition and legend. When something extraordinary happens, the circumstances are remembered imperfectly; over the years the story is gradually embellished and elaborated with imagined detail, gaining credibility in the retelling and also a halo of authenticity because of its survival from ancient times. In this way a wondrous superstructure built on a fairly humdrum event may become accepted as indubitable truth by those not given to scepticism and to an unprejudiced appraisal of facts on their merits. For instance, an important person may suffer a heavy fall from a height or perhaps from a horse, happily without sustaining much injury, to find that a turquoise he was wearing has cracked. To account fo his good fortune he or his circle may connect the two events as cause and effect and so give rise to the tradition, firmly believed during the Middle Ages, that wearing a turquoise was a sure protection against injury from a fall. The few doubters would hardly have gone to the length of putting the matter to an experimental test.

Mankind has an inquiring mind and must know the reason why things happen, yet unexplained phenomena still surround us on all sides, even after centuries of research and discovery. How much more ready must our ancestors in the ages of faith have been to snatch at any likely explanation than are we, who set up one theory only to supersede it by another. It is so easy to accept reasoning from analogy: green is a restful colour, therefore emerald must be good for the eyes; some serpentines have a mottled marking resembling the skin of a snake, therefore serpentine must be a protection from snake bit, for snake does not bite snake; red stones must obviously be good for haemorrhage, yellow stones for jaundice; diamond and white beryl sparkle, therefore they must make one alert and quick-witted. Many similar analogies gained credence and were handed down orally and in writing over the centuries. Moreover, each retailer of such tales added something from his own experience or imagination; the final result was most elaborate treatises, attested by saints and philosophers as well as cranks and charlatans. Based in part on Plato, Herodotus, Theophrastus, Pliny and Arab sources, important books on the medicinal and general virtues of gemstones were written from the eleventh to the thirteenth centuries by such men as Marbodus, Bishop of Rennes; St Hildegarde of Bingen; Albertus Magnus, the great philosopher; and at the turn of the sixteenth century by Anselmus Booth, physician to Rudolph II, the Holy Roman Emperor.

For example, St Hildegarde, who lived in the twelfth century, gives the following instructions concerning the use of jacinth: 'If anyone be bewitched by phantoms or magic spells, so that he has lost his wits, take a hot loaf of pure wheaten bread and cut the upper crust in the form of a cross – not, however, cutting it quite through – and then pass the stone along the cutting, reciting these words: "May God, who cast away all precious stones from the devil, cast away from thee, N., all phantoms and all magic spells, and free thee from the pain of this madness". The patient is then to eat the bread'.

By the time of Anselmus Booth (or de Boot) faith and reserve were strangely blended. In his *Gemmarum et Lapidum Historia* he writes: 'That gems or stones, when applied to the body, exert an action upon it, is so well proven by the experience of many persons, that anyone who doubts this must be called over-bold. We have proof of this power in the cornelian, the haematite and the jasper, all of which, when applied, check haemorrhage. However, it is very necessary to observe that many virtues not possessed by gems are falsely ascribed to them'.

Some scepticism survived at all times, but much of the lore surrounding gemstones is believed implicitly in many parts of the world to the present day and not only by 'backward' people. Both Napoleon I and Napoleon III wore a cornelian amulet. It was lost when Napoleon III's son was killed wearing it in the Zulu wars. Many such stones are worn by people today – and why not if it gives them pleasure and confidence.

From the writings mentioned we know that in antiquity and throughout the Middle Ages certain gemstones were credited with specific powers. This is still the case in India where each occasion and time calls for the wearing of a particular gemstone. In Europe gemstones could exert their curative influence most effectively in contact with the wearer's body, say as pendants or through the open setting of a ring. As an amulet, a gem protected the wearer while a talisman usually had a more positive action, conferring certain powers on its owner. Substances other than gemstones were of course also used for these purposes.

Later writers 'discovered' ever wider powers in gems so that each stone came to be used for quite a variety of purposes and the same protection could be obtained from a variety of gems. Thus evil spirits and the terrors of the night could be combated with diamond, peridot, green jasper, malachite, chalcedony, cat's-eye or a chiastolite, while the evil eye, so much feared in southern Europe, could be deflected by diamond, coral, cornelian or eye-shaped agate. These attracted the evil eye if worn prominently and acted like a lightning conductor.

Moonstone and diamond promoted love but onyx repelled it and caused discord. A medieval Arabic work, wrongly ascribed to Aristotle, states: 'Those who are in the land of China fear this stone (onyx) so much that they dread to go into the mines where it occurs. None but slaves and menials, who have no other means of gaining a livelihood, take the stone from the mines. When it has been mined, it is carried out of the country and sold in other lands'. This shows that some stones had negative qualities; amber, for instance, stood for tears.

Agate made one bold, agreeable, persuasive; it cured insomnia and gave pleasant dreams, as did jacinth (zircon or grossular garnet). It had the power to avert tempest and lightning, a quality also peculiar to bloodstone, which had the additional virtue of assuaging anger, protecting the wearer from deception and freeing him from imprisonment.

Carbuncles could be such powerful stimulants that they had to be worn with care lest they cause apoplexy! Cornelians and emeralds made one eloquent; for best effects these stones should of course be kept under the tongue. Chrysoprase was good for thieves: it made them invisible and preserved them from being hanged or beheaded. Among its many other virtues, coral cured madness and gave wisdom, but it lost its powers when broken. It was essential not to cut it, especially with metal.

Diamond made one strong, fearless and invincible, even against the devil! But it lost its virtue if the wearer were guilty of a major crime or sin. For full efficacy it had to be acquired as a gift and not bought by the wearer—a commendable course in any case.

Emerald thwarted witches and magicians; it enabled one to prophesy, an attribute shared by moonstone, and it strengthened the memory. It blinded poisonous snakes, was a guardian of the pure and was easily fractured by sexual passion.

Haematite brought success in lawsuits and made warriors invulnerable if rubbed over the body. Its iron content and red streak ('blood and iron') made it a favourite with Hitler's followers.

Jade was of course the magic stone par excellence in China, particularly when carved to form lucky symbols—a butterfly or the 'hand of Buddha' fruit. In China, Egypt, Central America and New Zealand it was buried with the dead to ensure a happy after-life. The virtues of jasper were many, but they tended to vary with its colour: green jasper, like serpentine and malachite, protected from poisonous snakes; yellow jasper cured jaundice; red jasper stanched the flow of blood.

Lapis lazuli cured melancholy and undulating fever—an odd combination—but its powers may have been confused with those of sapphire, whose name it bore for a long time. Children would come to no harm if a piece of malachite were hung round their neck.

An Australian opal miner at work.

*Top* 'Tiki' made of New Zealand greenstone (nephrite jade).

*Right* The second mummiform coffin of Tutankhamen, inlaid with gemstones, Egyptian Museum, Cairo.

*Above* Phoenician ivory plaque.

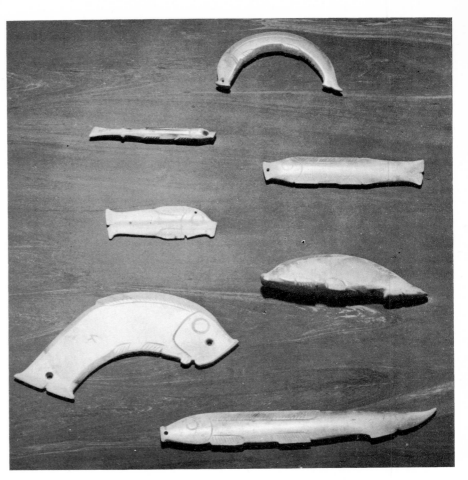

Chinese jade amulets.

Opal was once thought to combine the virtues of all other gemstones since it had all their colours. It was most highly esteemed by Queen Elizabeth I and considered exceptionally lucky, especially if dark. The current belief to the contrary is quite recent; some trace it back to Sir Walter Scott's novel *Anne of Geierstein* in which the great novelist featured a stone of somewhat equivocal powers: while making the heroine irresistible it killed her when it was sprinkled with holy water.

Ruby was another cure-all. It was an elixir of youth, particularly effective if rubbed over the face; nowadays we employ other forms of face massage. Ruby kept one in good health, reconciled disputes and guarded one's house and fruit trees. It was most effective if worn on the left side. It also conferred invulnerability, but only if inserted in the flesh. Its kindred mineral, sapphire, was the prerogative of kings and high ecclesiastical dignitaries, perhaps because it helped one to understand signs, omens and oracles for which reason it was also much favoured by witches. It was swallowed as an antidote to poison. In the East, star stones and cat's-eyes are considered exceptionally lucky, especially in games of chance.

Turquoise was worn particularly by men, perhaps because they were more likely to fall off horses. In the East it is used on horses' harnesses as a protection for the beasts. It was greatly venerated by the Mexican Indians and large numbers of stones have been found in their burials. They thought, also, that it aided the hunter or warrior if attached to a bow or a gun.

The potency of gemstones as amulets or talismans could be greatly enhanced by engraving. Even in ancient Egypt or Babylon, engraved seals had some talismanic as well as merely practical uses. In the Middle Ages cameos and intaglios were held in exceptional esteem, from stones crudely carved with signs of the zodiac to those showing the gods of ancient religions, reinterpreted in Christian terms. Thus Mercury became the Archangel Michael; Jupiter/Serapis, the patriarch Joseph; Zeus and Athena under an olive tree with a serpent at their feet were unmistakeably Adam and Eve. For some reason, cameos of Alexander the Great were thought to bring special luck. Old Mycenaean seals were similarly venerated by Cretan peasants, a lucky circumstance that has ensured the survival of many historic artefacts.

The use of gemstones in heraldry seems to have been peculiar to England, where the names of coloured gemstones were admitted side by side with the heraldic designations. Thus the heraldic term for red, 'gules', could also be rendered as ruby; vert (green) as emerald; or (gold) as topaz; argent (silver) as pearl; azure (blue) as sapphire; purpure (purple) as amethyst; tenne (orange) as jacinth and so on. The high nobility used these gem terms particularly often. They were naturally also used in blazoning (describing) the coat of arms of the Gemmological Association of Great Britain.

These armorial bearings also contain a very ancient heraldic device, the escarbuncle. Originally this is thought to have represented a bright gemstone from which emanated eight rays like the spokes of a wheel. The escarbuncle of the Gemmological Association has a gemstone set at the end of each ray, namely a pearl, ruby, jacinth, topaz, emerald, turquoise, sapphire and amethyst. These represent white light and its constituent spectral colours in the correct order. The escarbuncle was probably derived from a traditional Indian jewel of even greater antiquity, namely the Naoratna or nine jewels, a powerful talisman of the Hindus and Burmese. This has a ruby at its centre which is surrounded, like the escarbuncle, by eight gems; these are a diamond, jacinth, cat's-eye, emerald, topaz, sapphire, coral and pearl. Such a talisman would combine the virtues of all these stones, which would moreover reinforce each other, bringing good fortune to the wearer under all conceivable circumstances.

A charming way of imparting a special meaning to set gemstones can sometimes be seen in rings, particularly of the eighteenth and

*Below left* Naoratna.

*Below* Escarbuncle, used in the armorial bearing of the Gemmological Association of Great Britain.

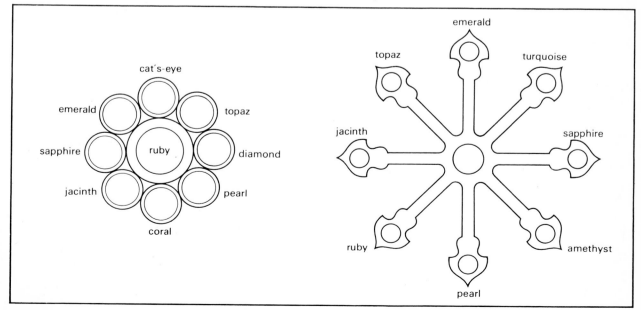

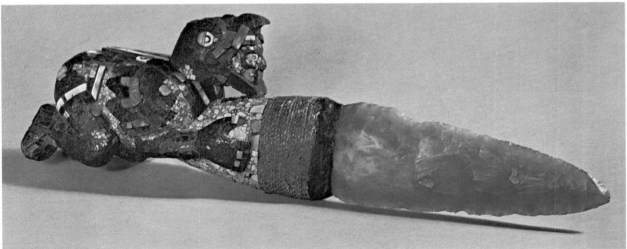

*Top* Imperial Easter egg, Fabergé.

*Above* Aztec sacrificial knife with chalcedony blade and turquoise, malachite and shell mosaic handle.

*Far right* Twelfth-century cross, copper gilt, decorated with enamel and precious stones, Musées Royaux d'Art et d'Histoire, Brussels.

*Right* Cameo of Roman Emperor Augustus by Dioscorides, British Museum, London.

167

nineteenth centuries. These rings hold a row of stones of which the initial letters spell out a message. Diamond, Emerald, Amethyst, Ruby, Emerald, Sapphire, Topaz spell out 'Dearest'; another favourite design spells out 'Regard' in the same manner and there are other variants.

The medicinal uses of gems have already been referred to as they cannot be separated from the talismanic. In both, merits of ever more varied kinds were imputed to gemstones so that in the end virtually any stone could cure any disease. The curative gems could merely be worn but became more potent if finely powdered and swallowed. Often they were steeped in water or mixed with a liquid which was then drunk. The liquid sometimes contained herbal ingredients, such as laudanum, which may have been effective. As a general rule, the rarer and costlier the gems, the more potent were they as a cure, but physicians could prescribe larger quantities of a cheap stone if the patient could not afford an expensive one. There are several stories of fraud and substitution by greedy apothecaries. Curiously, powdered diamond was thought to be a powerful poison though it was otherwise the supreme protection against poisoning. Benvenuto Cellini relates how his life was saved because a man bribed to poison him had substituted cheap rock crystal for costly diamond powder. Nowadays one of the favourite methods of stealing diamonds is to swallow them. Pliny, who passes on the medicinal traditions of his day (first century AD) was plainly sceptical about the efficacy of gems, but open derision was not voiced in Europe till the eighteenth century; the use of gems as medicines is recorded in Scotland as recently as one hundred years ago and it persists to the present day in India, China and elsewhere.

A widespread modern survival of the talismanic tradition is the use of gems as birthstones. This has a long and fascinating history. In many civilizations all round the world certain stones, not necessarily the same ones, became associated with the recurrent lunar cycles and hence with the zodiac. These lunar stones were then considered to be auspicious for wear during that month or, later, for wear by persons born under the planetary influences prevailing in the month of their birth. The stones were credited with transmitting sympathetic vibrations emanating from astral influences, with drawing strength and beneficent radiations from the sun, moon and the planets and with the ability to retain these by virtue of their hardness.

As long ago as 4000 BC the high priest at the temple at Memphis in Egypt wore twelve gemstones on his chest, which were probably connected with the zodiac. This may have been taken over by the Jews during the Egyptian captivity and have given rise to the venerated 'breastplate', a linen bag set with twelve stones worn by the High Priest as specified in the Book of Exodus, chapter twenty-eight. There is now considerable doubt about the original identity of these stones since there are substantial variations in the several Bible versions handed down to us and the translation of the names used presents difficulties. As has been pointed out before, gemstones have changed their names since ancient times. The 'sapphire' mentioned in the Bible was probably what we now call lapis lazuli, the 'sard' was cornelian, the 'topaz' peridot, and 'ligure' may have been amber. Yet a different array of twelve gems appears in the Book of Revelations as the foundation of the Heavenly New Jerusalem and these become associated with the twelve apostles.

The practice of wearing monthly birthstones was common at different periods among Romans, Arabs, Jews, Indians, Spaniards, Russians, Italians and other peoples, but only from the eighteenth century onward did the practice of wearing stones appropriate to the month of one's birth spread gradually from central Europe to the West. There was, however, no consistency and very different lists of monthly birthstones were advocated by different authorities. The confusion increased as time went on, conflicting advice abounded and in the end conferences were arranged between jewellers' associations and other bodies to settle on a standard list. Happily such a list was finally accepted and it has been in common international use for some decades, though a few objections are still voiced occasionally, for example, against the selection of turquoise for December, where it is felt that the warmer colour of ruby would be more appropriate, especially as it has more historic sanction. The list recommended sometimes has an expensive and a cheaper stone as alternatives and various possible substitutes and deviations are still found in some countries. The list recommended by international agreement and followed by most jewellers is:

January  Garnet
February  Amethyst
March  Aquamarine or Bloodstone
April  Diamond or Rock Crystal
May  Emerald or Chrysoprase
June  Pearl or Moonstone
July  Ruby or Cornelian
August  Peridot or Sardonyx
September  Sapphire or Lapis Lazuli
October  Opal
November  Topaz or Citrine
December  Turquoise

Gemstones are also connected with wedding anniversaries; diamond (sixty years) and ruby (forty years) are well known but there are also stones for the following anniversaries:

Twelfth  Agate
Thirteenth  Moonstone
Fourteenth  Moss Agate
Fifteenth  Rock Crystal
Sixteenth  Topaz
Seventeenth  Amethyst
Eighteenth  Garnet
Nineteenth  Jacinth
Twenty-third  Sapphire
Thirtieth  Pearl
Thirty-fifth  Coral
Thirty-ninth  Cat's-eye
Fifty-fifth  Emerald

There are also 'propitious' stones for days of the week and hours of the day, but no agreed list exists concerning these.

To follow the lore and superstitions concerning gemstones through the history of many nations is a fascinating study. A monumental task has been accomplished by the well-known mineralogist G. F. Kunz in collecting material from a vast range of sources in his book, *The Curious Lore of Precious Stones* – a book full of references for the interested student.

*Above left* Sixteenth-century French pendant formed round a pearl, enamelled and decorated with gemstones and pearls.

*Above right* A diamond crystal, a gold nugget and modern gold and diamond jewellery.

*Right* Victorian jewel box containing jewellery of gold, pearls, garnets, turquoise, jet and agate.

*Far right* Gothic crown of Princess Blanche (daughter of King Henry IV of England) made for her marriage to the Elector of Bavaria.

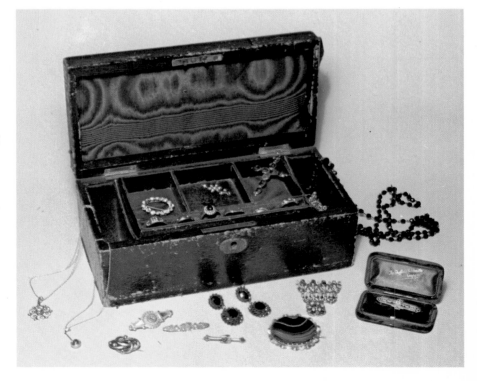

170

# Collecting and Looking After Gems

Those who love and are interested in gems will almost invariably wish to possess them, deriving satisfaction from being able to examine them closely whenever inclined so to do. Collecting is a highly individual pursuit, determined by personal likes and circumstances. Gem collecting need by no means be the prerogative of the rich. Interesting and beautiful specimens of the less precious stones are well within the financial reach of most people. Collecting may involve no more than the random acquisition of such gems as chance produces, but if it develops into a deliberate search, it is highly advisable to decide at the outset what kind of collection it is to be. Without a clear direction and standard procedures one is apt to be sidetracked into the impossible quest of a specimen of everything there is in the gemstone world. There are too many varieties and local variants; some form of selection or specialization will inevitably be forced on one.

As with most other forms of collecting, one guiding principle that should be firmly adhered to is to reject inferior specimens. Damaged, badly cut, flawed or merely small or common stones do not maintain their value, may be useless for display or demonstration and bring little gratification to the owner. Even rare and precious stones suffer appreciably in value if they are of poor quality, nor will they represent their species adequately. One may of course be prepared to make do with a poor specimen for the time being, in the hope that a good one may be found eventually but meanwhile one will have squandered one's resources on something of little intrinsic worth.

Defects may not always be obvious and it is a wise precaution to examine each stone carefully. Using a loupe of at least eight to ten times magnifying power on cut transparent gems, search for cracks, fractures, cleavages, scratched facets and edges, irregular cutting and deleterious inclusions. Sometimes such faults can be remedied by re-cutting or merely re-polishing a stone, but it will normally not suffice to repair the damaged area; to retain symmetry the entire crown or pavilion, or even the entire stone, will have to be remodelled.

An exception to the rule to admit only the best may be made where the collection is to serve for reference only, say for a student's use, and not for display or investment. Even poorly cut or damaged stones have the right densities and hardness, while for purposes of study a super-abundance of inclusions may be a bonus. The monetary value of such a collection may be small but it will serve its particular purpose.

On the other hand, where a collection is intended for investment or for special display, only the very best and largest stones that can be afforded should be admitted. In recent years fine gemstones have rather more than maintained their value in the face of inflation and the best specimens have appreciated outstandingly. Mediocre stones can be expected to appreciate slightly or merely to maintain their money value (which may or may not correspond to the price paid for them, for reasons to be explained presently). It does not, therefore, follow that every piece of jewellery will rise in value in the same ratio as fine stones. For investment, it is far better to acquire one really good stone than several smaller, less fine ones. The very largest and costliest stones present a problem in their disposal, in that there are very few buyers able to afford them, but this problem may not unduly worry most readers of this book.

As with most collectable articles, the gem market is divided into two sections – a trade section and a collector's section. They overlap to some extent, unlike the stamp trade, for example, where the post office does not deal in valuable stamps. Most gems are bought and sold for wear in jewellery but the same gems could also be acquired by collectors. On the other hand, some gemstone rarities lack any particular appeal to the eye and some are too soft for ordinary wear. They are bought only by collectors since it would be next to impossible to dispose of them over the retail jeweller's counter. Their trade value would be low, yet collectors will pay a high price for them. For example, taaffeite, though hard and fully transparent, is not particularly attractive in colour; yet since only five stones are known to exist, their value per carat runs into thousands of pounds. The gem collectors' market, though growing, is of course very much smaller than the trade market, so that it is not always a speedy and straightforward matter to dispose of collectors' stones.

This is a relevant consideration when a specialized collection is planned. A comprehensive collection of, for instance, all colour or locality varieties of a particular gem species and its imitations or of all the gemstones to be found in a particular locality will have great appeal to a museum or to a collector who will value them well beyond the trade price based on the wholesale value of each stone taken by itself. The same thing would apply to collections of, say, stones containing interesting inclusions throwing light on their origin, or of fluorescent stones or those showing good spectra.

Having decided the general purpose of a collection, the next step is to plan its contents. If investment is the main object, chance and opportunity will be the main determinant and the collector will have to rely on the advice of dealers whom he can trust. Unless he has considerable expertise and a good judgement, he will avoid much loss and disappointment if he confines his dealings to well-recommended, reliable and established firms or traders to whom he can confidently return with any difficulties or queries. To find such traders is in fact the main problem facing an investment collector, or for that matter any collector concerned with maintaining the value of his collection. Once a contact based on mutual trust has been established such traders can be of the greatest help. They will often go to considerable trouble to obtain the best advice and to find items suitable for the collection. They may be in touch with other collectors and with overseas suppliers; they may be willing to bid reasonably at auctions and revalue the collection from time to time, for example, for insurance. With the increasing number of artificial and 'improved' products now available it is not safe to buy from unknown sources, least of all abroad. There are tales of soldiers investing their service gratuities in gemstones in the East, only to find on their return home that the stones were synthetic; or of rough gems offered for sale with the soil still clinging to them that also proved to be synthetic; or of last-minute switches of better-looking synthetic stones for natural ones. Buying from known sources is a safeguard, as are the testing facilities offered by various trade institutions and museums. Legislation protecting buyers of gems against fraud exists in several countries and the penalties can be heavy but it is best to avoid difficulties before they arise.

The advice of dealers may be somewhat less helpful where a specialized

*Right* Imperial State Crown, displaying the Timur ruby and the second largest stone cut from the Cullinan diamond.

*Below* Birthstones: from left to right they are: garnet (January), amethyst (February), aquamarine and bloodstone (March), diamond and rock crystal (April), emerald and chrysoprase (May), pearl and moonstone (June), ruby and cornelian (top of picture, July), peridot and sardonyx (August), sapphire and lapis lazuli (September), opal and tourmaline (October), topaz (drop shape, November), zircon and turquoise (December).

*Far right* Coloured pebbles— agate, jasper etc.—polished ready for mounting, with others already mounted as pendants.

*Below right* Colourful tumbled pebbles.

174

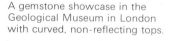
Interior and layout of the gemstone collection in the Geological Museum, London.

collection is being formed because the collector will aim at knowing more about his chosen field than most general dealers can be expected to know. The specialist will derive his information from studying the literature, including past and current issues of periodical magazines. He will seek the advice of museums and become familar with their exhibits. He will talk and write to scientific bodies and to experts in his and in related fields. In the process he will learn a great deal, meet many interesting people and have a lot of fun. The periodicals mentioned in the bibliography contain references to relevant societies and clubs.

Many collectors like to possess both cut and uncut specimens of each of the gem varieties they collect. Rough specimens are sold by traders in minerals and geological samples. There are also shops near many geological sites or in neighbouring towns. The guidelines which apply to acquiring rough specimens are similar to those for cut stones: the choice should fall on well-formed, well-coloured, undamaged specimens that are typical of their species. Close examination is again advisable to guard against chipped crystal edges or the cementing of broken crystal groups. If possible the specimen should still be attached

A gemstone showcase in the Geological Museum in London with curved, non-reflecting tops.

to a small part of the rock in which it was found, thereby permanently disclosing its origin.

Cut stones can be stored in little space but uncut crystals can present a storage and transport problem. If they are to be on display, they need to be well separated from each other. If they are kept in drawers, they must be protected from damage by bumping against each other for many of them are quite brittle. Rough specimens need not be larger than a very few inches; even so, a comprehensive collection can consume much space. A solution that has found much favour consists of the so-called 'micromounts'. They consist of tiny specimens, mounted in boxes one inch square. They can only be fully appreciated under a loupe or better, a low-power binocular microscope. Well-formed, undamaged crystals are much more common in these small sizes. They also have the advantage of being cheap and easy to store and transport.

In Europe few collectors are in a position to go and find gemstones of much value directly from their deposits. Few rich sites are left and these are under close control. Most of them are nearly exhausted and permission to collect is not usually given. There is nevertheless much

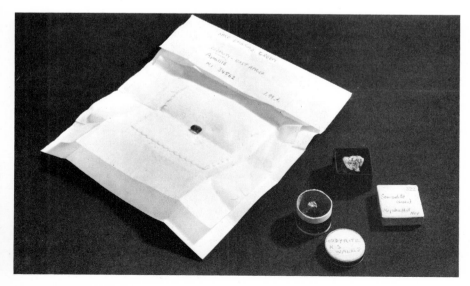

Gemstone in its paper and two micromounts.

scope for those who take pleasure in the less costly gems of the silica and feldspar families. These are distributed widely and handsome specimens are still to be found.

Conditions are rather different in the USA and other parts of the New World, in Australia and some of the more accessible parts of Asia and Africa. In these continents there are still some well-known localities where one may find good specimens of the rarer and more valuable gemstones with varying degrees of effort. Some sites are freely accessible, in others search is discouraged.

Finding gemstones for oneself is undoubtedly the most gratifying way of acquiring them. Interest in collecting and cutting gem materials has grown extraordinarily in several countries and in the western world places where gems and ornamental stones can be won have become the happy hunting ground of an ever-increasing number of lapidary clubs and 'rockhounds'. Their interest usually extends also to the collection of handsome non-gem minerals, the grinding and polishing of ornamental material and the making of simple jewellery. It is a fascinating and rewarding hobby that has many aspects.

The advantages of joining a lapidary club are considerable, especially for the beginner. Excursions to collecting sites will be organized under the guidance of more experienced members who can advise about productive spots and about worth-while material; access to sites not open to the public will be granted more readily if owners of such sites are assured that the club is under responsible leadership; guidance will be provided about the conditions likely to be met and hence about the clothing and equipment most suitable. In addition there will be lectures, demonstrations and discussions with members sharing their experiences and, if lapidary work is undertaken, it will be easier for the combined resources of the club to procure a more varied range of the somewhat costly machinery and other equipment required. The guidance of experienced members will be invaluable to the beginner.

In Britain and Ireland all land is owned by somebody and collecting is only possible with the owner's permission. This is, strictly speaking, true even of seaside beaches which usually belong to a local authority, but no objection will be raised to the removal of a few pebbles; only gathering on a large scale will require express permission. Beaches are in fact a very productive hunting ground and there are few that do not

Members of a club looking for minerals in Reedy Creek, Victoria, Australia.

produce at least some colourful jaspers, cornelians or flints. Several areas on the east coast and in Wales are noted for exceptionally varied and attractive pebbles. Jet may be found on the Yorkshire coast together with occasional Baltic amber which also occurs further south. Translucent chalcedonies are not uncommon on many beaches and it is easier to assess the potentialities of clean, wet beach pebbles than weathered pebbles found elsewhere. Collecting from beaches involves the least amount of preparation and equipment.

The simplest way of polishing beach pebbles is to 'tumble' them, but care must be taken to see that those selected are all of a sufficient and similar hardness. This process requires little skill but may take up to several weeks. The stones are kept in revolving drums in a slurry of carborundum and various cushioning materials. First the rough outer skin is ground away with coarse carborundum, then increasingly finer grades are used until a good polish is achieved.

Attractive gravels also occur on inland sites, usually on existing or extinct river courses but in such situations some digging is often necessary. The favourite haunts of collectors are, however, old mines and mine dumps, rock faces, quarries, pegmatite and other outcrops. Local knowledge is here the surest guide, though a good geological map and a little expertise may provide indications. Hours of fruitless search may be avoided by speaking to museum personnel in the locality, miners, school teachers, mineral shopkeepers and other cognoscenti. To find them is time well spent, if they can be induced to talk!

*Far left* Drum for producing 'tumbled' gemstones.

*Left* Marking out a slab of ornamental stone prior to cutting.

*Bottom* Sawing a mineral specimen.

179

Quarries and particularly disused mines are dangerous and should on no account be tackled by the inexpert or alone. Quite good pickings may be had with far less danger off the quarry floor or off spoil dumps outside the mines. The latter may, however, have been worked over several times and the material tends to be weathered. In all cases it is essential to obtain permission to enter from the owner (if there is such a person – some old mines have no traceable owner). Entry to other private land also needs permission and leave to remove specimens should always be sought. In Britain and some Continental countries the collection of gold, silver and markedly radioactive specimens requires special permission, but elsewhere there is no such general restriction. Greed can be a collector's most deadly sin; he must learn to be satisfied with filling his minimum requirements, for most British sites are now nearly exhausted and something should be left for posterity. No attempt must be made to remove a specimen if it or the site are likely to be damaged in the process. It is important to leave the site as neat and undisturbed as possible.

The equipment required depends on the site to be explored. Weatherproof clothing and comfortable waterproof boots are advisable, as are tough gloves and, in mines, a helmet and lamp. A geologist's hammer will suffice for small specimens but a pickaxe, sledge hammer, chisels and spades may be needed for excavating larger items or splitting geodes. Such work may also make the wearing of an eyeshield or goggles imperative. A loupe will often prove useful. A good supply of newspapers for wrapping and cradling specimens and a strong canvas sack for carrying them are essential. It is a good practice to number specimens (on the newspaper wrapping) on the spot and to enter such items as map references and descriptions of the site in a notebook. Do not trust to memory; some collectors make a habit of photographing sites. For further transport specimens can be arranged in shallow wooden boxes (for example, the trays used for packing fruit) carried in the boot of a car. At home the specimens can then be trimmed, cleaned, labelled, catalogued and displayed or cut as required.

Some of the main gemstones localities have been indicated in chapter four; more detail will be found in the books and journals listed in the bibliography. Apart from the classical sites there are deposits, too numerous to list, in which gemstones of all kinds and qualities may be found, albeit in small numbers; but this will not deter the resolute rockhound.

There are, of course, several other ways of collecting gems. Fine stones may be found in rings or other jewels offered for sale in shops and these may appeal to the collector aiming at investment. The collecting of jewellery is somewhat beyond the scope of this book since such considerations as the quality and period of the setting may be equally or even more relevant and these are subjects for separate treatment, but one important fact relating to the value of jewellery bought in a shop needs to be pointed out. It is that a retail jeweller has in most cases to work on a fairly high 'mark-up', that is, a sizeable difference between the price at which he buys and that at which he sells. This derives from the slow turnover of his stock. It is not unusual for his stock to turn over only once in a year or longer, a process which takes only a few days with a grocer or butcher. Each item therefore has to bear its share of the rent, insurance, salaries, taxes and other overhead charges incurred over a long period, as well as to provide a profit. For this reason the mark-up has to be rather higher than in many trades; half, or more, of the buying price is not unusual. This means that the private collector of jewellery cannot normally expect to resell his purchase to another jeweller quickly at the same price. It may take some years for the value of the article to rise sufficiently. Here again the collector of quality items scores, for the mark-up on jewels of high value can be a rather lower proportion of the buying price and still yield an adequate return. The length of time a particular jewel has been in stock and the trend in the prices of similar goods also has a bearing on the mark-up.

Loose, unset gemstones are often treated rather differently. Few jewellers trade in them; they may have the odd stone in stock and be prepared to sell it at a reasonable price since they are rarely asked for such items. Most specialist dealers in loose gemstones do not deal with the public directly. They can be contacted through jewellers who may then make only a nominal charge for their services since they incur little cost in the transaction.

Auctions are another source of collecting cut gemstones of quality. Unset stones are sometimes offered at these and some bargains may be secured, but competition from all parts of the world has increased recently and the prices of the choicer items have reached very high levels.

Having secured his specimens the collector must take some care about recording and storing them. It will not do merely to put them on a shelf or in a drawer; one soon forgets when, how and at what cost they were acquired and these are essential data for a subsequent valuation, sale or exchange. Many methods of cataloguing are in use. A very simple one is to give each new acquisition a consecutive number so that the latest number also indicates the total size of the collection. Alternatively the specimens may be grouped under each mineral species and con-secutive numbers may be allotted in such a manner that one can readily tell how many items of each species there are in the collection. The species can then be listed according to a recognized mineralogical classification such as that evolved by the great mineralogist E. S. Dana of Yale University; or simply in alphabetical order as in the table at the end of this book.

The most permanent method of numbering rough specimens is with Indian ink; on dark minerals a dab of white paint can be applied first. This is not easily removable and it may be considered preferable to use a small paper label attached with a good adhesive. The label can be colour-coded to indicate the locality or any other relevant fact. Obviously, the least interesting surface of the specimen will be chosen for labelling. If there is no convenient spot, the label can be attached to any material supporting the specimen or to a box containing it; in such cases self-adhesive labels will suffice, but they will not stick satisfactorily to the actual specimens. Acceptable supports can be made quickly from expanded polystyrene and they can be readily replaced if they get dusty. Dust will collect on specimens left in the open, hence covered display cabinets are much to be preferred. Alternatively the minerals can be covered with plastic sheets or bags when not actually on show.

Specimens kept in drawers must be preserved from fracture and abrasion through jolting. Deepish layers of cotton wool, polystyrene, plastic foam or tissue paper will prevent this. It is also a good idea to keep each specimen in an open box of cardboard ot transparent plastic. Its name, number and locality can then be recorded on a card also kept in the box. It is convenient to keep related specimens close together; the collection should therefore be arranged accordingly to a well-recognized system such as Dana's.

Cut and polished loose gemstones are best kept in the traditional stone papers which ensure that several thicknesses of paper surround the stone on all sides. The illustration on this page shows how to fold such a paper. Frequently a thin lining paper and a thicker outer paper are used together and a flat layer of cotton wool is kept in the centre. This is essential when more than one stone is kept in the same paper. The outer flap of the paper is used to record the reference number, name and weight of the stone to two decimal places. The stones can then be filed in their papers in very little space. Large stones can be kept in boxes – the trade name is 'cases' – made for the purpose and lined with velvet. For display, mounts can be made for cut stones from layers or sheets of plastic with holes small enough to support the stone just below the girdle.

It is most advisable to keep a detailed catalogue or register of a collection right from the outset. Such a document acquires increasing usefulness with time. The items to be recorded may vary according to the collector's interests but they should normally include the following particulars for cut stones:

Reference number, variety name, colour, weight

Shape (round, oval, square, oblong, drop, boat, kite, etc.)

Style of cutting (brilliant, rose, step, mixed, cabochon, cameo, etc.)

Locality of origin

From whom acquired and date of acquisition

Price paid (or estimated value if exchanged or given)

Any notable characteristics such as fluorescence, inclusions, spectrum or particulars of its history

Stages in folding a stone paper. The outside flap is used to record the contents.

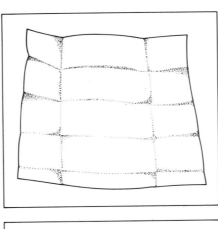
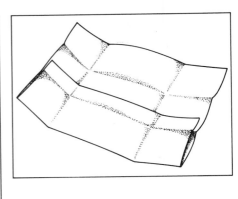
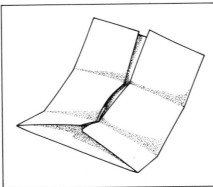
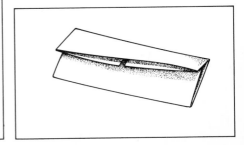

For rough mineral specimens the reference number, the names of the minerals present on the specimen, where, how and when collected, the value, and the approximate size (as $4'' \times 3'' \times 2''$) should suffice.

If it is desired to keep the values up to date entries can be made in pencil and altered periodically. This will also provide guidance for the value at which the collection is to be insured. Insurance should be on the basis of replacement value and this is likely to be an increasing figure. For specially valuable items a security problem arises; the best course to keep them in a bank's safe deposit.

As regards equipment, the most essential item is a good loupe magnifying about ten times and corrected for colour and distortion (an achromatic, aplanatic lens). When dealing with cut stones, a pair of softly sprung tweezers with fairly broad points, scored on the inside, is equally important. Some practice in their use is required, for polished stones have remarkable agility in flying off in unexpected directions when handled too firmly. They can be picked up most easily with tweezers if they are first placed on their table facet.

Equipment for more advanced work includes a microscope with an appropriate intensity lamp. The microscope need not magnify strongly as most work will be done at enlargements of twenty to sixty times. Powerful objectives have a short working distance which precludes examination of a large stone throughout its depth. For preference the microscope should be of the geological type, with a rotatable stage, polarizing equipment and a calibrated fine adjustment (for measuring vertical distances and refractive indices by the apparent depth method). A simple polariscope will be found useful for identifying anisotropic stones. It can be made from a watchmaker's eyeglass fitted with polaroid; the other polaroid disc can then be held in the crossed position in one hand and the stone turned between them in the other hand. An assayer's or chemist's balance weighing accurately to one hundredth of a carat (0.005 grams) is useful for checking weights and calculating density. Refractometer, dichroscope, hand-spectroscope, colour filter, hardness plates or pencils, a micrometer and an ultraviolet lamp complete the equipment of the more advanced worker. The microscope lamp can be used in connection with several of these. A photographic record of all items in a collection has much to recommend it.

Where the gemstones are set in jewellery careful attention should be given to its maintenance. Well-made jewellery will stand a lot of handling but it is far from indestructible. Like gemstones it should be stored in such a way that individual pieces cannot rub against each other. They may be wrapped in chamois leather or tissue paper and brooches should be pinned to the lining of cases. Valuable pieces and all rings should be kept in their own cases. Clumsiness and impatience must be avoided when handling jewellery but even then accidental damage occurs frequently, for instance by knocking a stone against a hard surface or by catching a jewel in clothing. Damage may pass unnoticed at the time and it is therefore wise to have jewellery checked over at least annually if it is worn frequently. Natural and cultured pearls should be restrung even more frequently if they are worn constantly. The claws of settings may get bent, the catches, hinges and links of necklets, brooches, bracelets and chains wear out in time. For this reason, safety chains or safety catches should be fitted to any valued jewel, but not if this involves a structural alteration to an antique piece. In doubtful cases expert advice should be sought, for today's second-hand cast-off may become tomorrow's treasured antique and liberties taken with the former may be regrettable in the latter.

It is usually possible to resize gem-set rings unless the stones are numerous, but care must also be taken not to damage the design or any hallmark or inscription.

Repolishing after some wear will make an astonishing difference to the appearance of precious metal jewellery and also to some soft gemstones such as opal or moonstone. Metal jewellery should be cleaned professionally but stones in open settings may be cleaned at home with a small stiff brush and detergent. The deposit of lime and soap inside rings can be removed with a bristle paint brush or one made by stripping about three eighths of an inch from a piece of electric flex. The fine wires will reach into all crevices but no force should be applied, lest stones are poked out or claws bent. Any detergent should be washed off thoroughly and drying, say with blotting paper, must be thorough. Cleaning the pavilion facets will enhance the brilliance of diamonds and other transparent stones but detergent should not be used on turquoise nor should other porous stones be left in contact with it for long.

Our review of the course of gemstones from their origin in the earth's crust to their placement in a jewel or a collection is complete. Much more could be said on all the subjects raised and a considerable literature is at the disposal of the serious student. If this book has given to the reader the most essential facts about gemstones, some useful hints about their acquisition and care, and a wish to learn more, its purpose has been fulfilled.

# Data Table

The data set out in this table relate to representative specimens of gem quality. Some deviations occur.

c.c. = crypto-crystalline   — = does not apply.

| Name | Composition | Crystal System | Hardness | Refractive Indices | Birefringence | Specific Gravity |
|---|---|---|---|---|---|---|
| Alexandrite see Chrysoberyl | | | | | | |
| Amber | Fossil resin | Amo | $3\frac{1}{2}$ | 1.54 | — | 1.08 |
| Andalusite | $Al_2SiO_5$ | Orh | $7-7\frac{1}{2}$ | 1.633–1.644 | 0.011 | 3.1–3.2 |
| Apatite | $Ca_5F(PO_4)_3$ | Hex | 5 | 1.63–1.64 | 0.003 | 3.18 |
| Aquamarine see Beryl | | | | | | |
| Axinite | $HMgCa_2BAl_2(SiO_4)_4$ | Tcl | $6\frac{1}{2}-7$ | 1.68–1.69 | 0.010 | 3.29 |
| Benitoite | $BaTiSi_3O_9$ | Trg | $6-6\frac{1}{2}$ | 1.75–1.80 | 0.049 | 3.64 |
| Beryl | $Be_3Al_3(SiO_3)_6$ | Hex | $7\frac{1}{2}-8$ | 1.58–1.59 | 0.006 | 2.72 |
| Aquamarine | | | | | | |
| Emerald | | | | | | |
| Beryllonite | $NaBePO_4$ | Mcl | $5\frac{1}{2}-6$ | 1.55–1.56 | 0.010 | |
| Bowenite see Serpentine | | | | | | |
| Brazilianite | $NaAl_3(OH)_4(PO_4)_2$ | Mcl | $5\frac{1}{2}$ | 1.60–1.62 | 0.019 | 2.94 |
| Bronzite see Enstatite | | | | | | |
| Cat's-eye see Chrysoberyl | | | | | | |
| Chalcedony see Quartz | | | | | | |
| Castorite see Petalite | | | | | | |
| Chrysoberyl | $BeAl_2O_4$ | Orh | $8\frac{1}{2}$ | 1.74–1.76 | 0.009 | 3.73 |
| Alexandrite | | | | | | |
| Cat's-eye | | | | | | |
| Cordierite (also called | | | | | | |
| Iolite or Dichroite) | $(Mg,Fe)_2Al_4Si_5O_{18}$ | Orh | $7-7\frac{1}{2}$ | 1.54–1.55 | 0.009 | 2.63 |
| Corundum | $Al_2O_3$ | Trg | 9 | 1.76–1.77 | 0.008 | 4.00 |
| Ruby | | | | | | |
| Sapphire | | | | | | |
| Danburite | $CaB_2(SiO_4)_2$ | Orh | 7 | 1.63–1.64 | 0.006 | 3.00 |
| Datolite | $Ca(B,OH)SiO_4$ | Mcl | $5-5\frac{1}{2}$ | 1.62–1.67 | 0.045 | 2.95 |
| Diamond | C | Cub | 10 | 2.42 | — | 3.52 |
| Diopside | $CaMg(SiO_3)_2$ | Mcl | 5–6 | 1.67–1.70 | 0.030 | 3.29 |
| Ekanite | $K(Ca,Na)_2Th(Si_8O_{20})$ | Tet | $6-6\frac{1}{2}$ | 1.60 metamict | — | 3.28 |
| Emerald see Beryl | | | | | | |
| Enstatite | $(Mg,Fe)SiO_3$ | Orh | $5\frac{1}{2}$ | 1.66–1.67 | 0.010 | 3.27 |
| Bronzite | | | | 1.67–1.69 | 0.011 | 3.35 |
| Hypersthene | | | | 1.69–1.70 | 0.013 | 3.45 |
| Epidote | $Ca_2Al_2(Al,OH)(SiO_4)_3$ | Mcl | $6\frac{1}{2}$ | 1.73–1.77 | 0.039 | 3.45 |
| Euclase | $Be(Al,OH)SiO_4$ | Mcl | $7\frac{1}{2}$ | 1.65–1.67 | 0.019 | 3.10 |
| Feldspar | | | | | | |
| Albite | $NaAlSi_3O_8$ | Tcl | $6-6\frac{1}{2}$ | 1.53–1.54 | 0.010 | 2.61 |
| Amazonite | $KAlSi_3O_8$ | Tcl | $6-6\frac{1}{2}$ | 1.52–1.53 | 0.008 | 2.56 |
| Labradorite | $(Na,Ca)AlSi_3O_8$ | Tcl | $6-6\frac{1}{2}$ | 1.56–1.57 | 0.010 | 2.70 |
| Moonstone | $KAlSi_3O_8$ | Mcl | 6 | 1.52–1.53 | 0.005 | 2.57 |
| Sunstone | $(Na,Ca)AlSi_3O_8$ | Tcl | $6-6\frac{1}{2}$ | 1.54–1.55 | 0.007 | 2.64 |
| Fibrolite see Sillimanite | | | | | | |
| Garnet | | | | | | |
| Almandine | $Fe_3Al_2(SiO_4)_3$ | Cub | $7\frac{1}{2}$ | variable 1.77–1.82 | — | variable 3.8–4.2 |
| Andradite (Demantoid) | $Ca_3Fe_2(SiO_4)_3$ | Cub | $6\frac{1}{2}$ | 1.85–1.89 | — | 3.8–3.9 |
| Grossular (Hessonite) | $Ca_3Al_2(SiO_4)_3$ | Cub | $7\frac{1}{4}$ | 1.73–1.75 | — | 3.5–3.7 |
| Pyrope | $Mg_3Al_2(SiO_4)_3$ | Cub | $7\frac{1}{4}$ | 1.74–1.77 | — | 3.7–3.8 |
| Spessartine | $Mn_3Al_2(SiO_4)_3$ | Cub | $7\frac{1}{4}$ | 1.79–1.81 | — | 4.1–4.2 |
| Uvarovite | $Ca_3Cr_2(SiO_4)_3$ | Cub | $7\frac{1}{2}$ | 1.87 | — | 3.8 |
| Haematite | $Fe_2O_3$ | Trg | 6 | 2.94–3.22 | 0.280 | 5.1 |
| Hambergite | $Be_2(OH)BO_3$ | Orh | $7\frac{1}{2}$ | 1.56–1.63 | 0.072 | 2.35 |
| Hypersthene see Enstatite | | | | | | |
| Idocrase (also called | | | | | | |
| Vesuvianite) | $Ca_6Al(Al,OH)(SiO_4)_5$ | Tet | $6\frac{1}{2}$ | 1.71–1.72 | 0.005 | 3.40 |

| Name | Composition | Crystal System | Hardness | Refractive Indices | Birefringence | Specific Gravity |
|------|-------------|----------------|----------|--------------------|---------------|------------------|
| Jadeite | $NaAl(SiO_3)_2$ | Mcl | 7 | 1.65–1.67 | c.c. | 3.33 |
| Jasper see Quartz | | | | | | |
| Jet | Fossil wood | Amo | $3\frac{1}{2}$ | 1.66 | — | 1.1–1.4 |
| Kornerupine | $MgAlSiO_6$ | Orh | $6\frac{1}{2}$ | 1.67–1.68 | 0.013 | 3.32 |
| Kyanite (also called Disthene) | $Al_2SiO_5$ | Tcl | 5–7 | 1.71–1.73 | 0.015 | 3.67 |
| Labradorite see Feldspar | | | | | | |
| Lapis lazuli (a rock) | varies | — | $5\frac{1}{2}$ | about 1.50 | c.c. | 2.7–2.9 |
| Malachite | $Cu_2(OH)_2CO_3$ | Mcl | $3\frac{1}{2}$ | 1.66–1.91 | c.c. | 3.8 |
| Marcasite | $FeS_2$ | Orh | 6 | not readily measurable | | 4.8 |
| Moonstone see Feldspar | | | | | | |
| Nephrite | $Ca_2(Mg,Fe)_5(OH)_2 (Si_4O_{11})_{12}$ | Mcl | $6\frac{1}{2}$ | 1.61–1.63 | c.c. | 2.96 |
| Opal | $SiO_2 + nH_2O$ | Amo | 6 | 1.45 | — | 2.1 |
| Pearl natural | $CaCO_3$ + conchiolin | — | $3\frac{1}{2}$ | not readily measurable | | 2.7 |
| Petalite (old name Castorite) | $Li_2Al_2O_4(SiO_2)_8$ | Mcl | 6 | 1.50–1.52 | 0.012 | 2.39 |
| Peridot | $(Mg,Fe)_2SiO_4$ | Orh | $6\frac{1}{2}$ | 1.65–1.69 | 0.036 | 3.34 |
| Phenakite | $Be_2SiO_4$ | Trg | $7\frac{1}{2}$ | 1.65–1.67 | 0.016 | 2.96 |
| Pollucite | $H_2Cs_4Al_4(SiO_3)_9$ | Cub | $6\frac{1}{2}$ | 1.52 | — | 2.92 |
| Prehnite | $H_2Ca_2Al_2(SiO_4)_3$ | Orh | 6 | 1.61–1.65 | 0.030 | 2.87 |
| Pyrite | $FeS_2$ | Cub | $6\frac{1}{2}$ | not readily measurable | | 4.9 |
| Quartz Monocrystalline: Amethyst Citrine Rock Crystal Rose Quartz | $SiO_2$ | Trg | 7 | 1.54–1.55 | 0.009 | 2.65 |
| Chalcedony: Agate Cornelian Chrysoprase Onyx Bloodstone Jasper etc. | $SiO_2$ | Trg | 7 | 1.53–1.54 | c.c. | 2.61 |
| Rhodochrosite | $MnCO_3$ | Trg | 4 | 1.60–1.82 | 0.220 | 3.6–3.7 |
| Rhodonite | $MnSiO_3$ | Tcl | 6 | 1.73–1.74 | 0.013 | 3.5–3.6 |
| Ruby see Corundum | | | | | | |
| Sapphire see Corundum | | | | | | |
| Scapolite | varies from $Na_4Cl(Al_3Si_9O_{24})$ to $Ca_6(SO_4,CO_3)(Al_6Si_6O_{24})$ | Tet | $6\frac{1}{2}$ | varies from 1.54–1.55 to 1.55–1.57 | 0.021 | 2.68 |
| Scheelite | $CaWO_4$ | Tet | $4\frac{1}{2}$–5 | 1.92–1.94 | 0.016 | 6.00 |
| Serpentine | $Mg_6(OH)_6Si_4O_{11}H_2O$ | Mcl | $2\frac{1}{2}$–4 | 1.50–1.57 | c.c. | 2.6 |
| Sillimanite (also called Fibrolite) | $Al_2SiO_5$ | Orh | $7\frac{1}{2}$ | 1.66–1.68 | 0.020 | 3.25 |
| Sinhalite | $MgAlBO_4$ | Orh | $6\frac{1}{2}$ | 1.67–1.71 | 0.038 | 3.48 |
| Sphalerite (also called Zinc Blende) | $ZnS$ | Cub | $3\frac{1}{2}$ | 2.37 | — | 4.09 |
| Sphene (also called Titanite) | $CaTiSiO_5$ | Mcl | 5 | 1.90–2.00 | 0.120 | 3.53 |
| Spinel natural | $MgAl_2O_4$ | Cub | 8 | 1.718 | — | 3.60 |
| synthetic | $MgAl_4O_7$ | Cub | 8 | 1.724 | — | 3.63 |
| Spodumene | $LiAl(SiO_3)_2$ | Mcl | 7 | 1.66–1.68 | 0.015 | 3.18 |
| Sunstone see Feldspar | | | | | | |
| Taaffeite | $MgBeAl_4O_8$ | Hex | 8 | 1.72 | 0.004 | 3.60 |
| Titanite see Sphene | | | | | | |
| Topaz | $Al_2(F,OH)_2SiO_4$ | Orh | 8 | 1.61–1.64 | 0.010 | 3.53–3.56 |
| Tortoiseshell | horny | — | $2\frac{1}{2}$ | 1.55 | — | 1.29 |
| Tourmaline | complex borosilicate of Al etc. | Trg | 7 | 1.62–1.64 | 0.018 | 3.06 ± 0.04 |
| Turquoise | basic CuAl phosphate | Tcl | 6 | 1.61–1.65 | c.c. | 2.6–2.8 |
| Zinc Blende see Sphalerite | | | | | | |
| Zircon | $ZrSiO_4$ | | | | | |
| high type | | Tet | $7\frac{1}{2}$ | 1.93–1.99 | 0.059 | 4.69 |
| low type | | Amo | 6 | 1.79 | — | 4.00 |
| Zoisite | $Ca_2Al_2(Al,OH)(SiO_4)_3$ | Orh | $6\frac{1}{2}$ | 1.69–1.70 | 0.007 | 3.36 |

# Bibliography

## Journals

*The Australian Gemmologist,* Quarterly. The Gemmological Society of
  Australia, Gemmology House, 24 Burton Street, Darlinghurst,
  N.S.W., Australia.
*Gems,* Bi-monthly. 29 Ludgate Hill, London, EC4M 7BQ.
*Gems and Gemology,* Quarterly. The Gemological Institute of America,
  11940 San Vincente Boulevard, Los Angeles 49, California, USA.
*The Journal of Gemmology,* Quarterly. The Gemmological Association
  Great Britain, Saint Dunstan's House, Carey Lane, London, E.C.2.
*Lapidary Journal,* Monthly. 3564 Kettner Boulevard, San Diego,
  California, USA.
*Zeitschrift der Deutschen Gemmologischen Gesellschaft,* Quarterly.
  Gewerbehalle, 6580 Idar-Oberstein, Western Germany.

## General Books on Gemmology and Mineralogy

Anderson, B. W.: *Gem Testing,* Heywood & Co., London, 1971.
Bank, H.: *From the World of Gemstones,* Pinguin-Verlag, Innsbruck,
  Austria, 1973.
Cavenago-Bignami Moneta, S.: *Gemmologia,* Hoepli, Milan, Italy,
  1965.
Dana, E. S.: *Textbook on Mineralogy,* Wiley & Sons, New York, 1949.
Evans, I. O.: *Rocks, Minerals and Gemstones,* Hamlyn, London, 1972.
Kraus, E. H. and Slawson, C. B.: *Gems and Gem Materials,*
  McGraw-Hill Book Co., New York, 1947.
Liddicoat, R. T.: *Handbook of Gem Identification,* Gemological
  Institute of America, Los Angeles, 1969.
Pough, F. H.: *A Field Guide to Rocks and Minerals,* Riverside Press,
  Cambridge, Mass., 1960;
  *The Story of Gems and Semiprecious Stones,* Harvey House, New York,
  1969.
Read, H. H.: *Rutley's Elements of Mineralogy,* Murby & Co., London,
  1970.
Shipley, R. M.: *Dictionary of Gems and Gemology,* Gemological
  Institute of America, Los Angeles, 1951.
Smith, G. F. H.: *Gemstones,* Methuen & Co., London, 1972.
Spencer, L. J.: *Key to Precious Stones,* Blackie & Co., London, 1959.
Webster, R.: *Gems,* Butterworth & Co., London, 1970.
  *Gemmologist's Compendium,* N.A.G. Press, London, 1964.
  *Practical Gemmology,* N.A.G. Press, London, 1966.

## Special Subjects

Ball, S. H.: *The Mining of Gems and Ornamental Stones by American
  Indians,* Smithsonian Institute (Anthropological Papers No. 13),
  Washington, 1941.
Beigbeder, O.: *Ivory,* Weidenfeld & Nicolson, London, 1965.
Bradford, E.: *Four Centuries of European Jewellery,* Country Life Ltd.,
  London, 1967.
Bruton, E.: *Diamonds,* N.A.G. Press, London, 1970.
Cooper, L. and R.: *New Zealand Gemstones,* A. H. & A. W. Reed &
  Co. Ltd, Wellington, New Zealand, 1966.
Desautels, P. E.: *Gems in the Smithsonian Institution.* Smithsonian
  Institution (Pub. No. 4608), Washington, 1968.

Evans, Joan: *A History of Jewellery 1100–1870*. Faber & Faber, London, 1953.

Firsoff, V. A.: *Gemstones of the British Isles*. Oliver & Boyd, Edinburgh, 1971.

Geological Museum, London: *A Guide to the Collection of Gemstones*. Her Majesty's Stationery Office, London, 1950.

Gübelin, E.: *Inclusions as a Means of Gemstone Identification*, Gemological Institute of America, Los Angeles, 1953.

Holmes, M.: *The Crown Jewels*, Her Majesty's Stationery Office, London, 1955.

James, B.: *Collecting Australian Gemstones*, Murray, Sydney, 1970.

Kunz, G. F.: *The Curious Lore of Precious Stones*, reprinted 1972, with *The Magic of Jewels and Charms; Gems and Precious Stones of North America*, reprinted 1968, both Dover Publications, New York.

Leiper, H.: *The Agates of North America*, Lapidary Journal, San Diego, 1968.

Leechman, F.: *The Opal Book*, Ure Smith, Sydney, 1968.

Quick, L. and Leiper, H.: *How to Cut and Polish Gemstones*, Chilton & Co., Philadelphia, 1968.

Ruff, Elsie: *Jade of the Maori*, Gemmological Association, London, 1950.

Sinkankas, J.: *Gem Cutting*, 1962; *Gemstones of North America*, 1959; both D. Van Nostrand & Co., Princeton, New Jersey.

Tolansky, S.: *The History and Use of Diamond*, Methuen & Co., London, 1962.

Twining, Lord: *A History of the Crown Jewels of Europe*, Batsford, London, 1962.

Williamson, G. C.: *The Book of Amber*, Ernest Benn Ltd, London, 1932.

Younghusband, G. J.: *The Jewel House*, Herbert Jenkins, London, 1921.

# Acknowledgements

*Black and White:* Alinari 147; Ashmolean Museum 141 top; Australian News and Information Bureau 120, 178; Bildarchiv Foto Marburg 144; Trustees of the British Museum 134, 139, 145 top, 164; Trustees of the British Museum (Natural History) 7, 51, 52; British Publishing Corporation 150; Camera Press 101; J. Allan Cash 25, 100, 102 top left, 102 top right, 124 left, 125, 128 bottom, 129 bottom; Crown copyright Geological Survey photographs reproduced by permission of the Director, Institute of Geological Sciences 9–16, 20, 21, 24, 37–42, 44, 45, 57, 62, 90–93, 176–177; Daily Telegraph 117 top left, 117 top centre, 117 top right; De Beers Consolidated Mines Limited 76, 80, 121, 124 right; De Beers Industrial Diamond Division 54, 55; Diamond Grading Laboratories Limited 137; Dumbarton Oaks, Washington, D.C. 145 bottom; General Electric Research and Development Center, USA 56; Hamlyn Group Photographic Library 138, 178 centre right; Denis Inkersole of Mineral Associates 178 bottom; Japan Information Centre, London 99; Larousse 61; Ian Berry-Magnum 111; National Archives of Rhodesia 108; Novosti 60; Sotheby & Company 142; Robert Webster F.G.A. 102 bottom, 103. The illustration on page 141 bottom is from *Engraved Gems: The Ionides Collection* by John Boardman published by Thames and Hudson, photograph by Robert L. Wilkins.

*Colour:* Australian News and Information Bureau 162; Banque de Paris, Brussels 167; Trustees of the British Museum 163 centre left, 166 centre; Crown copyright Geological Survey photographs reproduced by permission of the Director, Institute of Geological Sciences 18, 19, 26, 27 bottom, 30, 31, 66, 67 bottom, 71, 74, 75 top, 78, 79, 115, 118, 119 top, 122, 123, 126, 127, 174 bottom; Crown copyright, reproduced with the permission of the Controller of Her Majesty's Stationery Office 174 top; De Beers Consolidated Mines Limited 170/171 top; General Electric Research and Development Center 67 top; Hamlyn Group Photographic Library 114, 163 top left, 166 bottom, 170 bottom, 175; F. L. Kennet, © George Rainbird Limited 163 right; Scala 170 top, 171 bottom; By courtesy of Messrs Wartski 166 top. The Taaffeite, page 127 bottom, appears by kind permission of R. K. Mitchell, Esq.

# Glossary

**ABYSSAL ROCKS** *See* **PLUTONIC ROCKS.**

**ALLOCHROMATIC** Coloured by an inessential impurity contained in a gemstone, such as chromic oxide in ruby or emerald. Allochromatic gems can occur in a wide variety of colours.

**ALLUVIUM** Deposits of rock detritus in such forms as sand, mud or gravel, laid down by rivers in geologically recent times.

**AMORPHOUS** Without shape, having no regular atomic structure and no directional properties such as cleavage or dichroism.

**AMYGDALE** A cavity, usually in volcanic rocks, that has become filled with secondary minerals such as chalcedony. The term is also applied to pebbles formed in this manner.

**ANISOTROPIC** Having physical properties that vary with direction, for example, differential hardness, double refraction, dichroism. Anisotropy is characteristic of all crystals except those of the cubic system.

**ARTIFICIAL GEM PRODUCTS** Man-made, crystalline products that have gem-like attributes but which do not occur in nature, such as strontium titanate, lithium niobate.

**BOULE** The pear-shaped crystal of a synthetic gemstone produced by the Verneuil process.

**CARAT** 1. Unit of weight used in weighing the more precious gemstones. One carat (1 ct) = 0.2 grams. The weight of a gemstone is always expressed to two decimal places and the decimals are often loosely called 'points'.
2. Measure of the purity of gold. Pure gold is described as 24 carat, but this is too soft for normal use. The purest gold used commercially (as for wedding rings) is of 22 carats, 22/24ths of gold and 2/24ths of alloy. Eighteen carat gold is three quarters gold and one quarter alloy and so on.

**CHROMOPHORE** A metal compound that tends to impart colour to a gemstone. The salts of chromium, iron and copper are examples of chromophores.

**CLEAVAGE** The tendency of a mineral to split along certain planes which are always parallel to a possible crystal face.

**COMPOSITE GEMSTONES** Partly or wholly man-made products imitating gemstones and consisting of more than one part. Doublets, triplets and soudé stones are composite gemstones.

**CROWN** The upper part of a cut gemstone.

**CRYPTO-CRYSTALLINE** (micro-crystalline) Composed of crystals too small to be seen with the naked eye or a loupe.

**CRYSTAL** A solid body the constituent atoms of which are arranged in a regularly repeating, three-diemensional pattern and which is therefore usually bounded by regularly disposed, flat surfaces and possesses directional properties such as cleavage. Crystalline is the opposite of amorphous.

**CRYSTAL FACE** Any natural, flat surface of a crystal.

**CULET** A small facet sometimes placed at the bottom of the pavilion of a cut gemstone.

**DENSITY** The mass of a body divided by its volume. Density can be expressed in a variety of units, such as grams/cubic centimetre, pounds/cubic foot. *See also* **SPECIFIC GRAVITY.**

**DIAMOND PIPE** A diamondiferous body of peridotite rock, approximately cylindrical or funnel-shaped, reaching the earth's surface from unknown depths.

**DOP** A contrivance for gripping a diamond mechanically while it is being polished. A dop stick is a wooden stick to which (non-diamond) gems are cemented while being cut and polished.

**DOUBLETS** *See* **COMPOSITE STONES.**

**DRUSE** A cavity in a rock, hollow at the centre and lined with crystals, usually of the same minerals as the rock.

**DYKE** A relatively thin body, usually of intrusive igneous rock (often pegmatite), that cuts across the layers through which it has intruded.

**EXTRUSIVE ROCKS** *See* **VOLCANIC ROCKS.**

**FACET** A flat polished surface on a cut gemstone.

**GEMSTONE, GEM** A stone that is valued on account of its beauty. For preference it should also be rare and resist abrasion.

**GEODE** A hollow, rounded stone, flinty on the outside and lined with crystals projecting inwards.

**GIRDLE** The widest girth of a cut gemstone where the crown and pavilion facets meet.

**GRAIN, PEARL** The unit of weight for natural pearls. One grain equals $\frac{1}{4}$ carat or 0.05 grams. Weights are expressed to two decimals of a grain.

**HABIT** The characteristic shape or shapes in which a mineral species occurs.

**HARDNESS** The power of a gemstone to resist abrasion. Hardness is usually measured on Mohs's scale (see page 40).

**HYDROTHERMAL DEPOSITS** Rocks laid down, usually in the last stages of igneous consolidation, from magma rich in water and other volatile substances.

**IDIOCHROMATIC** Coloured by an essential ingredient of a gemstone, such as the ferrous oxide always present in peridot. Idiochromatic gemstones have a narrow range of colours.

**IGNEOUS ROCKS** Rocks formed by solidification from the molten or partly molten state of magma. These are also known as plutonic or volcanic rocks.

**IMITATION GEMSTONES** Man-made products resembling gemstones more or less closely in appearance but differing from them in chemical composition and/or in crystal structure. Glass and plastics are examples of materials from which imitation gemstones may be made.

**INTRUSIVE ROCKS** Igneous rocks that have forced their way into or between other rocks and solidified before reaching the earth's surface.

**ISMORPHOUS REPLACEMENT** Interchangeability of certain kinds of atoms (ions) in a crystal in such a way that the crystal's structure is not altered appreciably.

**ISOTROPIC** Having the same properties in all directions (no birefringence or dichroism) as in amorphous substances and crystals of the cubic system. *See also* **ANISOTROPIC**.

**LAP** A flat revolving disc on which a lapidary cuts or polishes a gemstone.

**LAPIDARY** One who cuts and polishes ornamental stones or gemstones other than diamonds.

**LOUPE** A pocket magnifying glass. One magnifying ten times is commonly used in examining diamonds.

**MAGMA** Molten or semi-molten rock material from which igneous rocks are derived by solidification. This molten mass is thought to contain some suspended mineral crystals (olivine, for example), liquids and gases.

**MATRIX** The natural rock or mineral in which a crystal is embedded.

**METAMORPHIC ROCKS** Rocks formed as a consequence of great changes in temperature and/or pressure from pre-existing rocks.

**MINERALS** The homogeneous, inorganic, naturally formed consistituents of the earth's crust.

**MINERAL SPECIES** Minerals which have basically the same chemical composition and crystal structure belong to the same mineral species.

**ORNAMENTAL STONES** The more common kinds of gemstones, usually opaque to subtranslucent. They are rarely faceted but are used for carvings, inlays or in slabs.

**PAVILION** The lower part of a cut gemstone, below the girdle.

**PEGMATITE** Igneous rocks of coarse grain, usually intrusive, and often containing rare minerals, including large crystals of gemstones.

**PERIDOTITE** Plutonic rocks consisting of olivine and other dark minerals such as amphibole and mica.

**PHENOCRYSTS** Relatively large crystals in some igneous rocks contained in a groundmass of much smaller crystals.

**PLACER DEPOSIT** An alluvial or glacial deposit, usually of sand and gravel, containing valuable minerals.

**PLUTONIC ROCKS** Igneous rocks that have formed beneath the surface of the earth from magma.

**PNEUMATOLYTIC DEPOSITS** Rocks and minerals, such as tourmaline and topaz, thought to have been formed from a gaseous phase.

**REFRACTIVE INDEX** The ratio of the speed of light in a vacuum to the speed of light passing through a gemstone; or the ratio of the sine of the angle of incidence to the sine of the angle of refraction in the gemstone. This is usually measured in yellow light of a wavelength of 5893A.

**ROCK** Any naturally formed mass of mineral matter forming part of the earth's crust. It can consist mainly of one mineral or of a mixture of minerals.

**SCAIFE** (scyve) Cast-iron disc, ten to twelve inches in diameter, used for faceting diamonds.

**SECONDARY MINERALS** Minerals formed by the alteration of pre-existing minerals. Erosion, disintegration or solution may give rise to secondary minerals.

**SEDIMENTARY ROCKS** Rocks formed from fragments of other rocks transported from their original sites (as sandstone, conglomerate); or formed by precipitation from solution (agate, opal); or formed from the shells of marine animals (limestone).

**SILICA** Silicon dioxide, the basic constituent of sand, gravel and the silica gems.

**SILL** A relatively thin body of intrusive igneous rock (such as pegmatite) lying parallel to the layers of rock between which it has intruded.

**SPECIFIC GRAVITY** The ratio of the mass of a body to the mass of an equal volume of pure water at 4 °C.

**SPECTRUM** An image formed by dispersing a beam of light (or other radiation) into its constituent colours (wavelengths). An *absorption* spectrum is obtained by passing white light through a substance and then dispersing it, say, through a spectroscope: this discloses any wavelengths absorbed by the substance.

**SYNTHETIC GEMSTONES** Man-made materials having the same or similar chemical composition and crystal structure as natural gemstones.

**TABLE** The largest facet at the top of the crown of a gemstone, always parallel to the girdle.

**TRIPLETS** *See* **COMPOSITE STONES**.

**TUMBLING** A process for polishing ornamental stones by rotating or vibrating them in a container with abrasives.

**TWINS** Twinned crystals formed by a non-parallel intergrowth of two or more crystals in directions determined by their crystal structure.

**VOLCANIC ROCKS** Igneous rocks that have been ejected and have solidified at the earth's surface.

# Index

Page numbers in italic indicate illustrations and page numbers in bold indicate the main reference.

Abalone 99
Abrasion 11, 40
Abrasives 133, 140
Absorption spectra 47
Achroite 95
Acicular 40
Adularescence 81
Agate 8, 28, *30*, 90, *119*, *147*, *174*
　superstitions 161
Aigrette 148
Albertus Magnus 160
Alexandrite 9, *18*, 33, 48, 69 *et seq*
Allochromatic 46
Alluvium 32
Aluminium jewellery 151
Amazonite 82
Amber 15, 28, 29, 33, 51, 59 *et seq*, 60, *61*, *70*
Ambergris 61
Ambroid 60
Amethyst 7, 34, 49, 89, *115*
Amianthus 90
Amorphous 35
Amulet 161, *164*
Amygdale 20
Andalusite 9, 32, 104, *127*
Andamooka opal 92
Anderson, B. W. 47
Anhedral 20, *20*
Anisotropic 48
Apatite 29, 40, 104
Aquamarine 6, 33, 34, 63 *et seq*, *71*
Art Nouveau 152
'Arts and Crafts' jewellery 152
Associated minerals 14
Asterias 65
Atomic pile colouring *31*, 49
Auctions 181
Australite 92
Austrian Yellow diamond 158
Aventurine 82
Axes of reference *36*, 37
Axinite 104
Azurite 29, 87

Bakelite 60
Balance for gems *42*, 183
'Balas ruby' 68, 93
'Baroque' 102
Benitoite 104
Beryl 6, 29, 32, 61 *et seq*, *71*, 120
Beryllium 6
Beryllonite 104
Billitonite 92
Birefringence 44, *44*
Birthstones 168, *174*
Black Prince's ruby 93, 158
Block cave mining 110, 111
Blood, Colonel 159
Bloodstone 90, *119*
Blue earth 60
Blue ground 73, *111*
Bonamite 107
Booth, Anselmus 160
Botryoidal 40, *114*
Boule 52, *52*
Bowenite 106
Brazilianite 34, 104
Breastplate, High Priest's 168
Brilliance 10, 47

Brilliant cut 77, *77*, 78, *80*, *128*, *130*, 131, *135*, 147
　variations on the *131*
Brillianteerer 129
Bronzite 105
Bruting 128, *129*
Burmite 59

Cabochon 10, 131
Cachalong 91
Cairngorm 89
Callais 96
Cameo 134, *134*, 143, 146, *166*
Carat weight 134, *135*
Carbonates 50
Carborundum 133
Carbuncle 58, 82
　superstitions 161
Castellani 151
Castorite 106
Catalogue, collection 181 *et seq*
Cat's-eye 10, *23*, 72, *72*, *126*
Cellini, Benvenuto 130, 146, 168
Cementation 28
Ceylon (Sri Lanka) 32
Ceylonite 93
Chalcedony 28, 29, 90, *119*, 140, *166*
Chatham, C. F. 54
Chemical damage to gems 12
Chemistry of gemstones 50
Chiastolite 104
Chloromelanite 86
Chlorospinel 93
Chromium colouring 46
Chromophores 46
Chrysoberyl 9, 11, 29, 34, 69 *et seq*, *74*
Chrysolite 87
Chrysoprase 90, *119*, 131
　superstitions 161
Church, Sir James 47
Cinnamon stone 83
Citrine 49, 89, *115*
Cleavage 40, *40*
Clinozoisite 105
Closed setting 94
Colour in gemstones 8, 45 *et seq*
　artificial *30*, *31*, 48
　change in varying light 9, *18*, 69
　filters *41*, 47, 183
Colourless 46
Compacted rocks 28
Composite stones 56, *56*
Concentration 28, 112
Conch, Giant 99
Conchiolin 99
Conchoidal fracture 40
Connemara marble 106
Coober Pedy 120
Copal resin 60
Copper, colour due to 46
Coral 15, *103*, 127
　superstitions 161
Cordierite *22*, 32, 104
Cornelian 32, 90, *119*
　superstitions 161
Corundum 6, 9, 29, 32, 64 *et seq*, *71*
　synthetic 52, 69
Costume jewellery 152
Crocidolite 90
Cross cutter 129
Crypto-crystalline 35
Crystal 14, *35*
　systems *36*, 36, *et seq*
Cullinan diamond 154, *154*
Cymophane 72
Czochralski furnace *53*

Damage to gemstones 11

Dammar resin 60
Dana, E. S. 181
Danburite 104, *127*
Datolite 104
Density 41, *42*
Devonshire emerald 63, 159
Diadem 143
Diamond 10, 20, 29, 32, 33, 41, 49, *67*, 72 *et seq*, 76, *80*, *113*
　'bearding' 130
　cutting 124 *et seq*, *124*, *125*, *128*, *130*, *131*, *132*
　facets *129*, 130, *130*
　grading 76 *et seq*, *121*
　'make' 130
　'natural' 130
　proportions *77*, *80*, 130
　'sights' 124
　sorting 116, *121*
　superstitions 161
　synthetic 54, *54*, 55, *67*
　valuation 80
Dichroism 9, *22*, 47
Dichroite 104
Dichroscope *41*, 48, *48*, 183
Diffraction 91
Diopside 105, *145*
Directoire jewellery 150
Dispersion *22*, 27, 47
Disthene 105
Dop 128, *129*
Dop stick 133
Doublets 56, *56*
Dravite 95
Dresden Green diamond 158
Druse 20
Dumortierite 90
Dykes 20, *21*, 24

Ekanite 33
Electron 61
Electroplating 151
Electrum 61, 140
Emerald 6, 32, 33, 34, 40, 47, 62, *62*, 66, *71*
　goddess 159
　mining 120
　superstitions 160, 161
　synthetic 54, 63, 66
Emery 65
Enamelling 143, 146
Engraving 134, 164
Enstatite 105
Epidote 32, 105
Escarbuncle 165, *165*
Etruscan jewellery 141, 151
Euclase 29, 105
Euhedral 17, *20*
Excelsior diamond 155
Extrusive rocks 17

Fabergé, P. C. 152
　Imperial Easter Egg 152, *166*
'Fabulite' 81
Faience 97
*Fei tsui* 85
Feldspar 29, *75*, 81 *et seq*
Fibrolite 106
Finger auction 135
Fire, damage by 12
*Flèches d'amour* 90
Florentine diamond 158
Fluorescence *27*, 47, 68, 76
Foiling 94
Fossil wood 91
Fracture 40

Gahnospinel 93
Garnet 29, 32, 33, 34, *78*, 82, *et seq*, *141*
　almandine 32, 83
　andradite 32, 84

demantoid 84
　grossular 32, 83
　hessonite 83
　pyrope 29, 83
　spessartine 29, 83
　uvarovite 84
Garnet topped doublet 56, *56*
Gem gravel 28
Gemmological equipment *41*, 47, 183
Gemstone, definition 8
　age of 13
　cutting *131*, *132*, 133
　drilling 134
　engraving 134, *134*
　from solutions 28
　locations 32 *et seq*
　organic 15, 98 *et seq*
　storage 177, *177*, *182*
　superstitions 161 *et seq*
　valuation 135
Geode 20, *21*
Geological processes 16, *17*, 21
Girandole 148
Glass 35, 51
　inclusions in 43
　natural 92
　scratching of 12
Golconda 32, 73
Gold 33, 140
'Goldstone' 82
Goshenite 64, *71*
Grail, the Holy 159
Grain, pearl 102
Grand Mogul diamond *156*
Grease belts 113, *113*
Greenstone 85, *163*
Guanine 101
Gübelin, Dr E. J. 43

Habit, crystal 39, *39*
Haematite 105
　superstitions 161
Hambergite 33, *105*
Hannay, J. B. 52
Hardness 11, 40
　tests 41
Hatton Garden 146
Hawk's eye 90
Heating, colour change 49
Heavy liquids 42
Heliodor 64, *71*
Heliotrope 90
Heraldry 165
Hiddenite 107
Hope diamond 158
Hyacinth 58, 97
Hydrothermal minerals 17, 28, 29

Idar-Oberstein 121
Idiochromatic 46
Idocrase 105
'Igmerald' 54 *et seq*, *21*
Igneous rocks *14*, 16, 29
Imitation gemstones *31*, 50
Inclusions 34, *43*, 64, 65
Indicolite 59, 95
Indochinite 92
Intaglio 134, *141*, 143
Intrusive rocks 17
Iolite 9, 104
Iron, colour due to 46
Irradiation, colour change *31*, 49, 81
Isomorphism 50
Ivory 15, *103*, *127*

Jacinth 83, 97
Jade 8, 29, 84 *et seq*, *139*, *145*, *163*
　Chinese 142, *142*, *164*
　Imperial 8, 85
　'Oregon' 91

superstitions 161, *164*
Jadeite 32, 33, 34, *78*, 84 *et seq*, 120, 149
Jamb peg 133
Jargoon 97
Jasper 32, 91, *118*, *174*
  superstitions 161
Jet 15, 28, 29, 103, *127*, *138*, *150*
Jewellery, history of 140 *et seq*
  maintenance 183
  making of 135, *136*

Kimberlite 73, 83
Koh-i-nur diamond 155, *157*
Kornerupine 105
Kunz, G. F. 98, 152, 169
Kunzite 107
Kyanite 32, 105

Labradorite 10, 82
Lamarie, P. de 148
Lapidary 132
  clubs 178, *178*
Lapis lazuli 29, 32, 33, 34, *75*, 86
  superstitions 161
Lasers 55
Lattice, crystal 35
Lava 17
Lazurite 86
Limestone 28
Lithium niobate 56
Loupe 43, 183
Luminescence 47
Lustre *9*, 10

'Madeira topaz' 58
Magma 16
Malachite 29, 33, 86 *et seq*, *114*, *166*
  superstitions 161
Manganese, colour due to 46
Mantle 101
Marbodus of Rennes 160
Marcasite 29, 87
Massive 40
'Matara diamond' 58, 98
Matrix 34
Medicinal use of gems 168
*Mere* 85
Metamorphic rocks *16*, 29
Microscope *41*, 43, 183
Minerals 13
Mining *108*, 109 *et seq*, *109*, *110*, *111*, *112*, *117*, *120*, *162*
Miseroni 146
Mixed cut 130
Mocha stone 90, *119*
Mogok 7
Mohs' scale *11*, 40
Moissan, F. H. H. 52
Moldavite 92
Moonstone 10, *81*
Morganite 64, *71*
Morion 89
Moss agate 90, *118*
Mother-of-pearl 15, *126*
Mourning jewellery 150, *150*

Naat 128
Nacre 99, *101*
Naoratna 165, *165*
Nephrite 32, 33, 84 *et seq*, *85*, 134, *139*, *163*
Nomenclature 58
Nosean 86
Nuclear fission 97

Obsidian 92
Odontolite 97
Olivine 16, 29, 32, 87
Onyx 90, *118*, *147*
  superstitions 161

Opal 11, 28, 29, 40, 91 *et seq*, *115*
  doublets 92, 131
  matrix 92
  mining 120, *120*, *162*
  superstitions 164
Open setting 94
Operculum 15
'Oregon jade' 91
Orient 32, 99
Oriental 58
Orlov diamond 157
Ornamental stones 8
Orthoclase 81
Oxides 50

'Padparadscha' 65
Pain, A.C.D. 7
Painite 6, *7*
Paste 51
Pearls 15, 33, 98 *et seq*, *103*, *126*, *170*
  cultured *99*, *100*, 101, *101*, *102*
  grain 102
  imitation 101, *101*, *102*
Pegmatite 17, 28, 29
Peridot 33, *74*, *78*, 87 *et seq*
Peruzzi 147
Petalite 106
Petrified wood 34
Petrology 14
Phenakite 106
Phenocryst 17
Phosphates 50
Photometer 59, 77
Picasso P. 153
Pinchbeck 149
Pinctada 99
Pipes, diamondiferous 20, 110
Piqué 77
Pistrucci, Benedetto 134
Pitt diamond 157
Placer deposits 28
Plasma 90
Plastics 51, 60
Platinum 140, 151
Play of colour 10
Pliny the Elder 61, 86, 88, 96, 160, 168
Plutonic rocks 17
Pneumatolytic rocks 17, 29
Polariscope *41*, 183
Pollucite 106
Polymorphs *37*, 38
Pompeii 150
Porcelain imitations 51
Pounamu 134
Prase 90
'Prasiolite' 49, 89
Precious stones 7
Prehnite 106
Pressed amber 60
Prospecting for gems 108 *et seq*, *117*, *120*, *162*
Pseudomorphs *38*
Puddingstone 91
'Pyralspite' garnets 83
Pyrgoteles 143
Pyrite 29, 87, *115*
Pyro-electricity 96

Quartz 20, 28, 29, 33, 88 *et seq*, *91*, *115*
  amethystine 90
  cats'-eyes 90
  milky 90
  rutilated 90
  smoky 89
  synthetic 56, *57*, 89
Queen Elizabeth I 7, 101, 146, 164

Rarity 6

Ratnapura 32
Ravenscroft 149
'Reconstructed' rubies 52
Refractive index 43 *et seq*
Refractometer *41*, *44*
Regent diamond 157
Renaissance jewellery 146
Repolishing gemstones 11
Retinite 60
Rhodizite 33
Rhodochrosite 106, *127*
Rhodonite 106
Ribbon jasper 91
Rivières 152
Rocaille 148
Rock crystal 88, *115*, *147*
Rocks 13
  types of 15 *et seq*
Rose cut 131, *132*
Rose quartz 89, *115*
Rouge, jewellers' 133
Rubellite 59, 95
Ruby 6, 11, 33, 64 *et seq*, *64*, *71*
  superstitions 161
Ruin marble 91, *118*
Rumanite 59
Rutile 65, 81, 90
  synthetic 55

St. Edward's sapphire 159
St. Hildegarde of Bingen 160
Sancy diamond 158, *158*
Sapphire 6, 11, 32, 33, 34, 64 *et seq*, 65, *71*
Sard, sardonyx 90
Saussurite 86
Scaife 125
Scan, D.N. 77
Scapolite *74*, 106
Scheelite 106
Schiller 10, 81
Schörl 95
Seals 141
Sedimentary rocks *15*, 21 *et seq*, *21*
Semi-precious gemstones 7
Serendipe 32, 108
Serpentine *79*, 86, 106
  superstitions 160
Sévigné 148
Shah diamond 157
Sheen 10
Shellac 60
Siberite 95
Silica gemstones 28, 50, 88 *et seq*
  glass 92
Silicates 50
'Silk' 65
Sill 20, *21*
Sillimanite 32, 106, *127*
Silver 140
Simetite 60
Sinhalite 87, 107
Smithsonian Institution 55, 158
Smithsonite 107
Sodalite 86
Soudé emerald 56, 57
Specific gravity 41, *42*
Spectroscope *41*, 47, 183
Spectrum 47
Spelling rings 168
Sphalerite 107
Sphene 107
Spinel 16, 29, 32, *74*, *93 et seq*
  synthetic 52, 86, 94
Spodumene 107
Staining of gemstones *30*, 48
Stalactites *25*
Stalagmites *24*, *25*
Star of Africa diamond 155
Star of Sierra Leone diamond 155, *155*

Star stones 10, *24*, 65, *65*, 83, 89
  superstitions 164
Stone paper *177*, 182, *182*
Storing gemstones *177*, 181, *182*
Strasser 149
Strontium titanate 56, 81
Stuart sapphire 159
Styles of cutting gemstones 130, *131*, *132*
Succinite 59
Sulphides 50
Sunstone *74*, 82
'Swiss lapis' 49, 86
Synthetic gemstones 15, 51, 52, *54*, 81, *90*
  their inclusions 43, *43*

Taaffe, Count 6
Taaffeite 6, *127*
Tabular crystals 40
Talisman 161
Tang 128
Tanzanite 107
Tassie 149
Tektites 92, *93*
Thermoluminescence 98
Tiffany 153
  diamond *156*
Tiger's eye 90, *115*
Tiki 85
Timur Ruby 159, *174*
Titanite 107
Titanium dioxide 81
Topaz 29, 33, 34, 46, 49, 89, 94 *et seq*, *122*
Tortoiseshell 15, 51, 103 *et seq*, *127*
Tourmaline 8, 9, 29, 34, 46, 95 *et seq* *122*
Transparency 45, *45*
'Transvaal jade' 83
Triplets 56, *56*
Tripoli 133
Tumbling 179, *179*
Turquoise 12, 29, 33, 34, 49, 96 *et seq*, *119*, *166*
  superstitions 160, 164
Twinned crystals 38, *38*

Ugrandite garnets 83
Ulexite 12
Ultramarine 86
Ultraviolet light 47
Uniondae 100
Unit cell 36

Vanadium, colour due to 46
Variscite 97
Venus hair stone 90
Verdite 86
Verneuil, A.V.L. 52
  flame fusion furnace *52*, 52, 53
Vesuvianite 105
Vivianite 12
Volcanic rocks 17

Water opal 92
'Water sapphire' 58
Wedding anniversary gems 169
Wedgwood, Josiah 149

Yellow ground 73
Yttrium aluminate (YAG) 81

Zinc blende 107
Zircon 11, 29, 33, 46, 49, 97 *et seq*, *123*
Zois, Baron, von Edelstein 7
Zoisite 7, 33, 107, *127*